Integrated but Unequal

INTEGRATED

─────────────────────────── BUT ─

UNEQUAL

Black Faculty In Predominately White Space

Edited by MARK CHRISTIAN

AFRICA WORLD PRESS
TRENTON | LONDON | CAPE TOWN | NAIROBI | ADDIS ABABA | ASMARA | IBADAN | NEW DELHI

AFRICA WORLD PRESS
541 West Ingham Avenue | Suite B
Trenton, New Jersey 08638

Book and cover design: Saverance Publishing Services

Library of Congress Cataloging-in-Publication Data

Integrated but unequal : Black faculty in predominately white space / edited by Mark Christian.
    p. cm.
Includes bibliographical references and index.
  ISBN 978-1-59221-867-7 (hard cover) -- ISBN 978-1-59221-868-4 (pbk.) 1. African American college teachers--Social conditions. 2. African American college teachers--Job satisfaction. 3. Faculty integration--United States. 4. Discrimination in higher education--United States. 5. United States--Race relations. I. Christian, Mark.
  LC2781.5.I58 2011
  378.1'208996073--dc23
                        2011034726

To my mentor for over 20 years
Dr. William E. Nelson, Jr.

and in memory of
Dr. William A. Little (1941-2008)

Two wonderful Pan-Africanist Scholar-Activists

Table of Contents

Acknowledgements

It is without doubt that the first persons I should like to thank are the contributors to this important volume. Without their collective courage and commitment to the project it would have floundered into obscurity. It is important to thank all the anonymous referees who read and commented on the chapters. Special thanks to Dr. Denise Taliaferro Baszile, who helped me organize a symposium that produced some of the chapters in this book. The symposium took place on February 18, 2011 at Miami University of Ohio and proved to be a resounding success for all who participated and attended. Denise was designated to work with me on this publication as a co-editor but due to the pressures of a new administrative position at Miami University and family commitments she had to step aside. I also have to give a special thank you to the Director of Diversity Initiatives at Miami University, Dr. Juanita Tate, who provided the funds for the symposium to take place. Also, thanks to Dr. Ronald Scott, Associate Vice President for Institutional Diversity, Miami University, who facilitated the symposium and helped make the day a resounding success. Moreover, I appreciate the encouragement and support of Ms. Valerie Robinson, Director for the Association of Black Faculty and Students (ABFAS) at Miami University. I would also like to thank all the students of color at Miami University, and the few progressive Whites, who came out to support the symposium on a late Friday afternoon (notorious for when students get out of town!), as it proved that there is a deep interest in this topic beyond the faculty cohort. In terms of my current position as Chair of African & African American Studies at Lehman College, City University of New York, I would like to thank Professor Timothy Alborn, the Dean of Arts & Humanities, for his outstanding support. In addition, I would like to thank Kassahun Checole of Africa World Press for his encouragement to have this volume published; and for his dedication to the empowerment of peoples of African heritage. Finally, without the spirit of resistance that is part of my DNA it would have been impossible to have taken on the arduous task of editor. So I give thanks to my grandfather, George Rupert Christian (1882-1952), a staunch follower of Marcus Garvey, and a writer for the *Negro World,* and a man who had passed long before I entered this world; I can only hope that his spirit lives on in me.

Mark Christian
Editor

Introduction

Mark Christian, Editor

L et me state categorically: THIS IS NOT A BOOK OF TALES BY VICTIMS. Rather, it is a collection of experiences from the pens of successful to very successful Black academics from the US and UK. Indeed, this volume of writers is unique, but universal; exceptional, yet everyday in occurrence. If this sounds like a contradictory conundrum then it is aptly and oddly a conglomeration of Black faculty workplace experience. The reader is in for a poignant, albeit triumphant, journey into the lives of *successful* contemporary Black faculty who have been employed, and most continue to be so, on predominately White campuses in the United States and United Kingdom. Indeed, they are a rare breed of human species: faculty of color in White space. They endure the weight of daily benign racism (Anderson 2010), via psychological assaults with relative aplomb. After all, they are only the second and third generation era of Black scholars to be integrated into mainstream universities since the late1960s. However, the term that most conjures up the reality of their collective experience is: *integrated but unequal.* By and large they are tolerated by the majority, but frequently covertly scorned, and most often treated unfairly when it comes to hiring, promotion and tenure, professional development, in the predominately White university workplace.

Some of the terms the reader will become familiar with while perusing this book are: *microaggression, mobbing, isolation, racial battle fatigue, passive aggression,* and *philosophical racism,* to name just a few. These concepts collectively give a caveat that there engenders much struggle and strife for the Black faculty member on predominately White campuses. Although there is a growing body of literature in regard to faculty of color, it is still relatively small. There needs to be more books like this whereby the writers speak truth to power without fear and without worry. They all write courageously and honestly concerning their individual experiences.

Notably, most of the writers in this volume are in some way connected to the humanities, liberal arts, and social sciences. One could argue that they are sensitive souls with a deeper comprehension for the meaning of life. Especially in comprehending how the human family should care for one another, in our vastly complex and evermore precarious world. Yet should not all scholars in the humanities and social sciences areas be worldly and humane, regardless of one's cultural background? If the answer to this question is in the affirmative then why does so much institutionalized racism exist in academia (Feagin 2002; Chesler, Lewis & Crowfoot 2005; Moore, Alexander & Lemelle 2010; Turner & Myers 2000)? To answer the question properly we need to comprehend the longevity of racism in the US and UK societies. Indeed both nations have a long history of racist ideology and practice that has suffocated human progress and the greater need for social justice when it comes to their racialized communities.

In this sense, Black faculty do not exist in a vacuum, they are part and parcel of a broader society. Even though they occupy positions in higher education, and one would expect a higher moral and ethical code among all whom occupy academic space in the area of liberal arts. However, a liberal education does not necessarily permit the best practice concerning racialized integration and harmony in the university. There are in fact too many horror stories coming out of academia that pertain to racism and bigotry (Lemelle 2009). Therefore a myth to dispel at the outset is the erroneous idea that the majority White liberal arts setting brings forth higher minded persons with no ill will or racial prejudice. The manifold experiences of Black faculty indicates that discrimination is alive and kicking in the most "liberal" of spaces in higher education (Chesler, Lewis & Crowfoot 2005; Feagin 2002; Moore, Alexander & Lemelle 2010). Sometimes it is unintended on the behalf of White liberals, yet just as devastating in outcome had it emerged from overt racists (Trepagnier 2006).

Black Female Faculty

The Black women in this volume speak to their individual struggles as Black faculty, in spite of the evident success in dealing with the obstacles that impede their entry into higher education. They are relatively small in number, yet outstripping their male counterparts in terms of gaining entry into graduate schools. Although presently in terms of full-time status African American males have a slight advantage in numbers, this will undoubtedly change in time with the increased participation of Black women in higher education, and the lessening impact of Black males entering graduate school.

What is particularly impressive about Black women faculty generally is in their seemingly enduring capacity to cope with the impediments to success compared to their male counterparts. Is this because they are less threatening to White supremacy than the Black male? Or is it due to their collective inner strength and determination to succeed against the odds? Not easy to answer these questions without future qualitative research. However, with the broader statistical data showing that Black males are under great strain with low graduation rates in terms of high school diplomas and high incarceration rates, there is strong evidence that the Black male is endangered in societies like the US and UK (Alexander 2010). In addition, his counterpart Black female is left taking greater responsibility to keep families afloat, and to get ahead in life. This could be one explanation for the sheer determination of the Black female presently succeeding in higher education. Moreover, given the increasingly low numbers of Black male participation in education at all levels, it is inevitable that Black women will provide the intellectual backbone to the African American experience within the next two decades.

Black Male Faculty

In the US, which is far more progressive than the UK in terms of opportunity for minority cultures in higher education, a major crisis is taking place in contemporary times with the diminishing enrollment of Black male graduate students. Clearly there needs to be a more gender-balanced in-take of Black graduate students that will provide the future cohort of professors in higher education. There can be little doubt that without concerted effort on behalf of colleges and universities to recruit and retain Black males this catastrophe will have imponderable negative outcomes for society over the next 25 years. A recent update from the *Journal of Blacks in Higher Education* reported,

> There were 243,600 black women enrolled in graduate programs [in 2009], compared to 90,500 black men. Thus, women accounted for a whopping 71.1 percent of all African-American graduate school enrollments...
>
> Ten years earlier in 2000, black women made up 67.5 percent of all African-American graduate enrollments...(1)

What is to be done? Where does the culpability lie for this societal tragedy? Certainly it is a combination of factors that account for the drain in Black male scholars coming into higher education. Yet, when all is said and done, pivotal to this phenomena is the continued significance of racism in society. Whereby "race" itself is now blurred under the rubric of diversity, most progressive thinking scholars know that it is a paramount variable in this exclusionary reality (Alexander 2010; Anderson 2010; Bonilla Silva 2003; Feagin 2010). To suggest otherwise is to live in a world of wonderland; one does not have a grip on reality if she dismisses the key factor of sustained racialized discrimination toward Black males in numerous forms, from kindergarten to the grave. The contemporary statistical data is overwhelmingly stating: "the Black male is a target to attack and destroy" by any means necessary. This is not hyperbole or irrational, it is based on the varied social realities of Black life in societies such as the US and UK.

Methodology

Autoethnography is at the heart of this volume, complemented with quantitative evidence to enhance the validity of the varied perspectives offered by the authors (Spry 2006). The writers herein are twelve in total; a qualitative group made up of eight African

American and four Black British scholars. There are seven female and five male authors, each writing with honesty, courage, and a commitment to social justice via their personal narratives of life in academia (some do, but a number are not necessarily writing about their *present* institution). They are collectively part of what I deem a "rare and endangered species" in mainstream higher education. Ten writers live and work in the US, while two reside in the UK and are employed insecurely in British universities. The editor of this volume is Black British and has worked in universities on both sides of the Atlantic, and often writes in a comparative analysis in relation to the UK and US (Christian 2002, 2005, 2010a, 2010b).

Crucially, this group of writers offer testimony that will be useful and relevant to policymakers and those with the power to make an intervention to tackle the growing calamity of largely White (but certainly not exclusively) faculty incivility—with regard to their interaction with underrepresented groups in academia (Chesler, Lewis & Crowfoot 2005; Moore, Alexander & Lemelle 2010; Twale & De Luca 2008). Indeed, for example, it favors no one to have such a low number of highly educated Black faculty in modern societies such as the US and UK. Nor does it profit society if highly educated Black women face major problems in finding a male counterpart (if they so desire) to share a professional life together. Fragmentation of the Black community is not good for society, and not good for the life of the university systems in the US and UK.

Outline of the Book

There are three parts to this volume. Part I looks at the experience of Black female faculty. Chapter one by Robin Hughes and Natasha Flowers offers, among other things, a critique in how Black faculty are doing more service-related activity than is reasonable to ask. Due to the low numbers in people of color on predominately White campuses the need for their "visibility" is paramount in giving the appearance of a diverse workforce. In chapter two, Alma Jean Billingslea Brown gives a historical account of the struggle Black women have countenanced to enter academia. The fight for entry goes back to the era during the Civil War (1861-1865) up to the present, in which Black women have encountered manifold barriers to their success. Moreover, she offers concrete case studies of resistance by women of color to the forces of "sameness" and in challenging the status quo. She presently teaches at Spelman College, the first historically Black college for women, yet can speak to the themes and perspectives of this book due to her long career in academia. Chapter three by Helane Adams Androne offers a very creative and personal insight into her journey as a student to associate professor of English, and in doing so shows how difficult the task is in juggling a family while being exploited by overzealous service requirements. In chapter four, Jeanette Davidson looks at the intersection of White privilege and institutional abuse of power. Her experiences relate to how difficult it is to trust within academia when one is in a culture that creates anxiety and pressure for faculty of color. Davidson challenges universities to make real the promises of equal opportunity, and that diversity should not be a buzz word but an authentic building block toward best practice. Finally, chapter five by Mary Phillips gives the reader an insight into the neophyte Black woman scholar whom loves her natural hair in an environment that scorns it. It is not only the dominant culture, too often it is Black faculty and administrators (men and women) *within* academia that frown upon the natural hair of Black women. This is an important exploratory study that deserves greater attention. For if Black women faculty are "advised" to straighten their hair for the betterment of career prospects, it bodes negatively for the future of Black women presence in predominately White colleges and universities. It is an unpardonable tragedy to learn that this insidious assault on natural hair is taking place in the second decade of the twenty-first century.

In Part II, Black male faculty reveal their inner thoughts and personal experiences in teaching, research, and service related activities. Yet there is also evident a number of new philosophies for survival to consider, and new ways for policymakers in higher education administrations to think about the crisis met by Black faculty. Chapter six by Michael Dantley offers much due to his longevity of experience in teaching and high-level administration; along with an abiding spirituality in the conviction of his words. In short, he asks for greater parity and inclusiveness of all peoples in predominately White universities, and for an eradication of various impediments to Black faculty self-determination and humanness. In chapter seven Mark Christian provides a link between the macro-world of Black male disempowerment and the manifestation of institutionalized discrimination via his use of the term *philosophical racism*. That is, the unsavory practice of hierarchical knowledge in modern universities fosters inequitable treatment and resentment *per se*. However, he adds to this by arguing how Black male faculty whom speak truth to power through their association with Africana/Black Studies face greater threats being mobbed and/or bullied; and that this can be detrimental to one's professional development and livelihood. Martell Teasley in chapter eight speaks to and gives notice to the ugliness of microaggression in academia as it relates to faculty of color. It is covert, sometimes unintended, yet can be psychologically devastating over a sustained period of time. Teasley also advocates the need for mentoring and support systems for faculty of color. In chapter nine, Mark Giles opens his chapter with a parable to express admonition to Black scholars not to compromise one's roots and linkages to the Black experience. Indeed, it is such connections with one's community that ultimately sustains the life of the mind in times of assault and abuse. To know thy self is an important antidote to psychological and philosophical racism.

Part III gives insight into the experiences of two Black British scholars employed in the British university system. Chapter ten by William Ackah is a visceral description of the cold, sterile, often inhumane existence of Black faculty in the UK. He explores this phenomenon through the lens of Whiteness studies and the White privilege paradigm. It is a heart-wrenching, yet inspiring, account of life for a Black academic in Britain in the twenty-first century. Sadly it is also an indictment on the British university system and its inherent institutionalized racism. Shirley Anne Tate in chapter eleven closes out by also sharing her largely negative experiences of the British university system as it relates to a Black feminist. Indeed, in terms of the depth of despair it is almost twin-like to William Ackah's study, therefore rendering further authenticity to their experiences. Yet, Tate works in Northern England at the University of Leeds, while Ackah is employed at a Birkbeck College in London. It seems that distance is not the issue, it is the university environment and the culture of exclusion and disrespect for people of color that binds them. I predict with confidence that these two chapters alone will provide excellent comparative analyses and discussion in college and university classrooms for many years to come.

Overall, this volume is audacious in tone, courageous in output, and valid for anyone interested in the experiences of Black faculty in predominately White universities and other institutions of higher learning. If there are any faults in the book then they should be laid at the feet of the editor. I am a man who has developed a thick skin in academia; and because I hold to the creed that *all knowledge is essentially provisional,* it is important to explore new themes, approaches, and perspectives to social problems. Therefore I am confident, at the very least, that this book will not only provide a platform for further discussion and debate, but in kind it should inspire action to avoid the crisis of intellectual exclusion, intimidation, and downright unfairness growing out of control in higher education.

Note

1. The *Journal of Blacks in Higher Education,* (June 9, 2011), reported new data from the US Department of Education showing that in 2009, there were 342,400 African Americans enrolled in graduate programs in the United States. However, the figure when broken down represents there being 71% African American women graduate enrollments. http://www.jbhe.com/latest/index.html [accessed June 14, 2011]

References

Alexander, M. (2010). *The new Jim Crow: Mass incarceration in the age of colorblindness.* New York: The New Press.

Anderson, K. J. (2010). *Benign bigotry: The psychology of subtle prejudice.* Cambridge: Cambridge University.

Bonilla-Silva, E. (2003). *Racism without racists: Color-blind racism and the persistence of racial inequality in the United States.* London: Rowman & Littlefield.

Chesler, M., Lewis, M., & Crowfoot, J. (2005). *Challenging racism in higher education: Promoting justice.* New York: Rowman & Littlefield.

Christian, M. (2002). (Ed.). *Black identity in the twenty-first century: Expressions of the US & UK African Diaspora.* London: Hansib.

Christian, M. (2005, March 4). Why do we go abroad? *Time Higher Education Supplement,* 20-21.

Christian, M. (2010a). Black studies in the UK and US: A comparative analysis. In J. R. Davidson. (Ed.). *African American Studies.* (pp.149-167). Edinburgh: University of Edinburgh.

Christian, M. (2010b). Notes on the dilemma of the Black scholar in predominately White universities: A personal perspective via postmodernist agency. In S. E. Moore, R. Alexander, Jr., & A. J. Lemelle, Jr. (Eds.), *Dilemmas of Black faculty at predominately white institutions in the United States.* (pp. 53-70). New York: Edwin Mellon.

Feagin, J. R. (2002). *The continuing significance of racism: U.S. colleges and universities.* Washington, DC: American Council on Education.

Feagin, J. R. (2010). *Racist America: roots, current realities, and future reparations, 2nd Edition.* New York: Routledge.

Lemelle, Jr. A. J. (2009). Social and economic organization of the Black professoriate at predominately-white colleges and universities. *Journal of African American Studies. 14*(1), 106-127.

Moore, S. E., Alexander, Jr., R., Lemelle, Jr., A. J. (Eds.). (2010). *Dilemmas of Black faculty at predominately White institutions in the United States: Issues in the post-multicultural era.* New York: Edwin Mellen.

Spry, T. (2006). Performing autoethnography: An embodied methodological praxis. In S. N. Hesse-Biber & P. Leavy (Eds.). *Emergent methods in social research.* (pp. 183–211). Thousand Oaks: Sage.

Trepagnier, B. (2006). *Silent racism: How well-meaning white people perpetuate the racial divide.* New York: Paradigm.

Turner, C. S. V., & Myers, S. (2000). *Faculty of color in academe: Bittersweet success.* Boston: Allyn & Bacon.

Twale, D.J & De Luca, B.M. (2008). *Faculty incivility: The rise of the academic bully culture and what to do about it.* San Francisco, CA: Jossey-Bass.

——————————————————————————————Part I

Black Female
Perspectives

Chapter One

Tracked for Life: Reflections from "Too Black" Professors

�֍

Robin L. Hughes & Natasha Flowers

Introduction

Turner and Myers (2000) reported that African American faculty at predominantly white institutions (PWIs) were of the opinion that visibility at their institutions was often based primarily on race rather than on scholarly activities or credentials. At the same time, the faculty expressed frustration over the belief that they were invisible and did not fit the view of what others considered the norm, based on what may be differences in their physical features. As a result, for faculty of color, the emphasis may be placed on their skin color and other visible ethnic features, while their scholarly achievements may be ignored. For women faculty of color, the challenge is an invisible marginality (Stanley 2006) which is attributed to being a woman as well as a person of color. When the number of faculty of color PWIs is low, those few individuals may face heavy service demands. A consequence of having significantly fewer numbers of faculty of color as compared to their White colleagues is that service responsibilities may become a burden due to the insufficient numbers; quite simply, "the few are doing the work of many" (Branch

2001, p. 181). Scholars of color also find that they are often asked to respond to requests for service that are imposed upon them due to the assumption that they are best suited for specific tasks because of their race and/or ethnicity (Turner & Myers 2000; Aguirre 2000), but may not have expertise in other areas. Furthermore, faculty of color are involved at significantly higher rates than White faculty with student groups who participate in service activities (antonio, Astin, & Cress 2000), so while teaching time was decreased, time allotted to service activities increased. The findings reinforce concerns that because the number of African American faculty at predominantly White institutions is low, these faculty may face greater demands for service than their White counterparts. Additionally, White faculty may be relieved of the responsibility, as well as the benefits that can be gained from working and interacting with a diverse student body.

This presents a dilemma for minority faculty since while there is the expectation to engage in service activities, that service is often, *not* recognized or rewarded in the promotion and tenure process. Padilla (1994) labeled this plight "cultural taxation,"

> The obligation to show good citizenship toward the institution by serving its need for ethnic representation on committees, or to demonstrate knowledge and commitment to a cultural group, which may even bring accolades to the institution but which is not usually rewarded by the institution on whose behalf the service was performed. (p. 26)

Turner (2002) specifically addressed African American women scholars and their having to often deal with a kind of multiple marginality in which they may be accorded a particular status, or subjected to certain treatments due to their race and gender. The intersection of the two factors can combine in subtle and unsubtle ways to create multiple obstacles in terms of the climate for African American women scholars in PWIs, who as a result likely experience the academy differently than their male counterparts.

Underneath the belly of this straightforward literature is the call for all of academia to consider the frameworks that battle for the survival and success for faculty of color. There are some fixed mind sets not unlike those that are seen in the kindergarten through high school classrooms. The essence of the damning tracking system my own field of study rallies against exists within the halls where multiple-degreed folk individually and collectively analyze process, persons, and places and their impact on achievement of learners. Academia has its own issues with privilege and oppression in the realm of ranking and promotion but there is still too much under-done in multicultural education and global studies that put these issues at the core (Leonardo 2002). While there are ongoing studies stemming from the early work of Sheila Gregory (1995) and Caro-line Turner (2000) that shed light on the tightrope of tenure and promotion in a "chilly climate," this kind of work is still peripheral to the other frameworks universities use to define their work and out-comes in faculty affairs. Offices for recruitment and retention still exist. Diversity officers are still hired. Targeted hiring and offices of equal opportunity are still critical. But how do we begin to push the conversation for those who are outside of the traditional trajectory: doctoral program to tenure track position. Is it important to ask the question of what is happening to those Black folks who are gradu-ating with doctoral degrees and confronting the harsh realities of academia off the tenure track?

While examining self in relation to others, the authors will use what Taliaferro Baszile (2008) offers as critical race testimony to move within the critical race theoretical framework, the "bearing witness" from the first person perspective where "the teller speaks not only on his or her behalf but in relationship to the group situa-tion from which and because of which she narrates" with this form revealing "feelings, or the extent to which what is or has happened has taken a toll on the lives of real people" (p. 253). As provocative and life-saving as the collection and sharing of counter-storytelling (Delgado 1989; Solorazano & Yosso 2002; Yosso 2006) and critical race narratives (Guitierrez-Jones 2001), the critical race testimony is one's own reflection of truth that releases one's own "traumas of racism" in their own words (p. 253). The two separate testimonies in this paper will not provide a formulaic pattern. The intention is to tell multiple truths related to the trauma of racism and some twinge of hope for recovery as seen from two individual Black female profes-sors, one recently tenured and one on the presently on the clinical track. The stories may overlap but there is no prioritizing the way in which we move and attack within this writing.

Relevance of this Study to the Existing Literature

While this chapter certainly intersects and supports some of the current, relevant literature regarding the experiences of African American women in the academy, it also includes some rather unique departures from the usual and the normal narratives of Black women experiences in higher education. In particular, one distinctive departure is some discussion about how each author took significant risk in negotiating and remaining academically and mentally authentic. We share intimate stories about how we tried to remain academically and mentally authentic to ourselves and our communities during the years towards tenure and long term contract in both narratives. Our discussion and therefore philosophical negotiations had to move beyond becoming passive aggressive types who play the game in order to move up into a system that is generally molded to create cookie cutter theory and players (Freire 2001; Turner & Myers 2000). We, instead, elected to subvert and transgress the dominant paradigm by employing new rules and changing the so-called game in order to live in this academic space (Solórzano & Yosso 2001).

More specifically, we articulate the experiences of two African American female faculty who have taught at different types of institutions. The experiences described here occurred in multiple contexts and settings, including those that have occurred in urban educational contexts, and those that have occurred in what we refer to as the traditional, "forever fall" campus settings (Natalicio 2001). These environments are particularly important in understanding the "flavor" of experiences of two Black female professors. These political environments play key roles in how we negotiated our own intellectual spaces. In this context, space holds multiple meanings such as the spaces in which our writing may appear, what we write, teach, and where we conduct our work, how one is supposed to act, and most importantly how to resist oppression and internalized racism.

Robin's Story

I have negotiated, and resisted certain constructions of tenure track-trickiness. I have written about topics that were important not only to me, but to the health and general concern for other African

Americans. Tenure tracking also has implications for where one is to share their work. For example, scholarly outlets represent the best locations and highest praise for faculty intellectual production although the readership tends to include other college faculty and perhaps small groups of practitioners. Yet, publishing in locations where readership is wider does not hold the same cache or prestige. The insular nature of what counts limits the voice and reach of faculty writing.

I also describe academic, political maneuvers—which sometimes meant speaking up during important policy gatherings and via other outlets even if my views seemed unfavorable despite the "threat of tenure" in the air. Speaking up also meant seeing the importance of including other voices and resisting the need to become a bully on the academic playground.

In this chapter, we also discuss the constancy of negotiating a reality that resembles that of the larger world context and not one narrowly defined by a select few who set and maintain the agenda for the rest of intellectual discourse in a small disciplinary space. In doing so, we visit the notions of paradigmatic shift lag (Hughes 2009) which is asymptomatic of what William Smith, Yosso & Solórzano (2006) refer to as racial battle fatigue. One suffers from shift lag when they try to fit a unique worldview into a discourse that is assumed static, unwilling, and unable to change or give to difference. Racial battle fatigue results from chronic exposure to discrimination. I also introduce the metaphor, college professor whispering (also referred to as prof—whispering). This is a professorial behavior modification technique that resembles many of the procedures used by that of Cesar Milan, the "dog whisperer," who uses behavior modification techniques, and good common sense to train badly behaving canines. The only difference is that the technique or theoretical framework is applied in academic settings where there may be badly behaving professors in regards to race and cultural competence who are in need of anti-racist training.

The Intellectual Meta-Narrative:
The Art of Intellectual War

My own academic journey can be described as an Art of Intellectual War (Machiavelli, 2001; Tzu, 1983). There has been, what I might describe as some intentional, psychological warfare. In a sense, I have had to arm myself with the necessary skills for intellectual and political combat. This included support from Special Forces (tenured faculty of color) and psychological heavy artillery (finding ways to maintain sanity while behind the enemy lines actions). I have been able to make decisions about how I should proceed across enemy territory. However, I am always surprised to find pushback in supposedly allied academic spaces. In fact, not only have I been a target of friendly fire on more than one occasion, but I can think of numerous incidents when allied forces seem to get confused. For instance, during a talk to critical educators, I stated that institutional and structural racist systems of opportunity and privilege still exist in the academy. Noticing the pushback—furrowed brows looked like neon signs plastered on folks' foreheads—the facial expressions alone told me that I should be prepared for an academic counter-strategy. I knew that I would have to engage the audience by providing raw intelligence and my own analysis of it. I had only moments to think about important composite examples that might lead them right back to their own academic and epistemological honesty. I assumed this maneuver to be fairly simple and successful. However, I did not anticipate that a few folks would refused to re-calibrate their thinking equipment. Racial and political roadblocks that I could make sense of with ease were difficult for them to see and understand. I explained that search committees are often the biggest political roadblocks for new hires of color in the academy. These committees often have difficulty trying to find faculty of color. It is then left up to socially conscious people of color or culturally competent others to re-train those committee members (Turner, Myers & Creswell 1999). We know that there are significant numbers of African American, Latino, Native American, and Asian American faculty who go untapped every year for positions in the academy. While this may have something to do with where one may be looking, we all know that it has even more to do with who is looking for whom, and why (Kulis & Miller 1988; Kanter 1977).

In fact, we know that the art of looking can be a difficult challenge for those scouts who have had little time in the field and who have spent even less time fully engaged with people from diverse groups (Katz 1991). The ability to see through a diverse set of epistemological lenses and a CRT lens are necessary to inform colleagues of the new ways in which racism may rear its ugly head. If committee members are ill-equipped to see systemic racism, or are culturally restrictive, then who gets in looks a lot like who has always been there (Kanter 1977; Chemers & Murphey 1995). Indeed, who gets invited inside the academy remains part of the ongoing framework of 21st century racism. Institutionalized racism is sophisticated and covert rather than the old days when racists burned crosses to demonstrate power and exercise social and cultural terrorism.

The new 21st century racism tends to exist in a complex field of hidden land mines, and coded languages. It represents a duplicitous process that needs to be descrambled and exposed by well trained racial justice oriented professionals. Institutionalized racism no longer focuses on separate eating establishments, signs on doors suggesting who is invited to sit at the table, or red-lining housing policies. Instead, 21st century racism leaves you questioning your sanity and ability to see what may be right in front of your own face. Institutionalized racism comes with a complete set of sophisticated and complex codes. The 21st century racial codes are more difficult to detect because they are embedded in diversity policy and welcoming language. For instance, with regards to search committees they tend to look for "right fit." This language could mean or imply a number of things, from research agenda, to personal temperaments and attitude, or ideology. However, when the same types of people are chosen repeatedly, the track record tends to speak for itself. Many institutions of higher education tend to believe that they have met their obligations by hiring one special person of color per department (Turner, Meyer & Creswell 1999). Interestingly, the same story does not hold for white women. They are the more widely accepted underrepresented group that benefits most from affirmative action policies (Staples 1995).

The Religious Awakening: Prove that Theory Exists

Many faculty of color are taken off guard when they find out that what they are supposed to write about and where it should get published has been predetermined by most promotion and tenure committees (Turner, Meyer & Creswell 1999). On the one hand, some faculty of color make what they feel are necessary adjustments in order to continue their travels to the mystical land of Oz by following the prescribed academic yellow brick road and yet others try to subvert it or leave it (Hughes and Giles 2009). However, in recent years, there has been a new discourse in which one may also be prepared to prove that particular ways of knowing are indeed valid or real.

During recent conversations across multiple settings, I have been asked to prove that Critical Race Theory exists. I am always befuddled by some of the questions that I am asked during presentations in certain academic settings. While I was taken off guard during the first encounter, I now tend to welcome the engagement. I can always use racism and whiteness and the scholarship from critical white scholars to make the case for the utility of CRT. Of course this occurs after a fairly lengthy speech on religious denominations, belief systems, epistemology, and why scholars tend to use particular methods, conceptual models, and theoretical frameworks. I typically suggest that folks read *Coloring Epistemologie*, by Drs. James Joseph Scheurich and Michelle D. Young, 1997 or Dr. Audrey Thompson's, *Tiffany: Friend of People of Color* (2003). I was particularly fond of these articles because these White scholars focus on whiteness and not folks of color. It is important for all scholars to realize that critical White scholars actually do pay attention to their own Whiteness and not what they can do for communities of color. In fact, the study of whiteness may just provide some insight to white people about white privilege, white supremacy and how to peal the multiple layers of the subtle nature of institutionalized racism to expose how it works through policy, administration, and life in general (Thompson, 2003; Leonardo, 2002).

Still, however, this sort of epistemological arrogance, dismissal of an entire line of research, history of social justice activism, and theory has surfaced more since I typically view my work through the lens of CRT. The response to my work and the work of others has lead me to respond both defensively and offensively. Defensively, I spend some time in conversations with "nonbelievers" engaging in conversation about the tenets of CRT, discussions about race, and how we all construct reality. I cannot say that I delight in the discussions, however, I am hopeful that newly minted Ph.D's who participate in this work will not have to cover this same ground in future years. I have learned to focus on my own sanity and what I have to do to better cope within hostile environments while doing this work. In doing so, I have found that using theoretical concepts, such as Gaslighting and behavior modification techniques borrowed from the theater and animal psychology, most useful.

A Word on Teaching an Old Professor New Tricks: The College Prof. Whisperer

While Cezar Milan, the Dog Whisperer, provides techniques to control and train naughty and unruly dogs, I found that similar methods could be tweaked to re-train the culturally and racially insensitive, unruly, and naughty college professor. Lessons on redirecting poor behavior and tolerance of diverse ideology and epistemology have proven to be most useful. Teaching naughty professors lessons that they may have missed early on in their training, like how to get along with others who may think differently, or how to approach different policies, procedures, pedagogy, paradigms, and ways of sharing information have all been introduced to some naughty and unruly professors with some success. Although this work is difficult and time consuming, I am glad to report that after a few years, there are a few people who have changed as a result of college professor behavioral training school with flying colors and little knowledge that they had been re-trained.

Other forms of psychological training have also proved beneficial. The 1940s Hollywood film *Gaslight*, seems to provide some psychological behavioral utility as well. The movie portrays, a money hungry husband, who tries to rid himself of a wife to get some jewels hidden in the house, by convincing her that she is mentally unstable, that her perceptions are not real, and that she has serious psychological problems. The wife, goes from strong-willed and confident to doubting her own self-worth and her own notion of what is reality. I have used the gaslight lens to not only assist ignorant and unyielding faculty members to consider and sometimes accept theories that come from a reality that not only exist, but help their own understanding of the legitimacy of diverse perspectives. I know examples of junior faculty of color who were gas lighted. They were gaslighted into believing that their word was inappropriate in any academic space.

I have witnessed three responses to gaslighting. First, faculty either find legitimacy or shift their own reality into that of an imminent White scholar's mainstream work. The junior scholar of color seeks to co-publish with the white scholar to become real and legitimate. Second, they change how they conduct and or report their work altogether. In other words, their style of writing changes, where they publish changes, and there is a total rejection of a once organic interest and research agenda. Third, on rare occasion, the faculty member will struggle to maintain their own organic and authentic sense of self by writing and publishing in spaces where their work is most appreciated—through readership and praxis.

Most importantly, however, all suffer through significant bouts of paradigmatic shift lag (Hughes 2009) and racial battle fatigue (Smith et al 2006). No matter what route one decides to take, the political discourse and rules change constantly to fit another reality—the reality of faculty of color working in white spaces. Similar to the manipulations of the husband against the wife in that movie, someone eventually might believe that they are insane.

Natasha's Story

Clinical Tracked

To complicate the matter, there is this minority group within the faculty of color base: the clinical faculty member. Described differently across schools and campuses, the clinical faculty member is mainly considered a faculty member with rank who is not on the tenure track. On my campus, the acronym, NTT, is often used and it does not need the letter "o" to emphasize the role's limitations.

Stuck between the hard place of pursing a long-term contract with slipping hope of a tenure track rank is not uncommon for the thousands of PhDs who have a perfectly formatted dissertation, a few campus visits, and a love-hate relationship with lectureships. A peek into *The Chronicle of Higher Education*'s discussion forum on non-tenure track or job-seeking experiences highlight the despair of juggling working to live and writing to find "real" work. What is missing is the silent voice of the hundreds of people of color with PhDs who are wondering what really stalled an appointment in a market where people of color are purportedly a prize commodity.

Instead there is a "damaged goods" shame that might describe a Black female faculty member's reflection on three or more years walking alongside the tenure track but not on it. This shame is not unique to Black faculty but any real consideration of racist structures makes it difficult to just focus on "individual merit, exceptionality and hard work" as many white Americans do (Leonardo 2002). One Black female clinical assistant professor's experiences can easily protest the notion of work ethic and intellectual prowess as sole barriers to positioning toward the tenure track. The forces of privilege and the higher education version of the "second-generation discrimination" are just as endemic to this woman's experiences as her own individual choices and misunderstandings about academia.

(W.W.R) Writing while Racing Alongside the Tenure Track

Pushing forward while not obsessing about the common practice to hire the "freshly minted" PhDs, there are many, like myself, who try to contribute to the field through essays and publications. In the back of my mind, I hear one faculty member's insight regarding writing, "Research is currency." In my clinical track position, I felt pressured to focus on K-12 literature and I felt that I had somehow pulled a wool over the eyes of others with a curriculum and instruction degree and a dissertation that had a strong bent toward college faculty development. What a mess! However, I slowly began to see that my own inquiry was not a mistake but part of my path toward contributing to various areas in education literature. With a dissertation on the classroom practices and teaching philosophies of Black faculty and a climate study of faculty of color, I had to claim my own perspective and my own passion. Frankly, I had to pay more attention to why I could not put down books such as Battle & Doswell's (2004) *Building Bridges for Women of Color in Higher Education* and articles by such as scholars Stanley (2006) on the experiences of faculty of color. These works are more than guidelines for me; it is important literature that should be read by more than just faculty of color.

However, after offering workshops and listening to faculty of color share how focus and passion are mistaken for narrow-mindedness and anger and how their expertise are questioned by students and white colleagues alike, I knew that there was research that faculty, chairs, deans, faculty development specialists, and graduate students needed to access. This literature needed to emphasize that these perspectives are not solely created in the minds of those who perceive them. Interactions, policies, and practices are just as critical to the perspectives of faculty of color and the lens we use to "see and hear" what is presented. Multicultural initiatives are not equipped fully to confront power and subordination. My experiences and what I repeatedly heard and read in the literature made it difficult for me to ignore the symptom of not wanting to face that race is a factor of inequity (Ladson-Billings & Tate 1995). I could no longer deny that the question of whiteness was still unexamined by me or by workshop participants. Whiteness lurked in and around the discussions but the etiquette of feel-good workshops suffocated any critical race dialogue or testimony. Sadly, when the opportunity to capture the voices of the university's faculty of color in the campus climate study I previously mentioned, the framework of critical race theory remained buried. I, along with the campus, was not ready to put the question of race and racism on the table as a part of the institutional policies and practices that impacted the promotion and tenure of faculty of color. Without this particular lens, any related work would be insufficient and superficial because any outcomes or lack of progress could not be pinned on "the absolute right to exclude" (Ladson-Billings & Tate 1995, p. 23) or the "whites only" construct that may still exist in the Obama era.

As I relate this to my own writing, I confess that my own attention to critical race theory is part of finding a voice that is not afraid to examine race as a part of the multicultural education. I was comfortable with showcasing talent, projecting statistics of faculty of color hiring trends, and supporting faculty at the initial phase of Banks' levels of integrating ethnic content. I focused on the inclusion of multicultural perspectives rather than persistently asking the question of why there is exclusion. I will continue to pose the question to myself and to my colleagues (professors and administrators): how can you write about Black folks and not consider a framework to help center race and racism especially when you are unfolding issues of equity and inclusion?

(T.W.R) Teaching While Racing

With the uncomfortable truth looming from the pages of the climate study, I moved into a faculty position knowing that many faculty of color may focus on exemplary teaching before setting up a solid research agenda (Cooper, 2006). Therefore, a teaching professor position would have a clear standard of teaching excellence that I would not be able to ignore during my first years. Any scholarship had to be prioritized within the realm of teaching and learning. Of course, I was a bit overly confident about my own reflective skills and my ability to resolve any issues in the classroom. I had a dissertation study focused on Black professor's philosophies and practices in multicultural classrooms and knew about the pressure to confront appropriately students' biases and resistance to new perspectives. The thrill of new challenges in a new environment was not to squelch the question of what the diversity course really meant to others and what the course meant to me.

Early on I saw the diversity course set ashore without an anchor. Interns were not seeing a direct connection between race and equity and state legislation was showing an even clearer confusion and disdain for too much "fluff" and not enough content.

Students and state leaders all expressed concern for the achievement gaps with three cheers for cultural competence. Nonetheless, there was still no sign of close attention to the complexity of race and reality of racism in terms of content, instruction, and assessment. Interns were even noticing a large number of Black students labeled with individual educational plans. However any conclusions built from a critical race theoretical perspective were not emerging. Yet I walked into classrooms hoping that a spark is lit by the end of sixteen weeks that will not be extinguished by the final course of the program. Knowing that there is so much conversation about what should be included in a diversity course but little conversation about what issues of race, equity and inclusion are missing from methods courses. As many other faculty report, there are tears, debates, and a distracting silence awaiting me each class session where values are challenged and not affirmed.

Frankly, those tears also position me as Leonardo (2002) noted, "as the perpetrator of a hurt" (Leonardo 2002). In so doing, admittedly

I have worked hard to reverse the repugnant positionality impressed upon me. I am in a few hours or days of a semester, thrown into a struggle to center race and decenter whiteness so that whiteness can be centered as a construct that impacts children's achievement and success in schools. I needed almost two years to recover from that intensity. Instead of journaling or jotting down ideas for papers, honestly, I narrowed my focus on how to challenge my students while still supporting their own identity development. With no semblance of the sentiment of one graduate student who wrote about how a critical race theory course changed her perspective on her role as a white person in a racist society (Morgan, 2006), my students' comments sounded more like, "I know there is a privilege to being Black. Why are we talking about white privilege?" Or questions like, "Does the other section of this class talk about black children and white privilege this much?" They never seemed to consider that every two weeks meant a new cultural dimension or issue of equity.

Ironically, only two or three students out of each course section mentioned the impact (positive or negative) of race-centered discussions in their final reflection paper. They spend so much time debating it until the end when they can easily forget it exists by not extending its life outside of those discussions. Like a therapist, I had to give them the white students the couch, keep the conversation going, and scaffold some important revelations. I did begin to share more than my state of origin but my experience as a child of a Black man who had spent time in prison and my own awakenings of what I had decided to hold dear and what I released as one of few Black college students on a predominantly white college campus. I had to let the story unfold and be clear about my own personal and scholarly understanding of race as a construct with its own set of rules. As Taliaferro Baszile eloquently proclaimed: "Essentially, although my pedagogical approach was consistent with academia's traditional ideas about proper pedagogies, it was mainly inconsistent with my pedagogical desire to teach about race and racism in ways that would change lives, or at least perspectives" (p.252). Like she lamented, neutrality does not exist from either the student perspective or the teacher's.

As a result of sharing some of my critical race testimony, I am also on the brink of what Berry (2005, p. 47) calls, a "personally engaged pedagogy," derived from her own critical race feminist perspective, that allows her to be accountable for all the students in the classroom, especially her Black students in the teacher education classroom. I had to recognize the hypnotic nature of my white students' resistance against race dialogue and how it negatively impacted my work and real integration of the few students of color in the classroom.

Getting Served by Service

Benjamin Baez (2000) instantly opened my eyes with his thoughtful paper on service from a Black faculty member's perspective. It was like the sermon that every sinner needs to hear. Instead of just focusing on teaching and writing, I could not resist the advocacy bone in my body. I had to know why policies and practices were upheld and some other issues were not openly discussed. I needed access to the truth of my own school. I agree with Dewey about learning by doing. I couldn't just sit in my office reading the emails and walking around in the dark. After one year of just teaching, I grabbed governance roles within the school (co-chair of faculty meetings), diversity committee, and after a year more, I reviewed course design and transformation as a member of the clinical faculty merit review. No one should doubt that I did not sign up for our school's diversity committee and help with multicultural recruitment efforts.

I could not in my own mind negotiate the desire to be a sanctioned member of my school's "family" and my own understanding of how service can become the slippery slope for so many faculty (Baez 2000).

While any mentor would have slapped the hand of a mentee who had a decent chance of getting an assistant professor appointment, I had no one even challenging my decisions. I knew the tenure track clock was ticking and my running shoes were wearing out, but I saw myself as a part of a small collective weeding out privileged spaces and extending the conversation past polite stagnancy. However, I still observed Black and Latino faculty within and outside of my department looking for the outstanding mentorship Amaury Nora received by a person in his field (2000). The extended description of his mentor reads like the true sponsorship of a person's professional development with the support of a privileged person's capital and that person's unwavering belief in the person of color's contribution to the field. Without knowing the specifics of the relationship between Nora and his mentor, the description still burns in my memory because it was such a fairy tale given what I knew about the hardship of faculty of color and my own lack of a mentor.

Again, questions bubbled to the top of my admiration for such relationships. Was there a critical race construct at the center of this relationship? Did notions of race or racism circle the wagons of Nora's success? I should mention that I have used Nora's details along with Stanley & Lincoln's upfront lessons of trust and openness in cross-racial mentoring (2005) as part of retention workshops' promises of what could be at any university, school or department. Those questions remain relevant as they mirror my own critical race testimony and could not be omitted from any present or future mentor-mentee relationship I hope to have.

Picking up speed

As I began to reframe and reset for next phase of my journey, I am not afraid to take responsibility for my own choices and I am not afraid to take the time to revisit my journey from a critical race perspective. This writing is not a shaming of any person but a part of the awakening that many scholars of color and critical white scholars like Thompson have tried to get across to all of us. We cannot just blindly interact, collaborate, mentor, and progress through the structure of higher education without some attention to the power and the oppression that the construct of race helps to illuminate.

We are not without the tools of critical race narratives and critical race testimonies to help conquer the anguish of racism, but we must be prepared to admit our own actions and reactions in the relationships we foster in the academy. As a clinical professor, I can focus on the limitations of the rank itself and I can revisit the perceived magnified marginalization of my faculty post. However, I must still maintain a sense of self-worth in any post and continue to challenge the power structures and structural racism that creeps into all ranks of faculty life.

Critical race theory can be so overwhelming to the scholar who has embraced Blackness as beautiful without really taking the time to look at what racism has done to negate the beauty by permitting celebration but little to no professional elevation. Critical race theory also gives me a stronger perspective on class and gender struggles that intersect with the victimization of racism. There is no looking for racism but putting the construct of race on the table as a powerful way to understand the weakness of meritocracy and fairness as the pillars of academic life.

As I began to broaden my perspectives and allow a more critical lens to take form, I was like that newly single person: ready for the experience of collaboration and authentic interaction. Two Black assistant professors specifically invited me to join them on two distinct research projects. I was no longer trapped by the small numbers of faculty of color or frustrated by the lack of mentorship for a clinical faculty member of color. I had to simply seek out folks who were comfortable with a discussion about the struggle and confident in their own role in contributing to solutions. My current rank and position is just part of what I needed to find my voice before someone told me what voice I needed to have. Just as Solórzano & Yosso (2001) and Freire (1970) warn, resistance can be the death of your own progress if it is leading you back to the subordination you abhor. I must be aware of how my own self-examination can promulgate a desire to be more like those who have the power when having their power in their context would not do anything for me or faculty of color. I have control of what mental track I am on, with or without a formal search process. I am free to write. I am free to teach. I am free to learn. I am free to examine.

References

Aguirre, Jr., A. (2000). Women and minority faculty in the academic workplace: Recruitment, retention, and academic culture. *ASHE-ERIC Higher Education Report, 27*(6).

antonio, a.l., Astin, H.S., & Cross, C.M. (2000). Community service in higher education: A look at the nation's faculty. *The Review of Higher Education, 23*(4), 373-398.

Baez, B. (2000). Race-related service and faculty of color: conceptualizing critical agency in academe. *The Review of Higher Education, 39*, 363-391.

Baszile, D.T. (2008). Beyond all reason indeed: the pedagogical promise of critical race testimony. *Race, Ethnicity, and Education, 11*(3), 251-265.

Battle, C.Y. & Doswell, C.M. (2004). *Building bridges for women of color in higher education: A practical guide for success.* Dallas: University Press of America.

Berry, T. R. (2005). Black on Black education: Personally engaged pedagogy for/ by African American pre-service teachers. *Urban Review, 37* (1), 31-48.

Chemers, M.M. & Murphy, S.E. (1995). Leadership and diversity in groups and organizations. In M.M. Chemers, S. Oskamp, & M.A. Costanzo (Eds.). *Diversity in Organizations: New Perspectives for a Changing Workplace* (pp. 157-190). Thousand Oaks, CA: Sage.

Delgado, R. (1989). Storytelling for oppositionalists and others: A plea for narrative. *Michigan Law Review, 87*(2), 411-41.

Freire, P. (2001). *Pedagogy of the Oppressed.* New York, New York: Continuum International Publishing Group. New York, New York.

Gutierrez-Jones, C.S. (2001). *Critical race narratives: A study of race, rhetoric, andinjury.* New York: New York University.

Gregory, S. T. (1995). *Black women in the academy: The secrets to success and achievement.* Lanham, MD: University of Press of America.

Hughes, R. L. (2009). Evaluating difference: Paradigmatic shift lag. *Teachers College Record, http://www.tcrecord.org/Content.asp?ContentID=15630*

Hughes R. L., & Giles, M. (2010). CRiT walking in higher education: Activating critical race theory in the academy. *Journal of Race, Ethnicity and Education, 13*(1), 41-57.

Kanter, R. M. 1977. *Men and women of the corporation.* New York: Basic Books,

Katz, J. (1991). White faculty struggling with the effects of racism. In P. Altbach & K. Lomotey (Eds.), *The racial crisis in American higher education* (pp. 187-196). New York, NY: University of New York.

Kulis, S. & Miller, K. (1988). Are Minority Women Sociologists in Double Jeopardy? *The American Sociologist. 19*(4), 323-339.

Leonardo, Z. (2002). The souls of white folks: critical pedagogy, whiteness studies, and globalization discourse. *Race, Ethnicity, and Education, 5,* 29-50.

Lynn, M. (1999). Toward a critical race pedagogy: A research note. *Urban Education, 33,* 606-626.

Ladson-Billings, G. & Tate, W.F. (1995). Toward a critical race theory of education. *Teachers College Record, 97*(1), 47-68.

Machiavelli, N. (2001). Cambridge, Mass: De Capo Press.

Morgan, A. (2006). Confronting myself: Looking through the lens of critical race theory. *Adult Learning, 17,* (1-4), 16-18.

Nora, A. (2000). Balancing research, teaching, and service. In M. Garcia's (Ed.), *Succeeding in an academic career: A guide for faculty of color.* Greenwood Publishing Group.

Padilla, A.M. (1994). Ethnic minority scholars, research, and mentoring: Current and future issues. *Educational Researcher, 23*(4), 24-27.

Scheurich, J. J., & Young, M. D. (1997). Coloring epistemologies: Are our research epistemologies racially biased? *Educational Researcher, 26*(4), 4-16.

Solórzano, D.G. & Yosso, T.J. (2002). Critical race methodology: Counterstorytelling asanalytical framework for education research. *Qualitative inquiry, 8*(1), 24-44.

Solórzano, D.G. & Yosso, T.J. (2001). Critical race and latcrit theory and method: Counterstorytelling chicana and chicano graduate school xxperiences. *International Journal of Qualitative Studies in Education, 14*(4), 371-395.

Smith, W.A., T.J. Yosso, & D.G. Solórzano. (2006). Challenging racial battle fatigue on historically white campuses: A critical race examination of race-related stress. In C.A. Stanley (Ed.). *Faculty of Color: Teaching in Predominantly White Colleges and Universities.* (pp. 299-327). Bolton, MA: Anker.

Stanley, C.A. & Lincoln, Y.S. (2005). Cross-race faculty mentoring. *Change. 37*(2), 44-52.

Stanley, C. (2006). Coloring the academic landscape: Faculty of colorbreaking the silence in predominantly white colleges and universities. *American Educational Research Journal, 43*(4), 701-736.

Staples, R. (1995). Black deprivation-White privilege: The assault on affirmative action. *The Black Scholar , 25*(3), 2-6.

Tatum, B. D. (1997). *The complexity of identity: "Who am I?" Why are all the black kids sitting together in the cafeteria and other conversations about race.* New York: Basic Books.

Thompson, A. (2003). Tiffany, friend of people of color: White investments in antiracism. *Qualitative Studies in Education, 16*(1), 7-29.

Turner, C. S., Myers, S. L., Jr., & Creswell, J. W. (1999). Exploring underrepresentation: The case of faculty of color in the Midwest. *Journal of Higher Education, 70*, 27-59

Turner, C.S.V. & Myers, S.L. (2000). *Faculty of color in academe: Bittersweet success.* Boston: Allyn and Bacon.

Tzu, Sun (1983). *The Art of War.* Boston mass: Shambhala Press. Translated by Cleary, Thomas.

West, C. (2001). *Race matters.* New York, NY: Vintage Books.

Yosso, T.J. (2006). *Critical race counterstories along the Chicano/Chicana educational pipeline.* New York: Routledge.

Chapter Two

Black Women Faculty in Predominantly White Space: Negotiating Discourses of Diversity

❋

Alma Jean Billingslea Brown

From Mary Jane Patterson, who in 1862 became the first African American woman to earn the B.A. degree, to Anna Julia Cooper, whose dissertation on the Haitian Revolution earned her a PhD from the University of Paris, Sorbonne in 1925, black women in white academic space have historically contested and challenged practices of racialized gender and class exclusion. One consequence of that challenge has been that black women in the professoriate, from the 19th century through the first decades of the 21st century, have been instrumental in mapping new intellectual terrain as well as sustaining what bell hooks calls the "revolutionary fervor" to gain access to and transform the academy (hooks 1989, p.50). However today with decreasing numbers of black women entering institutions of higher education as faculty and data showing that once hired, they are not being retained, promoted and tenured, the stories of black women challenging the strictures of racism and sexism in the academy now resonate with some urgency and need to be told.

What I want to do here is look at the stories and histories of black women faculty who have negotiated a culture of power not their own and how their stories substantiate that practices of dominance and exclusion in white academic spaces are still alive and well. At the same time, with some attention to the history and the complexity of diversity work in higher education, I want to also identify the strategies black women have devised to challenge exclusionary practices, isolationism, academic apartheid and other practices of racial and gender discrimination in predominantly white institutions.

Marian Wright Edelman, civil rights activist, founder of the Children's Defense Fund, and the first African American woman to pass the Mississippi State bar examination, often tells the story of how her family's social justice work in the small town of her birth, Bennettsville, South Carolina, shaped her activist work as a student and her leadership role in the 1960s Atlanta Student movement. Edelman also explains how the mentoring she received as a student and the influence of women whom she calls Great Black Women Mentors, Harriet Tubman, Sojourner Truth, Ella Baker and Septima Clark, helped her to make difficult career and professional choices. Despite her success as a civil rights attorney, Edelman has declared publicly that the United States, at this point in time, does not need any more black women lawyers. "What the country needs instead, is more black women law *professors.*" Referencing the power of the professoriate, whether in undergraduate liberal arts, graduate or professional schools, to map academic and intellectual terrain, Edelman's statement also recognizes the power of black and minority faculty to contest enclosed curricula and disrupt institutional authority. It is useful to note that Edelman prefaced her declaration for more black women in the professoriate with her own history and story. Stories, as narratives that mirror self and society in time and space, can be especially useful in the work of social justice. They communicate the ideas, memories and insights of the individual who recounts them and have the capacity to "transgress the structures of domination and can reproduce and affirm the struggle for voice by those on the wrong side of the power relationships" (Clough 1988, p.3; Denzin 1989, p.82).

Edelman, as representative and symbol of how the 1960s black freedom struggle forced white institutions to grant access to blacks and other minority groups, may have been one of the first to experience how black women in law, like black women in the academy, not only suffer inequities but also find that their perspectives, values, and voices are ignored, deemed irrelevant and excluded. One may speculate that such inequities may have influenced Edelman's decision to do social justice work in arenas other than law.

Karla Holloway, noted literary critic and theorist and currently Professor of English and Law at Duke University, has also written about the challenges black women face in having their perspectives, voices and work recognized in the academy. Holloway's story offers another compelling example of how marginalizing and branding black women's intellectual work, their research and scholarship as inferior, constitute a particular kind of segregation, an "apartheid of knowledge" in the U.S. academy. In 1987, Holloway co-authored and published an early and seminal study in literary criticism, *New Dimensions of Spirituality: A Biracial and Bicultural Reading of the Novels of Toni Morrison.* Holloway explains how her colleagues questioned the work she and her co-author, Stephanie Demetrakopoulos (1987), were doing and whether Toni Morrison was worthy of a full-length book study. She describes their experience,

> Our project was consistently denied financial support, its validity questioned; our critics queried not only the worthiness of the author we proposed to study ("Was Morrison really worth that kind of attention?" we were asked), but the worthwhileness of criticism that cared about the critic's social and political evolution (Holloway and Demetrakopoulos. (p.168)

To name and contest the practice of making black women's scholarship and the scholarship on black women writer irrelevant, Holloway not only exposes her colleagues but names the origin and source of the practice. "What other than racism, ignorance and incredible short-sightedness could fail to recognize the status of an author like Toni Morrison?"(Holloway and Demetrakopoulos 1987, p.169)

Holloway's story is a useful example of how race and gender intersect, interrelate, and transform each other in the experience of black women academics. Ordinarily a black faculty woman's collaboration with a white woman faculty member would have mediated, if not erased, race. But because the research was on another black woman, albeit a well-known writer, and because the study examined the influence of Holloway's and Demetrakopoulos' racial and cultural backgrounds on their respective readings of Morrison's fiction, the study situated race rather than gender as a primary marker. For that reason, as Holloway so accurately discerned, their work elicited racist and supremacist response. Gender, rather than erasing race, I want to suggest, simply caused a reconfiguration of the pattern of racism.

Another way in which the "apartheid of knowledge" operates for black women academics is described by Heidi Mirza in her study, "Transcendence over Diversity: Black Women in the Academy." Using the research from a number of sources, Mirza (2006) affirms a similar phenomenon experienced by black women faculty in predominantly white institutions in Britain who struggle, in a similar way,

> ...against the presumption that scholars of colour are narrowly focused or lacking in intellectual depth...whatever our history, what ever our record, whatever our validations, whatever our accomplishments, by and large we are perceived as one-dimensional and treated accordingly...fit for addressing the marginal subjects of race, but not subjects in the core curriculum. (p. 4)

Minimizing the value, quality and significance of the scholarship by black women faculty on both sides of the Atlantic remains a key strategy for denying them tenure and promotion. Looking at studies which indicate that minority faculty in general find promotion and tenure procedures to be ambiguous, inappropriate and unfairly weighed, Sheila Gregory (2001) explains that the result for U.S. black women especially is a "revolving door syndrome,"

> This syndrome manifests itself when minorities/women are appointed on tenure track, kept four to six years, evaluated unfavorably for tenure and required to leave. This

> up-and-out process may be repeated at numerous institu-
> tions until the unsuccessful participants opt to leave the
> academy altogether. (p.29)

The "unfairly weighed" tenure decisions that create this revolving door, Gregory goes on to explain, begin with regarding the work of black women faculty as irrelevant and inferior, particularly in U.S. research institutions where faculty members are required to produce a certain amount of research and publish in majority-dominated, refereed journals. Because black women faculty frequently conduct research and write on issues relevant to their communities and publish in journals that focus on minority issues, their publications are not regarded as scholarly work or as making significant contributions to their fields. Again, as Gregory (2001) explains,

> For black faculty women, this can create a complex chal-
> lenge because many tend to focus their research in the
> very areas where they teach and provide community
> service. (p.129)

The experience of one black woman faculty member at a research institution in the Midwest is exemplary. Tenured with a joint appointment in Women's Studies and her primary discipline, this faculty member used community-based research, a series of interviews and oral histories of black women in rural and semi-rural communities as the basis for a study documenting the experiences, perceptions and contributions of black women in a Midwestern state. Although the study was published by a university press, reviewed and well-received, it was deemed not relevant to the scholar's field. She was consequently denied promotion to full professor. Even more compelling is the story of the Afro-Cuban social scientist whose work on orisha-based religions and alternative spiritual traditions in Afro-Latin communities throughout the diaspora was not deemed scholarly because of her experiential background and family relations: a member of her family was a priestess/practitioner of the religion. When this faculty member changed her focus from her own ethnic group to another African Diaspora community, her work was still unfairly evaluated and she was denied tenure.

In many instances when black women are successful in negotiating hierarchical structures and supremacist practices to gain access to and secure faculty positions and even tenure in white institutions, they may still be confronted with another well-known strategy to deny women and minorities equity in the academic workplace. In such instances, although these women may be visible in tenure-track or tenured positions, but they are excluded from the mainstream of academic activity and "contextually entrapped", to paraphrase Sheila Gregory, into roles in which they are perceived and may even see themselves as tokens, anomalies and curiosities (Gregory 2001: 129). During the early days of affirmative action, the African American vernacular folk term used to name this role and strategy was the "onliest one," a role still fraught with danger.

The role of token or the "only" black or black woman faculty has been generally understood to be the role of gatekeeper whose primary purpose is to disprove, just by her presence, allegations of institutional racism and/or sexism and to justify not hiring or promoting minorities. But for black women faculty in particular, the role of token assumes yet another dimension because in the context of affirmative action, black women were "twofers." Occupying a singular, third space and fulfilling needs or quotas for race and gender representation, black women often assumed such roles without a clear understanding of how these roles were complicit with strategies of concealment and structures of subordination and constituted a kind of academic servitude.

It is important to note, however, that perhaps the greater danger of tokenism and gate keeping is that these roles move beyond complicity with the structures of domination and subordination. The greater danger inheres in the cost and the consequences to individual women especially in terms of identity. Theorizing how, in order to perform as scholars, black faculty in white institutions in the United States, have to embody the bigotries, exclusionary practices and rationales of the privileged white and male elite founders of these institutions, Anthony J. Lemelle Jr. (2009), has suggested that to undo the condition of this complicity or academic servitude, black faculty have to use what he calls "reflexive logic." They have to interrogate and ultimately refute the epistemologies of privileged and powerful groups. If they fail to do so, Lemelle goes on to explain,

...they perform before colleagues and students as if they are not a privileged or subordinating social class. They behave as if the knowledge they impart is not complicit in segmental degradation and humiliation in the professoriate and in society. In this pretense, individuals imagine favorable personal accomplishments when the facts do not warrant it... [and] mislead their students as "role models." (pp.17-18)

For those black women faculty who reject the role of token and refuse to affirm elite, white male categories of scholarly knowledge and judgment, the consequences can be costly. In both their personal and professional lives, isolationism is amongst the most common cost and consequence.

Consider the story of a black woman assistant professor who had been enthusiastically recruited by a large institution in the state university system of California. Notwithstanding the fact that having come to campus a few days early in jeans and sweatshirt to clean her office, she was approached by a white faculty member who expressed her gratitude at seeing that the university "had finally hired someone to clean the ladies room," this new junior faculty member was still able to see colleagues on campus and within her department as friendly and collegial. Within a few months, however, she noticed that two white male faculty members who had been hired in her same divisional cohort, albeit in different departments, would mention grant and research opportunities and faculty development workshops about which she had not been given any information. These same two men also soon became part of campus-wide, social and professional networks which she had been unable to penetrate. This black woman faculty member, who was married with school-age children, also experienced additional demands on her time from community and other service obligations related to her family and children.

But she was bright, energetic, and positive, so she persevered, publishing high quality scholarship in refereed journals and performing service at the departmental, campus and national level. Active in professional organizations in her field, she presented regularly at conferences but at the beginning of the sixth year began to experience some uneasiness. Her first concern was that, contrary to what she had been told at the time she was hired, there had been no effort made to build a program and hire more faculty in her area. After six years she remained the only one. The second concern, once she began to prepare her tenure portfolio, was how her work would be evaluated. And so she took the risk of approaching a senior colleague in her department to get some indication of the expected number of publications and how her teaching and service were regarded. She was shocked by the response. What she was told, albeit in indirect, nuanced language, was that neither the quality, quantity or place-ment of her publications nor her service or her teaching were of any real concern to her department. A visible, well-liked token, she was virtually assured of tenure. All she had to do was continue in her role as gatekeeper and protect the university from allegations of racism and sexism. Soon after she secured an appointment at a smaller institution with a more diverse faculty and student population, this assistant professor resigned before submitting her portfolio.

While this story of tokenism, isolationism, and exclusion, expe-rienced specifically as the inability to join existing networks or to form new ones, ultimately had a relatively favorable outcome for this faculty member, there was yet another dimension to her story that bears relation to this discussion. At the point that this black woman faculty member discovered she was being shut out from networks and opportunities afforded to her white male colleagues, she started to attend events organized by the campus office of diver-sity. But what she learned was that diversity at this institution was focused primarily to four manifestations of human difference, age, gender, sexual orientation and ability, all of which functioned, in a very subtle way, to erase race as a significant category of differ-ence and diversity. What she also discovered was that the diversity discourse had been recorded as a kind of non-threatening multi-culturalism which permitted the same structures of domination to operate. Realizing that the office of diversity would offer her no help and was in fact complicit with practice of diversity as another way of "doing advantage" rather than "challenging disadvantage" (Mirza 2006, p. 7), this assistant professor simply left the institution.

While scholars in both the United States and Britain have sub-jected the philosophy, practice and discourse of diversity to critique, charging that diversity programs have come out of a "thrust for global markets and aversion to accusations of institutional racism"(Mirza 2006, p.1), it is useful to consider that practices of diversity may represent "a bigger sea of change in how to conceptualize the attainment of racial and social justice in society" (Mirza 2006, p.4). In the same way, while Frank W. Hale, Jr. admits that "It is an illusion to believe that diversity in its genuine sense is alive and well in the academy" (Hale 2004, p.13), it is just as useful to remember that the U.S. academy historically has been and remains, as Angela Davis discerns, "an important site for political contestation of racism, sexism and homophobia" (Davis 1994, p. 423). These differing attitudes and assessments of diversity necessarily mean that questions arise. Who represents diversity? What is its origin and source in U.S. institutions of higher education? Is it possible for black women faculty to negotiate current attitudes, practices, and paradoxes with regard to diversity to actualize its potential for equity and fairness in higher education? How can black women subvert the practice of institutions proclaiming that they are "being diverse" to conceal the fact that they are not really "doing diversity"? (Mirza 2006, pp. 6-7). This discussion, seeking to frame the experiences of black women faculty in predominantly white institutions through individual histories and stories, cannot respond to all of the questions. I believe it is useful, however, to offer some background on the origin and source of the diversity discourse in U.S. higher education.

The term "diversity," as Raymond A. Winbush explains, for U.S. institutions of higher education became popular after the publication of the 1987 Hudson Institute study by William B. Johnston and Arnold Packer, *Workforce 2000: Work and Workers for the 21st Century*. Commissioned by the Department of Labor during the Reagan administration, the study found that if the United States intended to sustain its dominance of labor and trade markets, it would have to use its entire labor force and include those who had been historically marginalized because of race, gender, age, disability and sexual orientation. Winbush goes on to explain two other factors which influenced the shift to "diversity" as the new discourse for equity and fairness in higher education. The first was that U.S. workforce dominated historically by white males in the 19th and 20th century would not be the reality of the 21st century. The projection that white males would comprise fewer than 20% of the workforce by the beginning of the 21st century meant that enlarging the workforce would have to be a primary goal. The second was that because corporations and government agencies began to see universities as "farm teams" for educating a this diverse workforce, institutions of higher education "set as priority the expanded inclusion of women, students of color, physically challenged individuals and non-traditional students...(Winbush 2004, p. 33). Identifying one of the original complexities surrounding the discourse of diversity as it was articulated in the 1990s, Winbush (2004) concludes,

> It is a paradox that the recognition of diversity as important for maintaining the United States' competitive edge in the workforce occurred during the period when there was a simultaneous chilling affect plaguing the very strategy— affirmative action—that could accelerate its growth. (p.33)

Just as "race" suddenly became an unfashionable word ,"diversity" and "multiculturalism" just as suddenly became the preferred terms in the new lexicon. As Winbush (2004) states, "Eventually affirmative action in both word and deed was relegated to obscurity" (p.35). But as the death knoll for affirmative action was sounded in law, the media, the workplace and the university, thoughtful people knew and understood the real agenda of anti-affirmative action proponents. What the adversaries of affirmation action wanted was a return to the acceptance of inequities in U.S. society as routine or worse still to the system of masking white privilege. As Frank Hale, Jr. (2008) explains, there had always been affirmative action for white males in U.S. society.

> People of color did not invent affirmative action, which had been running full speed for whites long before the 1960s. Was it not selective admissions for whites for more than two centuries that kept black people out of white institutions of higher education? (p.19)

From the perspective of those who were kept out of white institutions, commitment to ideas of diversity and access to higher education, although inadequate, still constitute one way to challenge structures of dominance and subordination and bring about institutional change. So rather than respond to the question, "What work does diversity do in higher education?" this discussion raises another question. "What does it take to make diversity work in higher education?" In other words, if diversity programs actually produce and actualize a network of policies, practices, resources, traditions and sentiments that are used to promote equity and fairness as well as dismantle structures of domination in the academic workplace, what are the processes and strategies that make it work? For black women faculty, as it is for other minorities and target groups, one strategy and perhaps the most challenging, is to be intentional and visible in making sure diversity gets translated as excellence.

Diversity as Excellence

In virtually every field there are black women faculty and scholars who can assist in the project of linking diversity to excellence. Deborah Gray White's 2008 collection, *Telling Histories: Black Women Historians in the Ivory Tower*, is a useful example. Gray's collection of essays by seventeen contemporary black women historians shows how diversity and inclusion have mapped new intellectual terrain, offered new methodologies and expanded the canon in historical studies. Referencing the foundational contributions of black women historians like Marion Thompson Wright who earned the PhD in history from Columbia University in 1940 and Anna Julia Cooper who earned her PhD in 1925 from the Sorbonne, the black women historians in Gray's collection identify the strategies of mentoring and networking as primary resources for producing and demonstrating excellence in scholarship that could not be marginalized, deemed irrelevant or inferior. Historians like W.E. B. Du Bois and John Hope Franklin who preceded these women and served, in some instances as their mentors, are also examples of how diversity and inclusion ultimately generated extraordinary research and writing.

Collaboration and Activism

Academic collaborations and faculty activism have also enabled black women faculty to negotiate the diversity discourse for access, equity, fairness and institutional change despite the critique that the axis of sameness on which some projects are based constitute an "essentialist fiction." Cheryl Evans Green, a faculty member in the School of Social Work at the University of Central Florida and Valarie Green King, from the Office of Diversity at the same institution, developed a project called SISTERS, which used strategies of collaboration and what I call "strategic essentialism" to negotiate and the diversity discourse at their institution. Explaining how the project was designed to create a "village" of caring and supportive women of African descent with the skills, attitudes, and desire to mentor and be mentored by each other, Green and King (2001) identified the three-fold mission of the project,

> ...to foster challenging and rewarding experiences within an academic environment that is perceived by some as neglectful, antagonistic, and at times brutally threatening; to provide the SISTERS participants with a variety of effective techniques and strategies for nurturing one another; and to help these women address the realities of "glass ceiling" issues that often exist for women, particularly those women who are Black, in the academy. (p.156)

Offering a framework for career and leadership development, the SISTERS project was unique in several respects. First, the focus of the project was on the total population of black women at the institution across all employment categories: faculty, tenured, tenure-track, and adjunct; secretaries, office managers, clerks, custodial workers, program coordinators and middle level managers. Next, using the seven principles of Kwanza, the project included focus group sessions and mentoring group sessions to enable participants to study the institutional structure and develop personal and career goals. The outcomes of the project were substantive. As Green and King reported, several of the participants were promoted, a few continued working toward a degree and several became mentors to the growing population of black students who had enrolled at the university (Green and King 2001, pp.163-164).

At the University of Maryland, the Collaborative Transformations in the Academy: Re-Constructing the Study of Gender, Race, Ethnicity and Nation, a project developed and supported by Bonnie Thornton Dill, Sharon Harley and Deborah Rosenfelt, is an example of collaboration engendering multiple diversity work that has had a cumulative impact for faculty, students and the institution as a whole. The Collaborative Transformations project enhanced and combined the resources of three separate entities, the African American Studies department (AASD), the Consortium on Race, Gender and Ethnicity (CRGE) and the Curriculum Transformation Project (CTP). From a 2002 seminar focused on black women, fifteen local scholars including professors, museum specialists, artists and policy analysts, produced an prodigious amount of scholarship: fourteen major research papers, an annotated bibliography published as a working paper, and the anthology, *Sister Circle: Black Women and Work* (Rutgers UP 2002) edited by Sharon Harley and the Black Women and Work Collective (Mclaughlin, Thornton Dill, Harley and Rosenfelt 2009, p. 26). Speaking to the link between activism, collective and collaborative academic projects and institutional-izing diversity work, Bonnie Thornton Dill recognized that each of the three women had been motivated, in her academic training, to break with tradition and construct new knowledge. She goes on to explain that they were all "children of the '60s, of the civil rights movement, of the other movements that followed...Like so many of our generation, we believed and saw that change was possible, that activism could make a difference." Ultimately all three women, as authors of their own stories, conclude that engagement with social justice movements outside of academia gave them all "both the tools and the conviction they needed to make a difference on campus" (Mclaughlin,Thornton Dill, Harley and Rosenfelt 2009, p.27).

Collective Action

Collective action, whether inside or outside of the academy, has been a strategy long used by black women faculty in predominantly white institutions. Joanne Gabbin, Professor of English at James Madison University and Executive Director of the Furious Flower Poetry Center, tells the story of a simple but effective use of collective action while a graduate student at the University of Chicago. In order to persuade the graduate faculty in English to hire a faculty member in African American studies, George Kent specifically, Gabbin had first approached the chair of the department with her request but soon understood that alone, she was powerless. So she organized a petition campaign to get signatures from students all over the campus. In telling her story, Gabbin (2009) remembers,

> It really did not matter that they were not students in English. I convinced students in the medical school, in business, history, religion and social work that signing the petition would send a message to the administration that blacks demanded a serious commitment to black studies and to a black presence at the university. (p.55)

When Gabbin met with the English department a second time, petition in hand, she and the other student signatories prevailed. George Kent was offered the position of full professor with tenure. And with a permanent scholar in African American literature, serious scholarship in the field was possible .While the climate in the country in these first decades of the 21st century is radically different from that of the late 1960s and as several scholars have theorized, identity politics and collective political projects on the old modernist lines are no longer viable, collective action is still possible. But such action must be grounded in histories of struggle and focused to issues of social justice and human rights. Otherwise diversity gets recast as mandatory difference and operates as a mechanism for "technologies of concealment in the unfinished work of racism" (Ahmed 2005; Mirza 2006, p. 6).

Angela Davis (1994), discerning the necessity for black women in the academy to pay attention to the issues which have political implication for both their research and organizing strategies, and recognizing the "range of issues and contradictions and differences" informing these strategies has warned,

> We can no longer assume that there is a single monolithic force against which we position ourselves in order to defend our name...we can no longer ignore the ways in which we sometimes end up reproducing the very forms of domination we like to attribute to something or somebody else. (p.427)

If the future of the academy is dependent on its ability to nurture the talent of all its faculty, especially those black faculty women whose numbers, Sheila Gregory tells us ,are steadily decreasing, then black women faculty must bring pressure to bear on the leadership in higher education. In collaboration with others, they might very well issue a call to collective action to ensure that institutions of higher education in the U.S. make and sustain a commitment to the principles of democracy and diversity.

References

Brown-Glaude, W. (2009). *Doing diversity in higher education: faculty leaders share challenges and strategies.* New Brunswick: Rutgers University.

Davis, A. (1994). Black women in the academy *Callaloo 17*(2), 422-431.

Denzin, N.K. (1989). *Interpretive Biography.* Newbury Park: Sage Publications.

Gabbin, J.V. (2009). *Shaping memories:Reflections of african American women writers.* Jackson: University of Mississippi.

Green, C. & King, V. (2001). Sisters mentoring sisters: Africentric leadership development for black women in the academy. *The Journal of Negro Education 70*(3), 156-165.

Gregory, S. (2001). Black faculty women in the academy: history, status and future. *Journal of Negro Education 70*(3), 124-138.

Hale, F.W Jr. (2004). Introduction. In F.W. Hale (Ed.), *What makes racial diversity work in higher education: Academic leaders present successful policies and strategies?* (pp.2-23). New Brunswick: Rutgers University.

Holloway, F. & Demetrakopoulos, S. (1987). *New dimensions of spirituality: a biracial and bicultural reading of the novels of Toni Morrison,* Westport, CT: Greenwood Press.

hooks b. (1989). *Talking back: Thinking feminist, thinking black.* Boston: South End Press

Lemelle, A. (2009). Social and economic organization of the black professoriate at predominantly-white colleges and universities. *Journal of African American Studies. 14*(1), 106-127

Mirza, H. (2006). Transcendence over diversity: Black women in the academy. *Policy Futures in Education.* 1-18.

Winbush, R.A. (2004). A brief meditation of diversity and "duhversity." In F.W. Hale (Ed.), *What makes racial diversity work in higher education: Academic leaders present successful policies and strategies?* (pp.33-37). New Brunswick: Rutgers University.

Wynn, L. (September, 2010). Review of White, Deborah Gray, ed. *Telling Histories: Black Women Historians in the Ivory Tower.* H-SAWH, H-Net Reviews.

Chapter Three

The "Invisible Layers of Labor": Ritualizing a Blackwoman Experience of Service

❈

Helane Adams Androne

This chapter is a reflection and contemplation on the intersections of service—to my family, to my people, to my profession—as a common denominator of my identities within a predominately white university and how Toni Cade Bambara's *The Salt Eaters* speaks to/about that intersection. I argue that the common denominator of being black, female, mother, and professor in a predominately white academic space is the perception and balance of service, a particular conundrum in an environment where service typically ranks last in the conversation about hiring, tenure and promotion; however, much like healing fiction by black women authors, using ritual to understand the experience is both reflective and prophetic.

According to ritual studies scholar Catherine Bell (1992), ritual is a means for integrating thought and action, its value in its use as both a method for and object of analysis. Here, I seek to use ritual as an analytical paradigm through which to reflect upon and, in some ways, reconcile with, my experience as a blackwoman academic in a predominately white university. Bell has categorized the symbols and systems of ritual as fitting within several categories: formalism, traditionalism, disciplined invariance, rule governance, sacral symbolism, and performance. While it is impossible to consider every aspect of these categories within the context of this reflection, I consider these categories as the foundation for understanding the complexity of rituals within systems of power, in this case, as they are reflected in most predominately white institutions. For the purposes of my reflection, I will focus a performative aspect of ritual to better express a process of my experience—the rite of passage.

In *The Study of Liturgy* (1992), edited by Cheslyn Jones, et al., ritual is divided three ways: formally, in which ritual conduct is compared to other comparable activities; functionally, in which ritual "meets the needs of the person or people practicing it"; and symbolically, in which ritual is viewed as "an activity of communication from which meaning is derived" (pp.54-5). Within ethnic literatures, the figurative births, deaths, and transformations of characters are often ritualized; formally, they can occur in individual and communal processes such as cooking and composition; functionally in that authors typically use individuals to address the needs of textual and actual communities; and symbolically by establishing a greater depth of meaning regarding racial, economic, and social realities. A three-tiered methodology of ritual, as suggested by Leonel Mitchell (1988), reveals characters, communities, and their changes in literary works as triad, non-static and progressive activities. In my work as a literary scholar, I have articulated ritual structures in ethnic texts as coping and healing mechanisms for intersecting oppressions experienced by ethnic female protagonists. I argue that ritual acknowledges the psychic fracturing that plagues so many ethnic women in these texts, and how these authors tell us something both historic and prophetic about coping and healing from the traumas experienced in our own and larger communities.

Reflection upon my experience as a blackwoman in a predominately white university must mean a layering of resources, one of which must be Toni Cade Bambara's novel, *The Salt Eaters* (1980). In the novel, Velma Henry, activist, mother and wife, reels from the resulting psychosocial fracturing of imbalanced service, both within and for her community. She is submitted to patriarchal boundaries within an activist culture that struggles against systems of power that marginalize her within that activist culture and within a larger marginalized community. Velma is overburdened by the imbalances of this multi-layered, often minimalized service and she has attempted suicide as a result. What makes *The Salt Eaters* so poignant in reflecting upon my own inseparably black and female identity within a predominately white university is that I learn from Velma that intersecting oppressions combined with committed service sometimes leads to self-denigration and personal, psycho-spiritual destruction. I will attempt to show how Velma's experience of service is instructive of the experience of blackwoman academics operating within similarly layered paradigms of power. In so many ways, Bambara's narrative performs the testimony of this experience in the ritualized healing of Velma's initial unraveling. But it is the expression of Velma initial unraveling that is prophetic in its parallelisms to the experience of blackwomen academics in pre-dominately white institutions.

So, in view of the ritual lens I apply to literary and pedagogical work, the analysis of it is only appropriate for me to articulate my story through a similar lens. And from this critical lens I must reflect on my current status as a recovering, stronger, tenured black-woman academic with a moral and communal imperative to serve. Bear with me, then, if I seem to speak in multiple voices, perhaps a less than traditional tone, in an effort to testify through an interdis-ciplinary reading of an undeniably intersecting identity. As Farah Jasmine Griffin argues,

> Ours is a tradition, a literary tradition, certainly grounded in the autobiography, the conversion narrative, the spiri-tual narrative, and the slave narrative. It has never been a notion of autobiography that was just about me, myself and I. It's always been a notion of autobiography that also sought to give voice to an experience of people who seemed voiceless to the majority of society. So it was never just about inward navel-gazing. Therefore, it is only natural that as our criticism developed some of it would take on that autobiographical voice as well—and especially from women (Brown 2010, p.217).

Consequently, this chapter is more reflection than report or sociological analysis, one that seeks to share my testimony in the spirit of those who have testified before me. Moreover, if this entire experience toward tenure has been a rite of passage, then I must acknowledge the stages and elements I have found within it relative to service.

Within the initiation, separation, transformation and reintegration that typically accomplishes a rite of passage, there are moments that define purpose and reveal flaws, moments that cause reflection and pain, and moments that create in us a passionate spirit. I learn from an Othermother, Dr. Tawnya Pettiford-Wates, a theater performer and teacher-scholar who, ironically, performed in the Broadway version of Ntozake Shange's pivotal play about blackwomen's testimonies and triumphs, *For Colored Girls Who Have Considered Suicide When the Rainbow Is Enuf* (1975), to examine the elements of birth, death and transformation for articulating the complexity of events within events. What I now understand is how my identity as black and female within a context that is defined by its traditional commitment to all that has been identified with whiteness and/or maleness is that my various experiences of service, mingled with attitudes toward service, made the strongest impressions on me and how I navigate the terrain as a blackwoman academic in a predominately white institution.

My birth and initial understanding of service was personal. As the child of a recently divorced and too-proud-for-welfare single mother, she exposed me to the relationship between service and survival. I stood with her behind tables of boxed food in the Los Angeles heat, working for the SHARE program. We were to serve other hungry families to be served. Once we had worked our time slot, we could take home our own box of food. My mother was grateful and proudly instilled in me, at every opportunity, an understanding of our part in this cycle of service. From there, she continued make sure I was further exposed to service of the most vulnerable of populations, in keeping with the core of our Christian beliefs: the elderly, the sick, and the children of our communities. I went on to serve in a hospital and at state run child development centers. I would see for myself the desperation of poverty, the nobility of age, and practice respect for the humanity of those in need.

This birth was for me a gaining of perspective, empathy and practice in the service of others, my community, and ultimately my own character. There was no moment of self-righteousness for we had very little ourselves. Feeling "good" about helping someone else was not really the point; the mandate was about my character and my relationship to people of all kinds who were linked by their needs and by my opportunity. I didn't understand it all clearly at the time, though I had my humbling moments; I was typically immersed within a context that magnified a system that encouraged individualism, complicity, and secular definitions of achievement.

But something happened as I got older and moved on to college—and into my first real interactions with academia. The opportunities to reflect and recognize my subjectivity became a political act. My individual self necessarily died to the purposes of organized articulations of alignments with organizations and antagonism toward communities of power. I found myself active and political, at odds even with my own parents concerning issues of language, citizenship and authority. Instead of pursuing material gain, I sought opportunities to resist. When I was supposed to be at work, I was sitting in the middle of Interstate 5 protesting the Rodney King verdict. When I should have been clarifying my relationship to math, I was in meetings as an officer in the Black Student Union sitting alongside comrades from MeChA (Movimiento Estudiantil Chicano de Aztlan). I pledged a historically black sorority with a community service focus that proved to me the unique identities and concerns of blackwomen in the world. My service suddenly included the recognition of the oppressions that had, to me, caused the poverty, illness and maltreatment for which I had individually sought to soften the blows. Graduate school was much of the same; alliances, however, broadened and my service began to take on a less global and more strategically academic focus. Suddenly, my service would be in counter-measures against predominately white university policies that we, as a multicultural body of graduate students, felt were short-sighted and antagonistic to our presence and concerns of those of the surrounding communities.

My transformation into a blackwoman academic came rather unexpectedly since I had little interest in serving an institution that might look anything like the ones I had attended. While I had developed keen literary interests, I had also found a kind of personal angst at the possibility of serving so many of the deeply privileged in a predominately white academic environment. The idea of translating my attitude about service into an environment that would possibly tokenize me or marginalize me was at least discouraging, if not depressing and stressful. I had determined that, if I must again find a way to reconcile aspects of myself, the best place to do so would be at a community college, someplace where people would be who had not necessarily had the "best" of opportunities, where most of the people who had struggled with poverty, family illness, and structural inequalities of every kind and would be trying to articulate their stories as well.

But I was discouraged from this by academics and members of my own community. They were clear: I should press toward the most lucrative and academically rigorous of institutions; I should seek rank and privilege and job security. This was a difficult decision for me, since on the one hand, my community clearly saw me as a success story to serve as a motivation for those coming behind me; on the other, they were seemingly driving me to serve many who would, if they acknowledged my community at all, would do so in condescending ways, or worse, prefer to theorize the community's issues without any representation from it. These are, of course, essentializing and extreme characterizations, accurate only in my memory of the internal debate. In truth, there were nuances, allies, and important spaces to carve out in these academic spaces. These initial experiences and reflections upon who I was and who I would choose to serve professionally set the stage for my rite of passage as a professor entering a predominately white university on a tenure-track dominated by traditions considered the realm of white privilege. In the tradition of rites of passage, I view this divided into several stages (initiation, separation, transformation and re-incorporation); along the way, I have understood certain truths attached to each.

Initiation

You will always encounter opposition to your existence. When I tell people I grew up in San Diego, I can almost watch as their mind's eye sifts through the commercials and photographs of beaches and bikinis, high priced homes and celebrity destinations. Of course that is all true for some. For me, San Diego was military bases and one-bedroom apartments in working class and poor, distinctly ethnic neighborhoods. It was conservative politics and random racist reminders of the lines diversity efforts couldn't cross. It was my mother's non-stop work, remarriage and my sister's arrival that spawned the subsequent moving "up" to a house in a new development in the middle of an old Hood. I witnessed San Diego forcibly stretched out of this mold a bit by population influx and tourism goals. As an undergraduate, there were meetings and marches, forums and articles, in support and protest—all in determined service to the people of our communities, on campus and off. My hair was typically braided or cut short, in my ears hung large heavy earrings, and I was often found in sweatpants or baggy jeans. When I arrived in Seattle, despite the grungy atmosphere, in a graduate college scene, I was still an instant standout with the odd combination of my natural hair and distinctly southern California sun-kissed attitude. Despite owning nothing more than what I could carry, the perceptions of my San Diego upbringing made me instantly part of a strange phenomenon that Washingtonians considered a problem— apparently Californians were driving up their cost of living.

Still, I arrived in a kind of ethnic awe: despite the clear lack of black presence, there was an African American Mayor and an Asian American Governor. Norm Rice, the 49th Mayor of Seattle, would serve two terms and become Seattle's first and only African American mayor. Gary Locke, now 36th United States Secretary of Commerce under our now first black President, Barack Obama, was the first Chinese American in history to be a governor in the United States. This was a man who didn't learn English until he was five and went on to become the 21st Governor of Washington state. Coming from a place vastly more diverse where I could hardly imagine an African American in any real position of power, this urban environment of almost 2 million residents with barely a 30% combined minority population, and a black population that was scarce at best, was positively shocking (US Census Bureau: State and County, QuickFacts, November 4, 2010).

I found myself a temporary employee of the county and a consultant in my own newly formed consulting business, hired to refresh Transit Operators on principles of grammar and test-quality writing in preparation for their Supervisory exams. I worked with ethnically diverse women in powerful positions to hire and fire people. I had African American and white female supervisors and a Persian co-worker. The city boasted every kind of Asian presence and attempted to both address and hide its Native American poverty. In this life I was a graduate student with a quick smile and a positive attitude, despite my run-ins with the overt and subtle workings of racism and class privilege. I had shaken off my elementary school days as one of three blacks bused into an elite program in San Diego, where I was called a "nigger" every day and told by white women to ignore it. I had, in my own mind, crystallized my pride and had, I thought, come to acknowledge the variety of responses available to me as a blackwoman and student activist during my undergraduate years. In fact, I was both excited and honored to do this job as something meaningful, outside my heavily theoretical coursework, something I thought would contribute to the "real" economically and ethnically diverse working people of the community. I was working on my doctorate in English at the time, had completed my Masters in Teaching English, and considered myself more than privileged to be working for the county, much less having the opportunity to teach folks I felt so attached to and yet alienated from during my educational hours. My first day would be a triumphant opportunity.

When I was granted the job, I prepared for this seminar like it was an exam. I was told that this was a group of folks keen on supervisory positions, people the organization wanted to promote, but who were scarcely prepared to lead when judged by their writing skills. These were going to be folks that I understood and wanted to serve, people I wanted to give my absolute best because they would be my aunts and uncles, my parents and my cousins. I would go in there and do whatever was in my power to get them their well-earned promotions that had been to this point clearly slighted them because their written words were about to be more important than the driving and interpersonal skills that had gotten them to this point. I spent hours creating accessible handouts and preparing every word I would utter. I delighted myself in finding ways of explaining and exploring grammar and usage in professional documents without jargon or haste. I researched their tests, considered how I would prepare them for all the possible narrative elements of their responses on the test, and made copious notes on how I would make sure that this workshop would not be overwhelming or mind-numbing.

As I stood nervously looking into the bathroom mirror before going into the station room on the first day, the person looking back at me was so different than the one I had known before. This suddenly lack-of-sunshine skinned mid-twenty year old woman staring back at me was "attractive" in her navy blue skirted suit, nylons and appropriately high heels. She was curvy and petite at five feet tall and 120 something pounds. Her girlfriends would have said that her hair was "laid," with a fresh, bouncing press from the best hairdresser in town. I had a newly minted "professional" look, carefully detailed notes and plans, and a nervously excited smile. This other, appropriate and less guarded me walked into a room full of almost exclusively white and predominately male bus drivers to teach them how to write.

I walked into the room with a mix of excitement and trepidation. This new me had not yet developed that sense of security with my own knowledge base; I still carried the weight of educational opportunity programs that somehow labeled me among my peers as less adept, less worthy of my position in graduate school. I carried the worries attached to my black self, my female self and my upwardly mobile just-out-of the Hood self. When I walked into the room, I admit, I already had more than my usual burden. But as had become my custom, I called upon my experience in the arena of performance and put on the appropriate show. I brushed all chips off my shoulders and walked in as someone else, confident and smiling, welcoming without any preconceptions or expectations for anything but excellence. After appropriately introducing myself and engaging the audience with eye contact and all the beginning niceties of our purpose for the seminar, I got my first question from the back of the room—a white male perhaps in his mid-to-late fifties. "Are we going to talk about Ebonics?" Laughter. Then, the air when out of the room.

What happened next was a careful mixture of extremely brief, carefully employed academic fast-talking that suggested both the importance of African American Vernacular as a subject of study and the irrelevance of it for our purposes that day. And then I moved on. It was that thing my friends said I could do with words:

I made him small. Even so, what it felt like was the shrinking of my own self. The big-ness of all the issues I carried came back and poured out on me in that moment and I became small too. Both of us were afraid in that moment. I was afraid I would fail; he was afraid that I wouldn't. After the class, at least two other white participants stopped to speak with me and apologize for the question. It had made them uncomfortable and embarrassed. They reaffirmed their respect and their appreciation for the service I was providing.

In and of itself, the question of the discussion of African American Vernacular in a class about writing is not necessarily a problem—at least it is not the stuff of climactic stories. Further, the question itself was not a racially-charged question; it was only in the differences between us and how those differences were (correctly) perceived by the questioner and others in the room that made the question an issue. In this particular instance, I could be sure, based upon the particular reference to an ethnic linguistic practice, that his greatest discomfort was with my race, though he may have taken further issue with my gender and age, which likely triggered in him a sense of the historical perversion of my authority, given the intersection of my identities.

This was my initiation into the rite of passage that would be my academic life. I would, from there, enter into an environment that would be full of peers with similarly dichotomous feelings about my presence, similar mixtures of insecurity and discomfort, similar interactions that would require apology. I was going to be a blackwoman in a traditionally white space. Who would they expect me to become? It is in this moment I can reflect upon my understanding of the performance of my own self. As Ruth Farmer and others suggest, there is a performance dialectic in the identity of a blackwoman,

> It is difficult to talk about being Black in a White space, even though in the United States such is usually the case. The difficulty is to speak, to name, without appearing to whine, a near impossibility, since African American women are not expected to speak at all. It is particularly difficult to be heard, since despite the reality, the myth still prevails that African American women are making great professional strides. Enmeshed within this myth is the belief that even when African American women are

suffering, obstacles are faced stoically and handled with a
prayer, and a smile. In other words, we always overcome.
We African American women are reluctant to dispel this
myth for it is one of the positive stereotypes afforded us"
(cited in Davis 2008, pp.176-177).

There would have to be a negotiation of this new space, a way in which
to identify myself, to make choices about my role in the perception
of my teaching, research and service. How would I construct and
perform my identity in a space in which my authority was apparent
and negotiable at the same time? I would become part of the statistical reality revealed by the 2006 U.S. Department of Education data:
African Americans made up more than 12% of the United States
population but represented just over 5% of all postsecondary faculty.
And we are already keenly aware of the research that proves African
Americans experience "fewer opportunities for career growth and
advancement than their White faculty peers" (see, Moody 2000;
Perna et al. 2006; Watson, 2001; Weinberg 2008; Williams & Williams 2006 as cited in Modica and Mamiseishvili 2010, p.107). The
atmosphere would be rife with possibility and problems. Scholars
such as Darden, Kamel & Jacobs (1998), have decisively concluded
that more African American faculty means more African American
students; however, scholarship also reveals that African Americans
have the lowest rate of tenure (as cited in Modica and Mamiseishvili
2010, p.108). To imagine my ability to navigate these realities, I had
to reflect upon the examples that I had for success; I had to call upon
my memory of actual and metaphoric Othermothers, whom I perceived as successful representations struggle.

Separation

*You will be alone; more often than not you will be separate from
family, community and resources, operating in a necessary academic isolation to complete the work. But there will be guidance.*
As a graduate student, I had come to understand the difficulties of
being a blackwoman in a predominately white institution through
my research and friendship with my committee chair/"mentor."
Due to both the perceived expendability and clear scarcity of black
faculty in PWIs, she was constantly bombarded with every graduate

student in need of support for work on race, gender, sexuality and class. She was (and is) an amazing forerunner for those of us who stood on the shoulders of her fight into such spaces. She was one of my Othermothers—of "the mind" as Patricia Hill Collins would say. She would find ways to employ graduate students of color in research positions to help us with our obvious financial crises; She would pause, among her own piles of paperwork and research, to provide a tidbit of revelation about the realities of the kind of scholarship that involves people of color in education. She was completely over-extended by her role and identity and responsibility and she drew both my highest esteem and my personal consternation for it. What I couldn't understand at the time was the constantly teetering balance between her commitment to graduate students, her commitment to her partner who was a black male academic, her commitment to the ever-important contributions to research in her field which allowed her presence, and that with the continuous demands on her time from the university, the department, and her colleagues, to say nothing of the idea that she may, ever so often, have wanted to spend time with friends and family. The complexity of this kind of existence is inherent as Wolfman (1997) notes that "a typical African American woman is a very complicated conglomerate of many roles (i.e., daughter; sister, both as an actual sibling and part of the black sisterhood; wife; partner; mother; community activist; church leader; homemaker; so forth) (as cited in Harley, 2008, p.26). When she and others made their way into the academy, one had to choose which roles would take precedence; they had favored academic roles so that we might have the chance to be whole.

For our part, we graduate students crowded her life like so many books, piles and piles of us, begging her to open us up and tell us our own stories. She knew all of us, had seen us before, over and over again, could have written our stories herself, but she never made us feel any lack of uniqueness or importance. She gave each of us a place on her shelves, those in her office, in her home, and in her heart. This, I understand only in reflection: that she was not my professor or my mentor. She was my guide, my Othermother "of the mind," who could really see me—and every one of us—with softened eyes that mothers have toward their young ones; she had served all of us in an environment that could have easily taken us out. How strange it is to recognize your foremothers as only mentors, only people who answer questions and help you navigate the terrain. These foremothers were and are more than that; they are the ones who know you deeply, who care for you deeply, and who don't tolerate you allowing your insecurities or your identity to talk you out of what is possible because they invest themselves in you; they have, in fact, been you and would consider your failure a loss greater than you. She and others like her sacrificed the most sacred parts of themselves to serve us and we are their legacy.

Transformation: My Body, My Hair, My Image

Some lessons must be learned through trauma and devastation. Service and servitude are very different. Clearly, we live in the world with the expectation and indeed hope that we will be able to serve others; we seek out the kind of willed assistance that implies. Unfortunately, the perversion of this attitude that occurs at times with the experience of intersecting oppressions can leave blackwoman academics feeling more like their will has been transformed into expectation based upon lack—lack of other black people, lack of other women, lack of other representations of diversity available to the university, and that creates a situation that feels more like a kind of servitude. It is a strange and precarious balance to strike that maintains your service within your will and not within the realm of expectation based upon lack (servitude) because of the stated necessity of service articulated in many of our job descriptions. So how can our service convey a sense of our genuine commitment to students, to the university and to the community? In the introduction to *The Black Academic's Guide to Winning Tenure*, Kerry Ann Rockquemore and Tracey Laszloffy (2008) argue,

> While all new faculty struggle in the transition from graduate student to professor, faculty of color must learn how to simultaneously juggle the excessive and never-ending service demands that result from being the only black faculty member (or one of a few) in their department, college, or university in addition to the alienation and hostility they may experience on campus. (p.3)

Surely we have the right and opportunity to choose the kind of service we would like to perform, to keep it within our will to accomplish based upon a view of liberal education consistent with that of the university's stated mission and goals. I have found that the balance between the two becomes absolutely necessary and impossible as one pursues the vestiges of success at a predominately white university.

Let me admit that I am an outwardly outgoing and energetic person, known for a quick step and sometimes equally quick wit. I say so out of necessity so that it might be clear how the combination of personality and an intersecting identity as a blackwoman academic could result in my own trauma as it relates to my moral and communal imperative to serve. When I finally bothered to count, I realized that I was exhausted; I sat actively on 11 committees that met on three campuses, several of which were by direct request of administrators. By my third year review, an administrator candidly told me that I could stop participating in service projects because I had already exceeded the typical service duties of my colleagues who had achieved tenure. Harley accounts for it: "African American women frequently experience stress because of their efforts to do twice as much and to accomplish tasks better than expected" (Harley 2008, p.26). As a junior faculty member, the requests I received for my participation in particular service projects/events/committees did not often feel like service as much as servitude. While other faculty serve in a variety of important ways on every sort of committee, I wonder how many of them receive such pointed requests based upon the obvious and unspoken "contribution" their experience of intersecting identity rather than any correlation to their research would provide? If anything, the bonus of my intersecting identity quite overshadowed any intellectual contribution I may have had.

Somehow the educational opportunity programs that sought to level the playing field had transformed into diversity marketing management programs. Did I know that my identity was part of the reason for my hiring? Yes. Most universities want the most "bang for the buck"; and, to be fair, many of our allies in these spaces see an opportunity for advancing the causes that have the potential to mark the university as a diverse space of intellectually motivating and challenging opportunities. But that comes with a price. This has been theorized as a kind of cultural taxation,

> Cultural taxation is "the obligation to show good citizen
> ship toward the institution by serving its needs for ethnic

representation on committees, or to demonstrate knowledge and commitment to a cultural group, which may even bring accolades to the institution but which is not usually rewarded by the institution on whose behalf the service was performed" (cited in Harley 2008, p. 27).

There is a clear dynamic then that situates me between the stated diversity goals and the market share of students and ranking flagships attracted to such claims. And there it is. Suddenly I see the full picture of the intersecting systems that govern my country. If that seems far too broad, let me explain.

We know that there were two different groups of whites who came to America: those who sought to escape persecution on moral grounds and those who desired to make their fortune by whatever means. Money and morality have been at odds in our country since its very beginning and the university is a representative of that historical reality; and, in some way, it is a laboratory for how institutionalized white privilege survives whatever challenges may come. On the one hand, my service is a willed desire that emanates from my own moral imperatives. On the other, my service is part and parcel of the benefits guaranteed to the university by my intersecting identities. Unless I am willing to sacrifice my moral imperatives, the two different branches of service usually mean more work, rather than any real balance between them. But this is not a revelation since, as Harley (2008) contends,

> Ironically, African American women faculty members are not only the 'maids of academe' but the 'work mules' (i.e., carrying a heavy load) as well. Brown (2000) referred to the over extension of African American faculty as the 'mournful wail' (i.e., others making demands on our time and energy) of African American faculty, which doubles if not triples their workload and channels them into a series of activities not formally recognized or rewarded by the university structure. (p.25)

It is the race and gender-mediated construction of service that marks my experience as a blackwoman academic most significantly in terms of service. *The Salt Eaters* speaks to the complexity that results from unbalanced service through Velma Henry, a wife, mother and activist working in a liberation movement. Velma reveals the depth of physical and psychological stress of intersecting responsibilities to serve so poignantly,

> [it's] Like work and no let up and tears in the night. Like being rolled to the edge of the bed, to extremes, clutching a stingy share of the covers and about to drop over the side, like getting up and walking, bare feet on cold floor... climbing in and too mad to snuggle for warmth, freeze. Like going to jail and being forgotten, forgotten, or at least de-prioritized cause bail was not as pressing as the printer's bill. Like raising funds and selling some fool to the community...Like being called in on five-minute notice after all the interesting decisions had been made, called in out of personal loyalty and expected to break her hump pulling off what the men had decided was crucial for the community good. (p. 25)

In the book, Velma is undone by the consistently negative images that collide in her personal and political life. Her personal life with her husband, James (Obie), is invaded in the bedroom by metaphoric contemplations of her daily life and service. Politically, Velma is fighting the invisibility and objectification of her physical self, aggressive in her activism only to be ignored for the sake of other over-arching political agendas. She fights her guilt and anger at being patronized alongside expectations that she will agree and serve. Velma serves from a moral imperative and responsibility to her community despite internal gendered obstacles or at least lack of appreciation for women's contributions.

It is this pattern by which blackwomen academics are subject to be consumed if we do not heed the cultural wisdom afforded us and take the example of the women who have preceded us. For we now understand that only achieving balance is not really the point. Fletcher and Bailyn suggest that if we only seek balance, we "will tacitly accept work as it is and family as it is, and see our task as helping (some) individuals keep them separate and cope with the demands of each" (as cited in Townsley and Broadfoot 2008, p.176). Rather, we ought to seek an integration of work and family such that the reality of personal responsibilities can mutually enhance experience and performance of both (Townsley and Broadfoot 2008, p.138).

This kind of service, transformed into servitude when it becomes traumatic and a mechanism of lack, is the point at which physical, emotional and psycho-spiritual trauma can, in fact, take us out. But how does this transformation take place? How is it that someone like myself, a blackwoman who felt a sense of clarity about who and how I would serve, could come to the point of servitude? How is it that blackwomen find themselves in particularly gendered positions of servitude in academia? Explanations for differences between the experience of black men and blackwomen are clear according to Thompson and Dey (1998),

> ...women have lower professional status; men are more likely to have supportive home networks, which allow them greater opportunities to become part of the larger community social networks; women spend more time on household chores, which is related to time constraints; and faculty who have higher salaries (who are likely to be men) experience less stress related to home responsibilities (cited in Harley 2008, p.29).

We tend to achieve our service expectations at a high cost, much of which is the subtle transformation of this work into servitude. For example, we are more likely to exhibit hypertension, heart disease, obesity, impaired immune function, high levels of depression, anxiety, "and stressors related to the demands of academic life and the multi-marginality of being underrepresented by race, a scholarly agenda, and the larger academic and social communities" (Bradley 2005; Jones 2001; Neal-Barnett 2003; Thompson and Dey 1998 as cited in Harley 2008, p.26). But it took my own personal experience of desperate commitment to the privileged tenets of tenure to recognize it.

I constructed my tenure dossier on the counter of the Neonatal Intensive Care Unit at Good Samaritan Hospital. I typed and distractedly edited page after page, cut, pasted, and deleted, certainly not nearly as focused as I could have been because my eyes consistently darted and my ears strained to listen for the machines that kept my newborn son alive. He was seriously premature at twenty-seven weeks, a far cry from the full forty. Prevailing traditions suggest that I had made a mistake in imagining that I could have a child prior to achieving tenure,

The consequences of having "early babies," or babies boom within five years after earning a PhD, significantly hampers women's ability to earn tenure. Yet, as Williams notes, this "maternal wall" does not affect women and men evenly; and in fact, early babies actually increased men's chances of achieving tenure above both women and men without babies (cited in Townsley and Broadfoot 2008, p.136).

Others might say it was a ballsy move, at least. Still others would suggest that it marked my lack of understanding and commitment to my identity as an academic. True academics don't make babies; they make texts. What I must admit in retrospect is that my service to the university had transformed into a servitude that pressed me forward toward acquiring the "success" and steadfastness of the superwoman. After all, "Men within five years of their PhD and who have babies are 38% more likely to achieve tenure in 12-14 years than women at the same point in their career" (Kerber as cited in Townsley and Broadfoot 2008, 138)).

Somehow, within the dynamic of a system established upon white male privilege, I had become convinced that my whole self belonged to the academy as opposed to *in* the academy such that I had to prove that nothing, not motherhood—regardless of its accompanying stressors—and not family or my own health would be an "excuse" for lack of production. After all, I loved my job and had a flexible schedule that I counted as a privilege worthy of all my time and energy, beyond that which was contracted. I found that my autonomy and flexibility provided a great deal of possibility for coping with my time constraints, but, as research has shown, such a schedule does nothing to curb the stress and psychological demands of maintaining excellence in scholarship, teaching, and service—not necessarily in that order. This short-term flexibility does make the long-term flexibility of academia difficult to achieve when one is committed to both work and family (Townsley and Broadfoot 2008, p.135).

I had become convinced of the necessity of a superior commitment through my own trauma based upon the competition for job security in a place where I felt pressured to prove the worthiness of my presence. Without questioning how I got to that point, without considering the statistics that warned of the persistent relationship between stress and health deterioration that boldly announced my state's D grade in premature births and prematurity as the leading cause of death among black infants, and without careful consideration of my own well-being and healing beyond a prior miscarriage, I plunged forward. I would re-organize my children, my husband and my family's concerns around my tenure-track, not because the institution had explicitly asked it of me, but because within a PWI, somehow I had become a servant of the most audacious kind, convinced of my own lack of importance and the absolute necessity of acceptance as a tenured faculty member who achieved that status without excuse or special consideration (Gavin, Chae, Mustillo, & Kiefe 2009). It's not that I didn't believe the relationship between stress and chronic diseases (Alexander-Snow and Johnson 1999; Alexander and Moore 2008). My physical self was becoming subject to my psychological stress. I had come to believe I was not worthy unless I was better at serving; but I am not unique:

> ...even when coherent benefit policies, onsite child care, health coverage, tenure clock stops, and generous parental leave policies exist, cultural expectations about what is considered "appropriate work" remain deeply entrenched (Kerber as cited in Townsley and Broadfoot, p.137).

Even in retrospect I wince understanding how I participated in the development of my own destructive behavior. I could see myself through lenses that told me that: "Total dedication is the expectation in the academic workplace and those who work there must demonstrate that such work is their primary, sole, and uninterrupted focus" (Wilson as cited in Townsley and Broadfoot 2008, p.137). I cannot isolate the reason for my son's prematurity; what I know is that in the opportunity to reflect, the act of constructing my dossier on the counter of the NICU proves to me a kind of dysfunction.

And so there was transformation. The rules for the inclusion of women's health issues within PWIs have grown at a snail's pace in relationship to the population; issues that become particularly vital to blackwomen's health are at best third in rank. My interaction with the benefits department set precedent for handling an ever growing situation in women's health: how would they determine benefits for premature babies? This is an issue that simply happens more to black women; hence, their previous experience was absolutely limited, both because of the pressures on women not to conceive and the lack of blackwomen academics. In the meantime, a significant part of my psychological well-being came in physical, psychological and spiritual transformation. I happily transformed part of my identity into a physical marker for the miraculous well-being of my son, aptly named Legend, by deciding to lock my hair. I have no plans to cut it until he experiences his own rite of passage into manhood, at which time, I will pass him the scissors and invite him to cut my hair as a symbolic gesture of personal and public witness between us. My body had, thank God, made it through to this point, but my Spirit was still trying to manifest itself.

Re-Integration

You do this for yourself and for the generations before and after you. You do this as a witness to the community that you belong to. Re-integration into one's community after a ritual often comes with public acknowledgement of personal trauma. Somehow, the community must participate in the process by witnessing the walk toward healing and balance. Re-integration is not the final step of a ritual; it is the beginning. It means I'm coming to a community of witnesses to speak my testimony and suggest, in my word and deed the potential of my own and my community's healing. And, I come not only to witness to the pain, but to ask for help from every person willing to listen, to apologize for taking individualism as anything beyond a debilitating social construct. But re-integration does not insulate one from the ever-present reality of identity when serving.

Part of my process of re-integration was self-determination; I would expend my energies in those areas in which I finally could feel free to serve more actively. Even in this I found resistance, however, and my identity as a blackwoman academic was again shuffled. While I receive tremendous support from most of my colleagues, when I found myself at philosophical odds with certain male colleagues with what I had assumed were similar goals, I came under a different sort of attack. This time, however, I was firmly established within a community of witnesses and was able to respond with less fear and more spiritual fortitude. It is no secret that blackwomen academics with opinions are labeled as troublemakers and perhaps even conspiratorial if they do not align themselves in submission to male leadership and ideas (Harley 2008, p.23). I came to know what Harley has suggested: "As an already marginalized population, African American women faculty members are more often reprimanded by their dean and criticized by colleagues based on supposition, misperceptions, and on information without merit" (Harley 2008, p.24). My self-determination had a conspiratorial edge to it for a few who saw my service as thinly disguised ambition, though certainly such would be completely appropriate and unquestioned for a more masculine colleague—or at least the criticism of which would have been handled more respectfully.

From this experience, I can turn prophetically to Bambara (1980) again, thinking about how she situates Velma within a community, yet struck by her service to it, but moves her toward a very political and personal healing,

> For [Velma] found a home amongst the community workers who called themselves "political." And she'd found a home amongst the workers who called themselves "psychically adept." But somehow she'd fallen into the chasm that divided the two camps. Maybe that was the lesson. Maybe the act of trying to sever a vein or climbing into the oven was like going to the caves, a beginning... (pp.147-148).

Velma consistently struggles against organizational politics that reveal male leaders who have an "unmindful gap between want and done, demand and get" (p.31). She comes to a point of frustration at which she desires most to be, "unavailable at last, sealed in and the noise of the world, the garbage, locked out" (p.19). Velma finds herself unable to function as such a fragmented being, with compartmentalized realities of her various selves: black and female, mother and activist, wife and goddaughter. It is the fragmentation that persists though, leaving Velma a woman who appears and acts unstable, eventually attempting suicide. The fragments of her life that had begun to conflate begin to conflict and she is left in desperate need of healing.

Bambara issues the warning for imagining that such personal work is finished. Through Velma's struggles, I understand the distinct intersections between my self and the direction of my community and the importance of my careful and sustained well-being,

Thought she knew how to build resistance...stay poised and centered in the work and not fly off, stay centered in the best of her people's traditions and not be available to madness...not go under... Thought the vaccine offered by all the theorists and activist and clear thinkers and doers of the warrior clan would take. But amnesia had set in anyhow. Heart/brain/gut muscles atrophied anyhow. Time was running out anyhow...Something crucial had been missing from the political/ economic/ social/ cultural/ aesthetic/ military/ psychosocial/ psychosexual mix. (p.258)

By the end of her healing, Velma realizes the delicate balance of her own well-being, the well-being of her people and the status of service being rendered to protect both. Velma realizes she is not alone and that she is not able to carry that burden alone, that left unchecked, "amnesia had set in anyhow"; her service did not make her invincible, the work does not end with the "workers of the sixties", and that the "vaccine" will not prevent this kind of ailment. So, I learn that within my process of reintegration there should indeed be conflict; however, that conflict need not have the destructive force it might have had prior to my own recognition of my own ritual process. Recognition of a ritual process and the literary prophets who articulate the damage and the potential so astutely, my personal response can be re-directed from fear, loathing, and damaging behaviors because I can name this trauma, see its attachments and relationship to my self, while understanding the necessity to insulate my inner self. I remember that Lee and Armstrong (1995) state that "emphasis on the 'psychospiritual' goes beyond the mind and body, while binding together cognitive, affective, and behavioral realms of existence into an integrated whole" (as cited in Harley 2008, p.28). I can serve, in the way that I choose, regardless of the particular mix of politics and academic economy that may suggest deficits in that system and my worth. This is what re-integration earns—a distinctly personal and always communal view of the landscape, with the understanding that there is an inevitable necessity to heal.

The Performance of Healing

This walk is not only by your body, but through your soul. The body is vulnerable always, but the soul is yours to protect. Heintzman and

Mannell (2003) define spiritual well-being as "a high level of hope, and commitment in relation to a well-defined worldview or belief system that provides a sense of meaning and purpose to existence in general, and that offers an ethical path to personal fulfillment which includes connectedness with self, others, and a higher power or larger reality" (as cited in Alexander and Moore 2008, p.6). And Ashford, LeCroy, & Lortie, (2006) define well-being as "a person's emotional and psychological capacity to cope with demands across time, circumstance, and setting" (as cited in Alexander and Moore 2008, p.13). Malidoma Patrice Some's description of sacred ritual in *Ritual: Power, Healing and Community* (1993) is revelatory for establishing connections between spirituality and ritual,

> Visible wrongs have their roots in the world of the spirit... Ritual is the mechanism that uproots these dysfunctions. It offers a realm in which the unseen part of the dysfunction is worked on in ways that effect the seen. (p.43)

Akasha (Gloria) Hull reads spirituality as part of African American female poetics. Barbara Christian also advocates the spiritual aspects of African American literatures, which bring into play different cultural ways of knowing and healing (Abel 1997, p. 2). But this leads me back to Velma Henry's plight in *The Salt Eaters*. Velma's husband pleads with her when her commitment outside herself gets to be too much,

> ...It's got to be costing you something to hang on to old pains. Just look at you. Your eyes slit, the cords jump out of your neck, your voice trembles, I expect fire to come blasting out of your nostrils any minute. It takes something out of you, Velma, to keep all them dead moments alive. Why can't you just...Forget...Forgive...and always it's some situation that was over and done with ten, fifteen years ago. But here you are still all fired up about it, still plotting, up to your jaws in ancient shit (Bambara 1980, p.22).

What we struggle with is ancient—and contemporary. A review of the current status of blackwoman faculty at PWIs reveals that the current generation faces similar issues of the past one. We are replaced, but not increased in number. Programs that attempt to balance historical wrongs are resisted (Harley 2008, p.30). Our particular healing, however, is predicated on the recognition of a problem that is not about the numbers. Helpful in considering this is Ann Folwell Stanford's feminist medical ethic that works to reconsider how black women have known, are remembering and revising, and are articulating the secrets of how to acknowledge and deal with the realities of their intersectional identities and oppressions. Stanford (1994) recognizes that medical science and communities must function together for healing,

> Without biomedical diagnostic labels, these illnesses are out of medicine's reach and remain in the domain of those people and communities best equipped to understand them, those who have the wisdom and skill to facilitate a healing that is not and cannot be separate from social context. (p.31)

In Velma's case, healing an individual ceases to be a private endeavor, but rather it becomes a communal event, as in the gathering of various community members, medical authorities, spiritual and intellectual representatives for Velma Henry's healing ritual. The individual is healed, not only to effect personal recovery, but also to "move beyond a narrow understanding of individual illness to become potential world healers themselves" (Bambara 1980, p.31). But in order to move through this process, these female protagonists will "have to be whole to see whole" (p.92). Of course Stanford asserts the irony that the community operates as "both the disease and the cure" at times and requires "an inner journey" to achieve appropriate balance (Stanford, 1994, p.34). In some sense, I learn that even the recognition of my selves can present a challenging community of both dominant and other. I take to heart Velma's healing process because it reveals that,

> Maybe the thing to do was invite the self by for coffee and a chat. Share with her how she herself had learned to believe in ordinary folks' capacity to change the self and transform society (Bambara 1980, p.259-269).

Velma's desire to take on the responsibility of service to her people's causes, alongside the volatility and marginality of her identity as raced (and burdened by its dejection) and gender (as female and expected to serve male imperatives) identifies a dichotomous struggle between her individual self and her communal self. It is Velma's individual healing, her re-entry into service to others as a whole person that eventually prompts the healing of a fragmented community that is "So used to being unwhole and unwell, one forgot what it was to walk upright and see clearly, breathe easily, think better than was taught, be better than one was programmed to believe..." (p.107).

It is the understanding of a blackwoman's role, individually and within a personal and academic community, that defines how to serve, when to serve, and to what extent service is required, regardless of the circumstances. My understanding has become a spiritual one: I must have dominion over my selves and my service if I am to survive. My community has the right to respond to my successes and my mistakes even as they have every right to be served by me. Dominion over my service will ultimately be a responsibility articulated in my research and my teaching as I witness and model the difficulties and the triumphs of being a blackwoman academic in a PWI. I receive no small clarity about this in the translation of this through Velma's experience when she learns,

> To have dominion was not to knock out, downpress, bruise, but to understand, to love, make at home. The keeping in the sights the animal, or child, man or woman, tracking it in order to learn their way of being in the world. To be at home in the knowing. The hunt for balance and kinship was the thing. A mutual courtesy (Bambara, 1980, p.267).

Insofar as Bambara and other blackwoman authors are prophets of our time who remind us of age-old wisdom and the power we have, I feel more confident in the opportunity to witness to the real intersections that fell so naturally between my teaching, research and service. I have indeed discovered so much in the telling. So, this is hardly a litany against service—quite the opposite.

Service is uniquely revealing and absolutely necessary. It is our moral imperative to serve others and to be responsible to our communities by achieving our own success and being enthusiastic about inconveniencing ourselves for the purpose of the success of others. There is, in my view, no other meaningful reason for my success if there is no legacy or opportunity left in or for anyone else. My position in a PWI requires that I perceive of my significance more clearly, that I reflect upon it and follow the wisdom I find. Further, as I contemplate the invisible layers of my labors, I am actually suggesting that there is a necessity to recognize the careful inlay of what is least valued and not usually apparent in the dossier and to realize that it is what is unsaid that remains a significant factor in the understanding of a blackwoman's experience in academia. That experience is mediated by one's personal decision and responsibility to serve and not doing so can easily find one suffering from a similar distress. But in witnessing to the process, the ritualized acknowledgement and recovery, we gain insight for the future challenges, of which there will be many,

> Velma would remember it as the moment she started back toward life, the moment when the healer's hand had touched some vital spot and she was still trying to resist, still trying to think what good did wild do you, since there was always some low-life gruesome gang bang raping lawless careless pesty last straw nasty thing ready to pounce, put your total shit under arrest and crack your back—but couldn't. And years hence she would laugh remembering she'd thought *that* was an ordeal. She didn't know the half of it. Of what awaited her in years to come (Bambara 1980, p.278).

In this sense I take to heart the experience of Olga Idriss Davis that led to her revelation that we must work toward, "transforming oppression into strategies for struggle and survival in the academy, and [challenge] ways of conceptualizing reality and relationships outside and beyond the strictures of academic thinking" (Davis 2008, p.178). I join her in releasing an attitude of the burden of service when I acknowledge my own narrative, articulate my personal ritual performance that reveals to me how very necessary is my struggle and my survival and my service.

References

Abel, E., Christian, B. & Moglen, H. (1997). *Female subjects in black and white: race, psychoanalysis, feminism.* Berkeley & Los Angeles, CA: University of California Press.

Alexander Jr., R. & Moore, S. (2008). The benefits, challenges, and strategies of African American faculty teaching at predominantly white institutions. *Journal of African American Studies*, 12, 4-18.

Ashford, J., LeCroy, C. W., & Lortie, K. L. (2006). *Human behavior in the social environment: A multidimensional perspective* (3rd ed.). Belmont, CA: Thompson.

Bambara, T. C. (1980). *The salt eaters.* New York, NY: Random House, Inc.

Bell, C. (1992). *Ritual theory, ritual practice.* New York, NY: Oxford University Press.

Berry, T. R. & Mizelle, N. D. (2006). *From oppression to grace: Women of color and their dilemmas in the academy.* Sterling, VA: Stylus Publishing.

Brown, K. N. (2010). *Writing the revolutionary black diva.* Bloomington, IN: Indiana University Press.

Davis, O. I. (2008). A visitation from the foremothers: black women's healing through a 'performance of care'—from African Diaspora to the American academy. *Women's Studies in Communication, 31*(2), 175-185.

Dozier, R. (2010). The declining relative status of black women workers, 1980-2002. *Social Forces, 88*(4), 1833-1858.

Feagin, J. R. (2002). *The continuing significance of racism: U.S. colleges and universities.* Washington, DC: American Council on Education.

Gavin, A. R., Chae, D. H., Mustillo, S. M. & Kiefe, C. I. (2009). Prepregnancy depressive mood and preterm birth in black and white women: Findings from the CARDIA study. *Journal of Women's Health, 18*(6), 803-811.

Gregory, S. T (1999). *Black women in the academy: The secrets to success and achievement.* New York, NY: University Press of America.

Harley, D. (2008). Maids of academe: African American women faculty at predominately white institutions. *Journal of African American Studies, 12*(3), 19-36.

Heintzman, P., & Mannell, R. C. (2003). Spiritual functions of leisure and spiritual well-being: Coping with time pressure. Leisure Sciences, *25*, 207–230.

Hendrix, K. G. (2002). "Did being black introduce bias into your study?": Attempting to mute the race-related research of black scholars. *Howard Journal of Communications, 13*, 153-171.

Jones, C., Wainwright, G., Yarnold SJ, E., Bradshaw, P. (1992). *The study of liturgy.* New York, NY: Oxford University.

Mitchell, L. L. (1988). *The meaning of ritual.* Harrisburg, PA: Morehouse Publishing.

Modica, J. L. & Mamiseishvili, K. (2010). Black faculty at research universities: Has significant progress occurred?. *Negro Educational Review, 61*, 107-122.

Patton, T. O. (2004). Reflections of a black woman professor: racism and sexism in academia. *Howard Journal of Communication, 15*, 185-200.

Rockquemore, K.A. & Laszloffy, T. (2008). *The black academic's guide to winning tenure—without losing your soul.* Boulder, CO: Lynne Rienner Publishers.

Some, M.P. (1993). *Ritual: Power, healing and community.* Portland, OR: Swan and Raven.

Stanford, A.F. (1994). Mechanisms of disease: African-American women writers, social pathologies, and the limits of medicine. *NWSA Journal, 6*(1), 28 – 47.

Stout, P. A., Staiger, J. & Jennings, N. A. (2007). Affective stories: Understanding the lack of progress of women faculty. *National Women's Studies Association Journal, 19*(3), 124-144.

Townsley, N. C. & Broadfoot, K. J. (2008). Care, career, and academe: Heeding the calls of a new professoriate. *Women's Studies in Communication, 31*(2), 133-142.

Williams, J. C. (2004). Hitting the maternal wall. *Academe, 90*(6), 16-20.

Internet sources

http://diversitydata.sph.harvard.edu/Data/Profiles/Show.aspx?loc=1276; [accessed March18, 2011]

http://quickfacts.census.gov/qfd/states/53/53033.html; [accessed March 18, 2011]

http://quickfacts.census.gov/qfd/states/53/53033.html; [accessed March 18, 2011]

Chapter Four

Black Faculty Members in Predominantly White Universities: Challenges, White Privilege, Strengths and a Vision for the Future

Jeanette R. Davidson

Introduction

The subject matter of "challenges" for Black faculty in pre-dominantly White universities/ institutions (PWIs) is commonly discussed in the literature (e.g. Davidson & Davidson 2009; Kendall 2006; Hale 2004; Law, Phillips & Turney 2004; Mabokela & Green 2001; Thompson & Louque 2005), at academic conferences (National Conference on Race & Ethnicity, NCORE 2011) and in private discourse. It is understood that campuses are often racially biased environments and that, despite their lofty reputations, many universities are little or no better than other institutions in the rest of society, and in fact sometimes are worse. It is also commonly recognized that even the most successful Black faculty members in predominantly White institutions, achieve as they do *in spite of* racially charged obstacles, not because of the *absence* of obstacles.

It is obvious that the academy needs to be rid of racial bias if it is to reach its fullest potential. Thompson & Louque (2005) outline common problems identified by participants in their research, related to respect in the workplace, cultural sensitivity, racism, the hidden "rules", the need for a supportive work environment, whether or not Black professors' contributions are valued and what they call the ultimate issue of "to leave or not to leave" an institution (p.2). Other factors they discuss include hiring practices, campus climate and barriers to tenure and promotion, the fear of losing jobs for speaking out and covert strategies that silence or punish Black faculty members who do so, undervaluing community service, skepticism about the qualification of Black faculty members and disparagement of their research on "Black issues".

Special challenges exist within the academy for Black women (and other women of color). These are often described as "double jeopardy" because of the impact of both race and gender (Mabokela 2001; Thomas 2001; Turner & Meyers 2000). "Disturbing trends" are discussed by Mabokela (2001) as she notes the general underrepresentation of African Americans in higher education, and access and matters related to entry of African American women into the academic environment. Collins (2001), who observes that there are too few college courses on Black women and their history, also specifies issues affecting Black women in the academy including the climate of the environment, the need for a supportive peer culture, mentorship, role models, the need for more financial support, and retention and tenure. Similarly, Alfred (2001) discusses Black women's challenges of access and inclusion in predominantly White institutions. In this sense, Kirwin (2004) observes, three reasons that,

> higher education must do better—significantly better—in our efforts to create more inclusive campus environments: (1) the correction of past and present inequities; (2) the development of the high-quality workforce our nation will need in the coming decades; and (3) the value added to the education of all students when they learn within a diverse community. (p. xxi)

Despite the attention in the literature to these matters, much of it is ignored or disregarded by a majority of university personnel. This is evidenced by the academy's lack of urgency, and passive acceptance, of the dearth of Black scholars in its midst (Mabokela 2001; Thompson & Louque 2005), often less than five per cent of all faculty members (Hale 2004), and its resistance to proactive change to what should be regarded as a crisis situation. This can at least partly be understood by Hale's (2004) contention that, "no consistent set of rewards and sanctions has been encouraged as a means of holding people accountable in the area of diversity" (p.13).

This chapter will focus on the situation specifically for Black faculty members in the academy from the perspective of the predominance of problems related to White privilege. Following discussion of pertinent literature, some of my first-person experiences as a Black woman, early in my career within the academy, will be presented. Borrowing from social work, a strengths perspective related to Black faculty in PWIs will then be discussed, in the context of there being a need for these institutions to be multiracial and multicultural. Racial inclusiveness contributes to universities being at their collective best, academically, socially and morally. A vision of how universities *could* look in the future, and how this would contribute to their being relevant and sustainable through the 21st century, will be discussed._

White Privilege in the Academy

The context for Black faculty members in PWIs is somewhat varied. Some function with relative ease and have measurably strong support within their institutions. Leaders within certain universities *have* made significant efforts to diversify their campuses and have demonstrated their commitment to strengthening the educational milieu by so doing. Often, however, the academy continues to be described in terms of the prevalence of White privilege (Davidson, Davidson & Crain 2000-01; Kendall 2006) or White Supremacy (Davidson & Davidson 2009; hooks, 1996) or as the "White bourgeois academy" (West,1999). White privilege, perhaps the most commonly used term of the three, refers to the systematic, unfair and unearned, advantaging of White persons. Some believe PWIs are bastions of White privilege with systemic, institutionalized privilege that dominates and subjugates and is pervasive. As Kendall (2006, p. 63) discusses, White privilege refers to an institutional set of benefits granted to White people. This indicates the common problem of disparate treatment for Black faculty members and other faculty members of color within the academy. In PWIs, this is not difficult to understand given their collective history of being designed *by* White men, *for* White men (Collins 2001; Kendall 2006) and the strong general resistance to change the status quo.

One of the academics who first framed the discussion about universities in terms of White privilege, is Peggy McIntosh (1988). Almost a quarter of a century ago, she wrote about the unearned assets she was granted in the academy simply for being White. "Positive" privileges, (like being welcomed in settings or in an institution) she contended, should be entitlements for everyone. "Negative" privileges, (like the ability to dominate and oppress), she advocated should be dismantled. McIntosh listed statements about "privileges" she could count on as a White woman that colleagues of color could not. Sadly, many faculty members of color, in today's academy, would argue that little (if any) structural change has occurred since the time of McIntosh's original writing of these statements. Examples presented by McIntosh that are still often evident in the academy include,

> I can, if I wish, arrange to be in the company of people of my race most of the time.
> I can remain oblivious to the language and customs of persons of color who constitute the world's majority without feeling in my culture any penalty for such oblivion.
> I can go home from most meetings of organizations I belong to feeling somewhat tied in, rather than isolated, out of place, outnumbered, unheard, held at a distance, or feared.
> I can be pretty sure that an argument with a colleague of another race is more likely to jeopardize her chances for advancement than to jeopardize mine.
> If I declare there is a racial issue at hand, or there isn't a racial issue at hand, my race will lend me more credibility for either position than a person of color will have.
> My culture gives me little fear about ignoring the perspectives and powers of people of other races.

> I can arrange my activities so that I will never have to experience feelings of rejection owing to my race.
> I can easily find academic courses and institutions that give attention only to people of my race. (pp. 5-9)

Other writers also specifically address the academy as sites of White privilege. Frances Kendall (2006), a diversity consultant whose services are sought on a number of university campuses, notes that faculty members of color often do not have access to mentoring, promotions, hospitable work environments and senior role models and often experience a sense of isolation, alienation and resignation (p. 28) . She notes,

> ...while white people in the academy and in corporations have little understanding of the complexities of white privilege and how it affects their daily lives, people of color in all organizations are very clear that primary access to power and influence lies in white hands. The enormous difference between these perceptions means there is little common ground on which to build relationships and then create organizations that best use the talents of all the members of their communities. (2006. p.xii)

While other writers (see, Hale 2004; Mabokela & Green 2001; Thompson & Louque 2005), often articulate such problems through the lens of "institutional racism" or as problems related to the absence of "racial diversity", Kendall frames systemic problems in universities as problems engendered by the domination of White privilege. She notes that students often do not gain the knowledge and skill they need for the global marketplace and that universities often ignore the power and oppression of racism in their midst, their " hostile" environments and their " root causes"(p. 27). Kendall describes how White faculty candidates are generally assumed to be "qualified" and people of color are generally assumed to be "unqualified" until they prove otherwise (p. 52) and how constantly this overvaluing of White people and undervaluing of people of color occurs.

Perhaps ironically, it is sometimes the most "liberal" or "progressive" persons who are the most difficult to work with concerning their White privilege (hooks, 1996; Kendall, 2006). They are some of the people who may hold persons of color to a "different" standard for tenure and who, using their "white race card", present themselves as "well-meaning" and "above reproach" (p. 97). Purwar (2004), in the United Kingdom, discusses how "academia prides itself in being an open space" yet is characterized by systems of racialized patronage, marginalization of faculty members of color, ethnic pigeon-holing, infantalization and hyper-surveillance of Black academics. Also, perhaps ironically, even now when there has been a transition from the education of the elite to a much more diverse student population (Pilkington, 2004), this has not trans-lated to appropriate action responses in the academy to promote race equality or diminish systems of White privilege.

Davidson, Davidson & Crain (2000-01), writing about White privilege in university programs that educate helping professionals, focus mostly on the impact of White privilege on students. They specify problems related to White privilege concerning: (1) screen-ing, admission and recruitment issues; (2) decision making pro-cesses within the program; (3) factors influencing the educational milieu; (4) the vulnerability of students of color; and (5) the need for accountability of faculty members with White privilege.

Calling for a "true revolution of values" (1993, p. 6) hooks describes the life of the Black academic on the margins, with many White faculty members lacking in courage and commitment to matters of diversity, and interpersonal dynamics from White femi-nists toward Black women faculty members being characterized by fear, hatred and potential exploitation. She discusses Whiteness as the gold standard from which "difference" is discussed in the academy, or even more problematic, as the unexamined norm. She critiques most White faculty members as being without a radical consciousness of race or even much contact at all with people of color until a student comes into their classroom. Her perspective is that they want to "manage" studies in diversity in ways to perpetu-ate the current system and that the only Black faculty members they want to hire are those who think like them or are co-opted (David-son & Davidson 2009).

Specific actions to fight against White supremacy in the academy include:

1) Rejecting *the paradigm of the servant-served*

hooks sees the dynamics within the academy as echoing the relationship dynamics of White domestic settings with Black hired help, and indicates that, when White women in the academy are challenged on the matter, they typically assume "a posture of innocence and denial" (Davidson & Davidson 2009, p.72; hooks 1994, p.103). hooks' rejection of the role of hired hand in the academy reminds us of the need for Black faculty members to assert ourselves in positions of intellectual and administrative leadership (Davidson & Davidson 2009).

2) Affirming *a presence as a Black body in the White Academy*

Here hooks reminds us that the academy is not accustomed to Black faculty members' presence or physicality in the system and that the privilege of being accepted as "a mind and not a body" is generally reserved for White men in the academy (1994). She likens campuses to plantations where Black persons' interests are not promoted (Davidson & Davidson 2009, p. 72; hooks 1992, p. 84).

3) Overturning *the colonized mind*

hooks understands that the academy needs Black scholars who are outspoken and independent thinkers. Other matters that are important in this context include working for change in the university power structure and affirming multiple Black identities (to challenge colonial, imperialist paradigms of Black identity as one dimensional). There are also strong implications for Black faculty members who undermine and oppress their peers and have colonized minds themselves (Davidson & Davidson 2009).

4) Resisting *a White commodification of Blackness*

hooks challenges White intellectuals when they want to function as owners, interpreters or overseers of Black ideas and images. In such situations, White faculty members often want to be involved in research about race, but in doing so may divorce their studies from the harsh realities of racism and want to privilege their ideas over those of the subjects of their scrutiny, the very people who are being oppressed (Davidson & Davidson 2009).

A First-Person Account

Despite the fact that these recognized institutional problems related to race (and gender) in the academy are well known, I still find it daunting to articulate even a few of the challenges I have faced. I would much prefer this information remain private, even though there is no shame in it for me. In addressing these matters I recognize the risk that I take of sounding as if I am "whining", or "weak." This in itself is demonstration of the absence of White privilege I share with my colleagues of color, when speaking truth to power puts us in the line of fire for criticism. In fact overcoming such challenges contributes to our having the "earned strength" that comes from struggle, spoken of by McIntosh (1988). I am therefore compelled to disclose some of my experiences if my first-person knowledge, voice and visibility can be used to facilitate positive change (Alfred, 2001; Collins, 2001). Many other Black scholars have fallen by the wayside, and many that could have joined the academy have been excluded; but some of us have survived and even thrived. Many of us have done so typically by standing up for ourselves and on occasion having principled, courageous allies, of different racial backgrounds, who were willing to work together in the face of inequity to be more racially inclusive in the academy. Now, our task is to mentor the next generation of scholars, hoping to make universities, across the nation, stronger, more functional, honorable, savvy and ultimately sustainable.

Background Information

As a Black, Scottish woman, my experience in the United States sometimes plays out differently than for American-born Black faculty members, at least when I first meet some people. Born and raised in Scotland, I met and married my American husband there when he was a doctoral student at Edinburgh University. After marrying, we moved to the United States. Even before I entered the academy, actually on my first day of employment as a social worker in the US, a White woman colleague itemized her perception of how

I was viewed, during the hiring process, by some of her peers. High-lighting what she called "strikes" "for" and "against" me, she indi-cated with a finger count, that being Black was a strike "against" me, being from Scotland and having a "cute" accent were strikes "for" me, and so forth. Other variables deemed "positive" included having been educated in Scotland and having medium toned skin (versus darker skin). For some people, my colleague asserted, these added up to the notion that, "She's Black... but not *really* Black... and she's not like *our* Blacks". Thus people may have preconceptions about me, some real, some imagined; some with a possible sub-text. These include: that I am well educated (possible subtext: not like under-educated African Americans who, if successful required Affirmative Action and are not *really* qualified); I speak well (possible subtext: speaks standard English; does not "sound Black" and is not like African Americans who may slip back into Ebonics). One serious misconception sometimes projected upon me is that, coming from Scotland, I will not be strongly affiliated with African Americans (possible subtext: philosophically or politically not expected to be a strong advocate for African American concerns; possibly "Black" on the outside and "White" in the inside; someone who will be assimi-lated and will not cause "trouble", and definitely not "radical").

Hence my first challenge! Incorrect assumptions about my phil-osophical, ethical and political being, made by *some* White persons in the workplace who may have met me briefly and have projected characteristics they *hoped* I would own, inevitably result in my having to deal with their reactions once they realize that I am not at all as they assumed. These reactions include disappointment, anger, sometimes even fury, as those making the assumptions process their feelings, believing they have been duped! Of course they misled themselves. I am always very clear about who I am—a Black woman, of Scottish heritage, who has lived most of my adult life in the United States and who identifies very much with African Americans. In contrast to how some White people perceive me incorrectly at first, African Americans generally recognize our affinity very quickly.

Situation 1

My entrance to the academy began when I was asked to teach an undergraduate social work class, on race and ethnicity, at a local university in the Southwest, as an adjunct instructor. I was probably selected not so much because of my academic record (though I had a 4.0 GPA in my Master of Science in Social Work studies) or my positive reputation as a social worker, but because I was the only person of color in the vicinity with an MSSW, apart from one very senior woman, the only other Black social worker in town. At the time I was working as a social work supervisor and was not focused on entering the academy. To cut a long story short, I negotiated to teach two classes: the aforementioned race and ethnicity class and another on research methods. I already recognized that I did not want to be perceived in a restricted way within the academy i.e. as if I should simply be an "add on" faculty member to teach about race and ethnicity and nothing else. Working hard during that first year, I found that I loved teaching and was very well received by the students. Within a year, the only other woman on the faculty retired. After a national search, I was hired for the full time tenure track job in the program. This was at a time (1986) when, though many faculty members in social work taught with Master of Social Work degrees, there was a growing expectation for new candidates to have doctoral degrees. I therefore promised I would enroll in the social work PhD program at a university located about one hour's drive away. Earning my doctorate therefore, was an additional requirement for tenure.

As promised, I started on my social work doctoral studies, first taking summer classes and evening classes. At the same time I was accruing a very strong teaching record. I taught "across the curriculum" (that is, I could teach practice courses, social policy, research etc.) and always taught five days per week. I also served, at different times, as student advisor and field work coordinator, service intensive functions that took great commitments of time. My workload, designated by the program administrator, required that I was on campus all day, every day. Also, as the only faculty member of color and the only woman in the program, I mentored many students, Black, White, Hispanic and Asian; men and women. At the same time, I began my research and publication agenda. Given the fullness of my daily schedule, and my doctoral studies, my research and writing activities generally had to wait until winter and summer university holidays, but these were progressing nonetheless.

I cannot remember when or why the chair of the program started to articulate negative responses to me, and frankly I do not care to dredge up old memories. I do remember that he made comments frequently about my being "too ethnic" looking. I remember he bemoaned the plight of so-called White victims of "reverse discrimination" and tried (in vain) to insist that I include his perspective on that topic, in my teaching; I remember his rude and inappropriate comments about my body when I was pregnant; and I remember he made comments about women students of color being "great pieces of meat" who thus would "easily get jobs". Whatever the reason for his negative attitudes toward me, I am sure it was because I stood up for myself and for students. These kinds of observations I have noted about him were in keeping with his overall reputation in the local social work community and people of different racial backgrounds, including Whites, routinely assessed him to be racially biased.

After I had completed all the evening and summer classes offered in the doctoral program in which I had enrolled, the aforementioned administrator became insistent that I could not have "time off" to enroll in the remaining classes I needed that were scheduled on weekday afternoons. He also began to schedule evening appointments for me with students requiring advising. At around the same time he also started telling people publicly that I was not going to get tenure. When he stated this to social work faculty members (all White) from the neighboring university in our hometown, friends and colleagues with whom I had positive relationships, they told me immediately, believing his comments to be unfair and inappropriate.

I did not know where to turn. I felt isolated, exhausted, had little socialization within the academy, did not know the "ropes" and had no mentor. I had Black colleagues—friends—but we were all untenured. We were all in the same situation—the "only one" in our respective units. The only two senior Black faculty members that I knew of seemed to be inaccessible, worn out and, from what I had heard, were involved with their own struggles with the university. My answer to all the work expectations I had been given previously had been to keep on working as hard as possible to get everything done, but now I needed a strategy to continue my studies, and earn my doctorate.

After considerable suffering in silence, I approached a senior White woman faculty member whom I had met from another academic unit, and, taking a leap of faith, told her of my situation. She was warm and responsive and promptly arranged a meeting with the dean of the college, and accompanied me to the meeting. Only then did I realize that the reputation of the administrator, with whom I had to work, was well known (yet generally tolerated) at the higher levels of administration. The college dean proved to be very understanding and appeared not to be the least bit surprised at my predicament. He stated he would mandate that my teaching and service schedule would allow me the time to leave campus to attend required doctoral classes, which generally amounted to one or two afternoons per week. Further, upon reviewing the workload I had been given by the administrator in the unit, the dean calculated that it was excessive and inequitable. In fact, he thought it must be prohibitive for research and creative activities. He therefore deemed that my tenure publication requirements would be reduced by half. Though under the circumstances that was a rational and fair decision for him to make, in the long run it would have been difficult, perhaps impossible, for me to live with. I therefore made sure that by the time I was a candidate for tenure I had the normally expected number and quality of publications (plus my doctorate) and no mention of a special arrangement about reduced expectations for publications needed to be placed in my dossier. I successfully completed my doctoral studies in 3 ½ years. This included one semester off from doctoral studies when I had a baby, though I taught all of my classes throughout except for a few weeks of maternity leave. Shortly after earning my doctorate, I was also successful in earning tenure and promotion.

Situation 2

Almost immediately after I earned tenure in the setting described above, I was heavily recruited by a number of "top" social work programs. To take the job I was most interested in would mean moving my family to the Northeast. My husband had a very successful private practice as a psychotherapist and we had two young sons. We were in the middle of building our "dream house". However, we decided this was a great opportunity and would afford us more time together as a family.

Our family income would drop considerably. However, I was being offered what I considered was a good salary. The practice at that particular school of social work was to count the full time salary as payment for 4 days per week. To entice recruits, an offer could be made for "fifth day" salary (i.e. this would amount to an additional 20 per cent in salary during the traditional 9 months academic year) plus "summer salary". This was the offer I received. I was extremely pleased.

I was told by the administrator in authority that the summer funding would be linked with a new, incredible research "trajectory" for me because, in addition to what I was already doing with my own research, he asserted that I would be mentored and would work with a nationally and internationally renowned researcher with whom I would co-write and publish.

I was also told that this particular school of social work did not automatically give tenure to new faculty even if, like me, they already had tenure from another institution, but that I would have associate status. I was then told I could go up for tenure in two years. This was presented in a way such that I perceived it to be the normal process and expectation. Finally, I also was told I could have my children enrolled at the university, tuition free, for their undergraduate degrees once they were college age.

Even though my husband was giving up his successful practice, we thought it was all going to work out, even financially. We had office property we could sell, money we could invest and my husband could easily get an advanced professional position (which he did). We moved to our new location still not having sold our home in the Southwest.

When I arrived on campus, I eagerly tried to arrange a meeting with the researcher with whom I was scheduled to work. After a number of failed attempts because of his busy schedule, I finally did meet him. The setting, in his home (he was between luxurious off-campus offices) was very bizarre. Multiple phones were ringing almost constantly (and one that he answered was placed in a cupboard). A number of graduate students were in various rooms and my host was interrupted so often by them that we could barely finish a sentence each, far less hold a substantive conversation. Most disturbing, he did not seem to have any expectation of working with me. He was not overtly rude or unpleasant. In fact he was friendly. He just seemed not to be invested in the plan or even to have much awareness that there *was* a plan. After other futile attempts to connect with this senior researcher, I returned to the administrator who had initially described the arrangement and had used it to recruit me. We discussed the situation and though vague, he indicated he would say something to the researcher involved.

I was embarrassed. I wanted to fulfill what I perceived as a contractual obligation and I wanted to be involved in the research projects that had been a considerable recruitment "carrot" when described. Troubled by the lack of progress, I mentioned the situation to a colleague, a White woman who had been on the faculty for some time. She looked at me aghast, obviously horrified. I still remember the distressed look on her face as she said of the administrator, "Oh no! You didn't believe him did you? He says it to all the people of color when he tries to recruit them--but it's not true. It's just to get you here! He says anything to get you here, and then does nothing once you are here!" Referring to the researcher, she went on, "He never works with any of the faculty members who are told this. He just wants to put their names on grant applications so it looks like he has a diverse team and so he'll get these huge grants. He just wants to work with his own White graduate students". She then proceeded to list off others who had been told the same as I had about the "research opportunity". Apparently we had all been misled, and everyone seemed to know it except for the latest person being recruited at any given moment. This time I was the person being recruited with the lure and I had moved my whole life and family believing what I had been told.

After two years of not selling our house, and having renters who caused considerable damage to it, (other things happen in addition to what goes on at work), we decided to go back to our home in the Southwest. We spent the third year of our stay in the Northeast organizing our return and interviewing for jobs at a university within commuting distance of our home. I left my position "in good standing", with the administrator who had initially recruited me still wanting to entice me to say! The matter of going up for tenure was moot, since I was not staying at the school of social work, though I did find out later that the process was not exactly as had been presented to me, and the institution had a dreadful record of failing to award tenure to faculty members of color, even to those who were very accomplished, and still does today.

Analysis of Work Situations

A brief analysis of the two situations described above illus-trates the predominance of White privilege in both settings. In the first setting, I felt isolated, in a hostile environment, without role models, mentorship or any immediate supports from a critical mass of Black peers except for others who, like me, were without power status in the university at large. Further, I experienced the typical "double jeopardy," as a Black woman, of being thrust into the role of excessive service expectations. I experienced the "indignities" of comments about how I looked both as a person of color and as a woman. In the second setting I was deliberately misled in the same way as other new faculty members of color reportedly had been at that institution. A pattern had apparently been established where the administrator and the senior researcher had an agreement that advanced a serious White privileged agenda. Clearly there was a pattern of tolerance within both institutions for racial bias in the behavior of the White men who wielded most power in their respective units and a blind eye was turned to their acts of impu-nity. In both settings, I was treated somewhat as a commodity to be exploited and my best interests were certainly not privileged.

Fortunately, in both situations I did have White women col-leagues to whom I could turn, one who gave me guidance and support in reaching out to the dean of the college, and one who explained what was going on! Their input at the time was crucial. I am appreciative of the positive experiences I gained in both set-tings: developing as a teacher; embarking and continuing on my *own* research agenda; gaining a strong positive professional reputation; and establishing wonderful personal and professional relationships. The emotional costs of worrying about how to survive and keep my job in the first setting and the social, emotional and financial costs of moving my family back and forth between different regions of the country, my husband giving up his practice and of being delib-erately misled, are ultimately incalculable. However I recognize that I am one of the fortunate survivors. I have a supportive husband and wonderful family and grew in strength through it all, being able to process my experiences, move on, survive and thrive. I am happy and fulfilled in my work and have had more success in my career than I ever even wished for, so I can review this material without being overwhelmed. I have the satisfaction of knowing I have continuously fought the good fight for more inclusiveness in the academy, motivated and informed by my experiences. At the same time, I know that some people never get over their negative experiences related to race in the academy. Their marriages break up because of the stress; their health breaks down; they do not get tenure; they are broken financially. Some even die prematurely.

These incidents from early on in my career should not lead anyone to think that at some point the challenges stop! Unfortunately, there are many other incidents that underscore the problems of White privilege, as identified in the literature, that I have witnessed or experienced over the years. Even while completing this paper I was obligated to go out of town for a series of meetings with a group of leaders in the academy. The challenge in that situation involved dealing with the remarks of a senior member of the academy using the word "darkies" in the course of his panel presentation. And yes... I had to deal with it publicly. And no.... No-one else publicly rose to the occasion to give me support.

A Strengths Perspective

There are a number of constructive ways to address the problems related to the dominance of White privilege. Elsewhere in the literature, hooks and others call for collective action to facilitate improvement (Davidson & Davidson 2009; hooks 1995). Thompson and Louque (2005) present recommended changes that emerge from their study participants related to improving campus climate, increasing support of Black faculty, more balance in professional duties, better compensation and other incentives and they call for courageous leadership. Pollard (2004) emphasizes the need for institutional initiatives and financial strategies (pp. 273-291).

A problem-oriented approach to White privilege in the academy could be supplanted by a strengths-based, solution-focused approach. Even when problems are clearly "diagnosed" and appropriate "treatment" is prescribed, often the results are not as substantial as anyone had hoped. A strengths perspective (Bartle, Couchonnal, Canda & Staker 2002; Boyle, Hull, Mather, Smith & Farley 2006; Saleebey 2009) places the major focus on the process of dealing with challenges and difficulties faced by individuals, families, groups and communities, not underestimating problems, but building on inherent strengths. In social work and other helping professions, taking a strengths perspective can be a quicker way to success in changing the conditions in which people are living, with greater potential for healing, empowerment and ultimately liberation. Further, when strengths are identified, the task of prioritizing goals is more easily accomplished.

As Saleebey (2009) describes it, there are several working assumptions in a strengths perspective. These include the assumptions that people have untapped, undetermined reservoirs of mental, physical, emotional and spiritual abilities that can be expressed, and that growth is enhanced by attending to these positive abilities. Assumed also is the notion that the inner wisdom of people can be brought into more conscious use by helping people recognize their capacity and the positive power that it has in their lives. Strengths in fact provide the fuel and energy for empowerment.

It should be noted too that focusing on strengths and empowerment is political. Strengths are linked with equitable distribution of societal resources, and the assumption here is that a focus on strengths encourages social-environmental (or systems) explanations (versus blaming the individual) and encourages collaboration with communities. There is also a sustainability factor with a strengths perspective. Individuals and communities are encouraged to be future-oriented and to build on successes rather than past-oriented with a sense of earned helplessness. With their inherent capacities energized, in members of all races in the academy, the academic community could be transformed.

In this context, then, the university community is the "client". Pathology and dysfunction are present. Old ways and patterns of being are destructive. Strengths, resources, capabilities, competencies, wise experience and positive energy directed toward becoming a more inclusive community remain largely untapped. Critical thinking, hope, heroic action and promise, possibility and purpose are underutilized. Caring about inequity for a group of faculty members, which should be central to democratic ideals, is seldom demonstrated and a communal spirit with a goal of community building is frequently missing.

The strengths perspective is valuable, then, when we examine the state of the academy. In social work it has become clear that capitalizing and building on strengths begets other strengths. A louder and clear articulation and outlining of the strengths of having Black faculty members (and other faculty members of color) is a good place to start. Often the majority of faculty and administrators frankly do not know what is going on in the teaching, research and service of Black faculty members, in Black Studies/ African American Studies and other disciplines and are unaware of their strengths within the community. Many are not aware that students *of all races* often voice their discontent with the deficits of the Eurocentrically focused education they are being presented in most of their classes and very much want the kind of content presented by culturally competent Black faculty, recognizing how that better prepares them for today's multiracial workplace. Many members of the academy are unaware, perhaps because they "anesthetize" themselves about White privilege (Kendall, 2006, p. 81), that corporate personnel, social service administrators and practitioners, and other potential employers of our students, are deeply concerned with the gaps in knowledge, the limitations in being able to discuss racial matters and the lack of training in critical thinking exhibited by students when they graduate, if they have been denied a broad, racially and culturally rich education.

Of course, a focus on our collective strengths as Black faculty members would in itself strengthen us, giving much needed affirmation and encouragement. The potential benefit for everyone in the academy, if all were to pull together with a spirit of community, full membership and common goals (as do communities embracing the strengths perspective) would be to bring authenticity and credibility to PWIs with hope for an improved future and an enriched sense of personal and professional meaning.

To illustrate a strengths perspective in the academy, attention in this paper is now directed to (1) focusing on three selected strengths of Black faculty members: intellectual capital; the impact on students; and interaction with communities, and (2) asking and answering three "miracle" questions: How would your lives as Black faculty members be different if there truly was equal opportunity in the academy? What would be the implications for students if there were more Black faculty members? How would universities better achieve their missions if they were more inclusive of Black faculty members? One of the strategies utilized, when taking a strengths approach, is to ask and respond to "miracle questions" (deJong & Berg 2001; Saleebey 2009). This is helpful in order to visualize the change that is desired and to clarify the goals that should be targeted. Frances Kendall (2006) notes that she has seen "an increasing propensity" in colleges and universities to "shrink from the truth about themselves" (p. 124). She goes on to say they want to "create hospitable climates for diverse employees, students and faculty" but "don't really know what that looks like" and "don't know where to start" (p. 124). These questions could help everyone envisage what the academy *could* look like in the future and related goals and objectives could stem from that vision.

Intellectual Capital

Scholarship in the Black intellectual tradition (Davidson, 2010; Davidson & Davidson 2010; Hall 2010; Marable 2000) has increased exponentially in recent years and is a tremendous strength brought to the academy by Black faculty members. Marable presents examples of the exciting intellectual contributions of contemporary Black academics in various fields including the social sciences, literature, political science, and history and also notes the fruitful collaborations of Black scholars with colleagues in Ethnic Studies and Women and Gender Studies (Davidson 2010). Nell Painter (2000) talks about the stunning sophistication of Black scholarship and its focus, not only on histories of peoples and cultures of the African Diaspora but on the meaning of race and difference in general. Bobo, Hudley and Michel (2004) describe the recent scholarship of Black academics as expansive, inclusive, and socially engaging. In fact, this scholarship not only *challenges* the academy it *revitalizes* it and in many instances it retains its function of speaking truth to power (Davidson & Davidson, 2010).

Impact on Students

Another strength brought by Black faculty members is the life altering impact they may have in the classroom upon students. The opportunity, to be taught by a Black faculty member, is significant for students of all racial and ethnic backgrounds. It is informative, potentially liberating and psychologically important. In the best situations, studying with excellent Black professors can help students understand who they are, their meaning, significance, place and agency in life and opens the door potentially to improved critical thinking with new insights, broader contextual understanding, higher order reflection, and increased emotional reasoning (Davidson & Davidson 2010).

Interaction with Communities

At the heart of the best Black scholarship is a connection with the real world and the commitment to social transformation (Davidson & Davidson 2010; Jones & Muhammad 2010; Marable 2000; West 1999). Just as the Black faculty member can facilitate transformation in universities with scholarship and in the classroom with important content and relationships with students, so too can we link universities with various levels of the community. This includes local African American communities that are often ignored by universities on their doorsteps, Black communities throughout the country and in Africa and the Diaspora. There are obvious strengths, including credibility, authenticity and commitment for example, that Black faculty bring when interacting in research initiatives, service learning activities, and other collaborative relationships with such populations. (Marable in Davidson 2010, pp. 96-126).

How the Academy *could* Look for Black Faculty Members

An academy without White privilege would involve a transformation of campus culture for Black faculty members. First, the setting would evolve into one in which Black faculty members would feel as welcomed as White faculty members. All would feel comfortable, "at home", and would have a sense of belonging. Presence on the faculty would be normative. There would be a community of Black scholars. Each professor would be able to count on having support systems, would not be isolated or marginalized on the basis of race and would not be perceived as the "token" Black faculty member in a unit or college. Further, excellent Black faculty members could reasonably expect to succeed in each of the routine processes of recruitment, retention, tenure and promotion and could have equal opportunities to achieve positions of leadership and roles in the upper levels of the administration structures. Scholarship—even about Africa and the Diaspora or about the African American community—would be respected, valued and supported. Black faculty members would find the academy to be a haven, a political sanctuary and there would even be room for so-called "radical" or "transgressive" scholarship (hooks, 1994). Black scholars and scholarship would be at the center of the university's functioning and mission, in an equitable position to that of White scholars and their scholarship.

What the Implications *could* be for Students in Universities

With a representative number of Black faculty members on campuses, emphasizing worldviews other than Eurocentric ones, students could have a plethora of rich text materials and research in the Black intellectual tradition infused in their studies. Course content would be much more inclusive in focus and could present an integrated focus on Black culture, arts, humanities, language, history, the social sciences and professions and, for the first time, students could find sufficient classes in which they could enroll that would move the academy past its PWI status. For field practica and service learning, students would more easily access opportunities to work with Black populations.

Furthermore, students would enroll in class with a Black teacher as a normative experience. They could then benefit from instructors' experiential knowledge and Black students in particular could have teachers who would better understand their struggles and challenges related to race/ background. In such a learning environment, the kinds of class discussions open to students would likely increase their potential for developing empathy for persons different from themselves and all would be enriched by the synergy in the classroom. Importantly, students would also have many Black role models and mentors, a true advantage for students of all racial backgrounds whether these relationships were same-race or cross-racial.

The preparation of students for multiracial/ multicultural interactions with others is a valid concern. With racially diverse faculty members in the classroom, and a representative number of Black faculty members, students would likely have more opportunities to discuss race, and to experience the benefits of racial inclusiveness. Critical thinking skills related to race and emotional reasoning about race would be enhanced (Davidson & Davidson 2010). In the best situations, students would develop cultural competence which would benefit them personally and professionally.

Achieving the Universal Missions of Universities

Most universities, even those that are more progressive in their campus culture, policies and procedures relating to Black faculty members, could benefit from being much more inclusive of Black faculty members. If they did have more diversity, they could take the higher moral ground on race relations in the US. Among organizations, universities could take a leadership role in demonstrating fairness, equity and true adherence to principles of equal opportunity. Further, universities could be fiscally prudent, politically savvy, adaptive, and current, utilizing "best practices" for running 21st century multicultural organizations. With representative numbers of Black faculty members (and other faculty members of color) in their midst, universities could have the personnel and the brainpower to *truly* provide the best education for students. Thus faculties and universities at large could extend opportunities for engaging in extensive, productive collaborations with local Black communities, simultaneously addressing the needs of both by bridging the gap that currently exists. Universities could address social ills affecting large segments of US populations and could reach their mission of serving all groups within their respective states as well as impacting society at large.

Conclusion

To move forward, we need multiracial, multicultural universities. Hale (2004) begins with a question, and then probes more deeply,

> How can any institution of higher learning, calling itself a university, be legitimate in its focus on liberal education unless it is committed to "universality"? True education should address the multiple and complex ways and contributions of various races and cultures in creative, credible, and authentic ways...... The strength and quality of a

university can be judged, in some measure, by the extent to which it is willing to acknowledge the quality, value and integrity of the contributions of people of color as part of American historiography, as well as their vital role in helping the nation achieve its democratic goals. (p. 20)

The current anachronistic model of the academy is dysfunctional. Even though there has been some modest improvement in multicultural, multiracial and international representation at PWIs, students of all racial backgrounds are being drastically shortchanged in their education by those university faculty members and administrators who refuse to move forward and address their needs, and so are the citizens of this country and the world at large. If we are to move forward in our universities, and be sustainable (in the fullest sense of the word) in the 21st century, there has to be radical change that involves inclusivity of all racial groups as faculty members in the academy. Understanding the strengths that Black faculty members and other faculty members of color bring to universities, and appreciating that inclusiveness of faculty members of all racial groups can transform our institutions, enhancing their credibility and legitimacy within and outside the campus environment, is paramount. Tremendous energy within the academy as a system is lost through racially-charged bias and out-of-date thinking. The human resources necessary to make change are there, ready to be nurtured and developed.

References

Alfred, M.V. (2001). Success in the ivory tower: Lessons from Black tenured female faculty at a major research university. In R.O. Mabokela & A. Green (Eds.), *Sisters of the academy: Emergent Black women scholars in higher education.* (pp. 57-70). Sterling, Virginia: Stylus.

Bartle, E.E., Couchonnal, G., Canda, E. R., & Staker, M. D. (2002). Empowerment as a dynamically developing concept for practice: Lessons learned from organizational ethnography. *Social Work, 47*(1), 32-43.

Bobo, J., Hudley, C., & Michel, C. (Eds.) (2004). *The Black Studies reader.* New York: Routledge.

Boyle, S.W., Hull Jr., G. H., Mather, J. H., Smith, L. L., & Farley, O.W. (2006). *Direct practice in social work.* Boston: Pearson

Collins, A. C. (2001). Black women in the academy: An historical overview. In R.O. Mabokela & A. Green (Eds.), *Sisters of the academy: Emergent Black women scholars in higher education.* (pp. 29-41). Sterling, Virginia: Stylus.

Davidson, J. R. (2010). Black studies for the public: Interview with Manning Marable. In J.R. Davidson (Ed.), *African American Studies* (pp. 96-126). Edinburgh: Edinburgh University.

Davidson, J. R., & Davidson, T. (2010). African American Studies: Vital, transformative and sustainable. In J. R. Davidson (Ed.). *African American Studies* (pp. 281-308). Edinburgh: Edinburgh University.

Davidson, J. R., Davidson, T., & Crain, J. (2000-01). White skin and sheepskins: Challenging the status quo in the education of helping professionals. *The Journal of Intergroup Relations 27*(4), 3-15.

Davidson, T., & Davidson, J. R. (2009), bell hooks, White supremacy, and the academy. In M. Davidson & G. Yancy (Eds.). *Critical perspectives on bell hooks* (pp. 68-81). New York: Routledge Press.

DeJong P., & Berg, I.K. (2001). *Interviewing for solutions.* (2nd Ed.) Belmont, CA: Wadsworth.

Hale, F. W. (Ed.). (2004). *What makes racial diversity work in higher education: Academic leaders present successful policies and strategies.* Sterling Virginia: Stylus.

Hale, F. W. (2004). Introduction. In F. W. Hale (Ed.) *What makes racial diversity work in higher education: Academic leaders present successful policies and strategies.* (pp. 3-23) Sterling Virginia: Stylus.

Hall, P. A. (2010). African American Studies: Discourses and paradigms. In J. R. Davidson (Ed.), *African American Studies* (pp. 15-34). Edinburgh: Edinburgh University.

hooks, b. (1993). A revolution of values: The promise of multi-cultural change. *The Journal of the Midwest Modern Language Association, 26*(1), 4-11.

hooks, b. (1992). Black looks: Race and representation. Boston: South End Press.

hooks, b. (1996). Blacks must recognize and fight oppression. In B. Szumski (Ed.), *Interracial America: Opposing viewpoints* (pp. 72-81). San Diego: Greenhaven Press.

hooks, b. (1995). *Killing rage.* New York: Henry Holt.

hooks, b. (1994). *Teaching to transgress.* New York; Routledge.

Jones, C. E., & Muhammad, N. (2010). Town and gown: Reaffirming social responsibility in Africana Studies. In J. R. Davidson (Ed.), *African American Studies* (pp. 55-75). Edinburgh: Edinburgh University Press.

Kendall, F. E. (2006). *Understanding White privilege: Creating pathways to authentic relationships across race.* New York, Routledge.

Kirwin, W. E. (2004). Foreword. Diversity in higher education: Why it matters. In F. W. Hale (Ed.) *What makes racial diversity work in higher education: Academic leaders present successful policies and strategies.* (pp. xxi-xxiv) Sterling, Virginia: Stylus.

Law, I., Phillips, D., & Turney, L. (Eds.) (2004). *Institutional racism in higher education.* Stoke on Trent: Trentham Books.

Mabokela, R.O. (2001). Introduction: Soaring beyond boundaries. In R.O. Mabokela & A. Green (Eds.), *Sisters of the academy: Emergent Black women scholars in higher education.* (pp. xiii-xx). Sterling, Virginia: Stylus.

Mabokela, R. O., & Green, A. (Eds.) (2001). *Sisters of the academy: Emergent Black women scholars in higher education.* Sterling, Virginia: Stylus.

Marable, M. (2000). Introduction: Black Studies and the racial mountain. In M. Marable (Ed.) *Dispatches from the ebony tower: Intellectuals confront the African American experience.* (pp.1-28). NY: Columbia University Press.

McIntosh, P. (1988). *White privilege and male privilege: A personal account of coming to see correspondences through work in Women's Studies.* (Working paper No. 189). Wellesley, MA.: Wellesley College Center for Research on Women.

National Conference on Race and Ethnicity (NCORE). San Francisco, June 2011.

Painter, N. I. (2000, December 15). Black studies, Black professors, and the struggles of perception. *The Chronicle of Higher Education,* pp. B7-B9.

Pilkington, A. (2004). Institutional racism in the academy? Comparing the police and university in Midshire. In I. Law, D. Phillips & L. Turney (Eds.), *Institutional racism in higher education* (pp. 15-26). Stoke on Trent: Trentham Books.

Pollard, L. N. (2004). Foundations for making racial diversity work. In F. W. Hale (Ed.) *What makes racial diversity work in higher education: Academic leaders present successful policies and strategies.* (pp. 273-291). Sterling, Virginia: Stylus.

Purwar, N. (2004). Fish in and out of water: A theoretical framework for race and the space of academia. In I. Law, D. Phillips & L. Turney (Eds.), *Institutional racism in higher education* (pp. 49-58). Stoke on Trent: Trentham Books.

Saleebey, D. (2009). Introduction: Power in the people. In D. Saleebey (Ed.), *Strengths perspective in social work practice* (pp.1-23). (5th Ed.). Boston: Pearson.

Thomas, G. D. (2001). The dual role of scholar and social change agent: Reflections from tenured African American and Latina faculty. In R.O. Mabokela & A. Green (Eds.), *Sisters of the academy: Emergent Black women scholars in higher education.* (pp. 81-91). Sterling, Virginia: Stylus.

Thompson, G.L., & Louque, A. C. (2005). *Exposing the "culture of arrogance" in the academy: A blueprint for increasing Black faculty satisfaction in higher education.* Sterling, Virginia: Stylus.

Turner, C. S. V., & Myers, S. L. (2000). *Faculty of color in academe: Bittersweet success.* Boston: Allyn & Bacon.

West, C. (1999). The dilemma of the Black intellectual. In C. West, *The Cornel West reader* (pp. 302-315). New York: Basic Books.

Chapter Five

Black Hair Politics in White Academia: With Reference to Black Studies

Mary Phillips

. . . I hit the barber shop real quick
Had 'em give me little twist and it drove 'em crazy
And then I couldn't get no job
Cause corporate wouldn't hiring no dreadlocks
Then I thought about my dogs on the block
Kinda understand when they chose to stealin' rock
Was it the hair that got me this far? . . .
'Cause success didn't come 'till I cut it all off

When the cops wanna harass cause I got braids
Ain't seen nothin' like that, not in all my days.
Man, you gotta change all these feelings
Steady judging one another by their appearance
Yes India, I feel ya girl!

– India Arie featuring Akon, *I am not my hair* (2006)

In the song *I am not my hair* rapper Akon highlights the limited access and negative treatment he received by community members, corporate America, and police enforcement in embracing his natural hair. While India.Arie proclaims that she is not defined by her hair Akon illustrates the social implications of wearing natural hair. This essay addresses black hair politics specifically in academia. I begin with a discussion on black feminist thought and its relationship to body politics. I discuss two major hair stories in illustrating internalized racism as it relates to hair politics in Black Studies programs/departments and support service units targeted toward students of color.

My hair is important to my identity as a black woman, as a black feminist. Feminist activist, Pearl Cleage (1994) defines feminism as "the belief that women are full human beings capable of participation and leadership in the full range of human activities-intellectual, political, social, sexual, spiritual and economic" (p.28). In the article, "What's In A Name? Womanism, Black Feminism, and Beyond" (1996) sociologist Patricia Hill Collins asserts that "feminism constitutes both an ideology and a global political movement that confronts sexism, a social relationship in which males as a group have authority over females as a group" (p.12). She argues that feminism challenges economic injustices associated with women including global poverty, political rights, marital and family concerns, and women's health issues. Black feminism allows "African American women to examine how the particular constellation of issues affecting black women in the United States are part of issues of women's emancipation and struggles globally" (1996, p.13).

Moreover, Collins (2000) argues that black feminist thought "aims to empower African-American women within the context of social justice sustained by intersecting oppressions" (p.22). Black feminist thought recognizes the lived experience while also encouraging black women to create new definitions surrounding self-identity. Black feminism as a political practice, counters the oppression of black women.

As a black feminist, the Combahee River Collective's manifesto on black feminism also resonates with me. Their manifesto recognizes racism, sexism, heterosexism, patriarchy, and capitalism as interrelated forces that affect black women. They argue that "sexual politics under patriarchy is as pervasive in black women's lives as are the politics of class and race"; thus, race, class, and gender cannot be addressed as separate entities (1995, p.243). As socialists, they believe that the economic, sexual, and racial oppression of the working class must be verbalized and addressed. The oppression central in the personal lives of black women makes necessary a political force toward liberation; therefore, the women of the collective assert that the personal is political. Personal matters as it relates to body politics particularly hair and weight are political issues. Black feminist thought is useful in that it places meaning and validates the lived experience of black women.

Hair Story #1

I was a master's student in the African American and African Studies Department at a Big Ten University and I wore natural hair. In *Hair Story: Untangling the Roots of Black Hair in America* (2001) Ayana D. Byrd and Lori L. Tharps mention that "the Natural was unstraightened Black hair that was not cut close. It was a less sculptured, less maintained version of the rounded, perfectly actualized Afro" (p.57). I created a crinkly version of the traditional Afro by braiding my hair at night in a bunch of small braids and unbraiding them in the morning and finger picking my hair into my style. I had learned to love and appreciate my natural hair from my mother. She taught me how to properly take care and manage my natural hair. As a student in Black Studies, I believed my natural hairstyle would be embraced, and certainly did not expect to get any criticism about my hair from a black professor in the department. One day, a familiar Black female professor, approached me while I reviewed some material in preparation for class in the departmental lounge where many of the graduate students congregated. She said, "What's wrong with your hair? You need to do your hair." She then touched my hair and further commented, "You need to go to the salon to get your hair done. Girl, you need a perm!" From her perspective my natural hair desperately needed a chemical alternation to fit the european trope of beauty. The conversation left me in shock that a black female professor in a Black Studies department would encourage me to look European.

Hair is extremely important within the black community. The social significance of hair has deep cultural and spiritual roots. In many African countries hair served as a form of communication and a source of empowerment. Juliette Harris (2001) suggests that "African women appreciated the nappy texture and hard density of their hair because these qualities made it capable of being molded into elaborate forms that could speak in all kind of ways" (p.153). During slavery in the Americas slave holders used hair to reinforce slave status. Bryd and Tharps (2001) suggest that "white slave owners sought to pathologize African features like dark skin and kinky hair to further demoralize the slaves, especially women . . . When the slave women internalized the slave owner's racist rhetoric, which was almost inevitable, it wasn't long before they passed the pathology on to their sons, daughters, and future generations" (p.14).

Consequently, a long-standing caste system in the black community stratified people particularly by their hair texture. The black community utilizes terms such as "good hair" and "bad hair" in their rhetoric and common language. Scholar Ingrid Banks (2000) defines these terms as follows,

> Nappy; kinky; 'bad hair': Hair that is tightly coiled or curled. This type of hair is referred to as 'natural' black hair because it is not chemically altered . . .'Good hair': hair that is naturally straighter in texture. However, 'good' hair can be quite curly but it is not tightly coiled or curled such as nappy hair. 'Good' hair is defined in relationship to 'bad' hair and is perceived as more manageable and desirable. (p.172)

The Black Studies professor imposed these European beauty standards on me by suggesting that my hair was nappy; therefore, inappropriate. For me, Black Studies existed as a space in which I could express my naturalness and feel safe without fear of ridicule. Black Studies celebrated blackness and worked in an effort to center and validate the black experience.

Black Studies manifested out of the Black Power Movement. Black Power is the belief that by rejecting mainstream American social constructions of racial identity, adopting an African-centered selfhood, and by creating a sense of urgency the black community can protect itself from institutional antagonism, elevate itself from economic despair, and transform the overall socio-political system. Black Power manifested in numerous places including college campuses. On predominately white campuses black students felt isolated and separated from the college environment. Their dismay and frustration caused students to challenge the University system in numerous ways. Students started demanding revisions to admission procedures, an end to police harassment, separate courses and programs that addressed the black experience, separate dormitories and student organizations, and an increase in black faculty and staff to name a few. This marked the beginning of the Black Studies Movement. The purpose of Black Studies is to challenge European discourse, develop critical thinking skills, instill race-pride and self-definition, and promote social change. Nathaniel Norment Jr. defines Black Studies as an "academic discipline which seeks to investigate phenomena and interrogate issues of the world from an Afrocentric perspective" (Norment 2007, p. xxxiii). The production of knowledge on the Black Diaspora works in an effort to emancipate the Black community.

Black Studies scholar, Maulana Karenga in *Introduction to Black Studies* (2002) defines Black Studies as the "critical and systematic study of thought and practice of African people in the current and historical unfolding" (p.3). He emphasizes the need to connect the community with the college campus in a "mutual exchange, where knowledge is shared and applied in the service of liberation and development of the Black community" (2002, p. 20). He stresses that Black Studies provides agency to Black people across the Diaspora. This agency is articulated in various ways including hair. Hair denoted a political allegiance to Black Power politics. The Afro served as a clear rejection to white beauty standards. It represented a direct affront to the white power structure. Scholar Noliwe M. Rooks (1996) stresses that "the Afro was understood to denote black pride, which became synonymous with activism and political consciousness" (p. 6). The Afro served as a proud symbol of blackness.

Specifically Black Studies was a unique discipline that bridges knowledge production with social responsibility (theory and practice). Hair became intricately tied to social responsibility. Banks (2000) asserts that "the long straight and curly hair that had been idolized by blacks in the 1950's and earlier was rejected by a generation of blacks influenced by the Movement" (p.127). I fully embraced this theory in practice and exhibited my politics through my hairstyle. Although many faculty, staff, and students no longer wore natural hairstyles, it remained important for me to link my hair to my Black Power politics. As a black feminist scholar of Black Studies hair, about self-determination, served as a constant reminder of the history of the black struggle and a form of resistance to opposing messages via advertisements, commercials, and popular culture that emphasized that society deemed straight hair most appropriate for black women. Black Studies provided me solace from these messages. The ill-treatment I received due to my natural hairstyle is counter-revolutionary to this mission of Black Studies.

Growing up I read many stories about hair discrimination in the workforce specifically as it related to braids. In the 1980's and 1990's many black women endured heavy criticism and condemnation in the workforce for wearing their hair in braids and other natural hairstyles. Many employers felt threatened by black women's hair. Banks (2000) mentions that, "in the late 1980's, black female employers went to court to challenge a policy by Hyatt Hotels and American Airlines against wearing braids. These companies couched their policy in terms that related to 'appropriate' grooming practices, which they argued braids violated" (p. 16). The discord surrounding black hair within corporate America dehumanized blacks and reinforced white domination.

Now in the twenty-first century this form of prejudice still prevails in society particularly within various sectors of higher education.

Hair Story #2

I have experience working in a student affairs unit that supports and assists students of color in transitioning to college. Regularly I proudly wore my hair natural to work. Naively, I believed that my hair would be embraced in a cultural office. One day I came to work preparing for one of my daily staff meetings when a co-worker pulled me aside. We walked outside of the meeting space and she told me that most of the co-workers believed I did not groom my hair in the morning. She told me that many people felt that my hair was unkept and looked "too wild." She explained that everyone had been gossiping about me and my hair for some time.

Closing the conversation, she mentioned that she could not take these mean-spirited statements anymore and wanted to make sure I knew about these discussions. I was mortified. After our conversation I walked back into the meeting room to rejoin my co-workers. I planned to keep it together until after the staff meeting but I started tearing up and everyone knew that the co-worker had told me about the discussions. Many of the people involved in these conversations I worked with as a student leader during my undergraduate years. They stated that this very personal issue had been difficult for them to address with me. A male staff member mentioned that he approached several different female administrators to talk to me about these concerns. He hoped that they had talked to me and did not anticipate that I would find out in this manner. Clearly so disturbed by the situation, they excused me from the meeting. As I departed, I told them that the way I had been treated was not right.

When I came to work the next day the director wanted to address this issue without any regard for my well-being. He immediately met with me and a senior staff member. Enraged, I explained that my mistreatment centered on my hair and my full figure and argued it was an injustice. Theoretically the office marketed an openness to cultural difference but they did not put this mission in practice. In reality, cultural difference terrified them. They practiced a politics of assimilation and my black female body threatened their conservative notions. I recognized the hypocrisy and feared students would be impacted by their negative attitudes and behavior.

The following day a female senior staff member told me to look at the hairstyles of other black women in the unit (most of them wore straight hair or a straight weave) and use that as a marker for appropriate hairstyles at work. To wear my hair like them, I explained to her, would contradict my core values. Instead, I would negotiate by wearing kinky-twists and I refused to compromise any further. All but one person in the office is a person of color. They have internalized stereotypes about their own people as ugly, deviant, and sub-human. The office is shaped by institutional white supremacist ideology and commonly practices cultural insensitivity. My hair performed "a black aesthestic that is linked to an authentic or radical blackness in the imagination of many whites", which caused them to reject this style (Banks, 2000, p.17).

My fear in their treatment negatively impacting students of color came true; I often received complaints by African American female students regarding nasty comments about their natural hair from staff members. I took the issue to the legal office on campus but they told me that the legal process would be long, painful, and humiliating. They suggested that I document everything; however, very little would probably come out of the case. I was told to put the manner behind me and move on. The office sent a short article to me regarding rights involving black hair in the workplace but they did nothing else about the issue.

Throughout history, black women's bodies have been constantly under assault and exposed to institutional violence. Black women's bodies have been controlled and stripped of humanity. Communities of color have often stigmatized other community members for not adhering to certain patriarchal norms set by white America. Bryd and Tharps (2001) discuss the comb test and brown paper bag test practiced within the black community in the late nineteenth-century. They write,

> In some churches a fine-toothed comb was hung from the front door. All persons wanting to join the church had to be able to pass the comb smoothly through their hair. If their hair was too kinky membership was denied. This was known as the comb test. There was also the brown-bag test, by which the skin was measured for lightness against a paper bag. During this time, historically Black colleges and universities like Howard (established in 1867), Hampton (1968), and Spelman (1881) were founded to educate the Black elite, but . . . judging from photographs of the early graduates, it seems as if one of the unspoken requirements for admission was a skin tone or hair texture that showcased a Caucasian ancestor. (p. 22)

In many ways modern versions of the comb test and paper-bag test are practiced in various sectors within black and other communities of color. I experienced not only hair but weight discrimination. Societal messages reinforce that women should be thin, fragile, and weak. Scholars Dina Giovanelli and Stephen Ostertag (2009) assert societal gender codes are that "a woman must be smaller than a man, demure, and take up little space. Fat women are, then, the antithesis of what it means to be appropriately feminine" (p.290). My hair and plus-size weight served as a double threat to the staff members.

Many nationalists believe when black people alter their natural hair they exhibit forms of self-hatred. Although I have nationalist leanings, I believe these issues are much more complicated. While self-hatred may be the case for some black people, others may have a strong sense of race pride and still choose to straighten their hair for other reasons such as social acceptance. Mariam Kaba (2001) insists that "Black women are in search of some of the privileges that the 'dominant' culture enjoys—a piece of the pie. And in the United States, where white men continue to control the institutions of consequence, they rightly associate whiteness with power" (pp.104-105).

In a society in which white domination is maintained, hair as well light skin can provide access to resources. Although racism limits these opportunities in some cases, hair and light-skin can provide certain comforts and mobility. While I protest these constructs of white supremacy by choosing not to chemically alter my hair, I do not judge other people for their hairstyle preferences; however, I strongly believe that the staff members discussed possess a strong sense of self-hatred about themselves and their community. I label these staff members as brainwashed not because of their hairstyle choices but on the grounds of their persecution of me. bell hooks (1992) suggests that "forms of representation in white supremacist society that teach black folks to internalize racism are so ingrained in our collective consciousness" that we sometimes ostracize people in our community that oppose these standards.

Black Women's Hair and Popular Culture

The mainstream narrative often excludes women in the Black Power movement. When women are mentioned their activism is often reduced to surface discussions. In particular, it is problematic that Angela Davis' afro has become more famous than her actual activism in the movement. In recognizing her icon status Davis, discusses the ways in which the image of her afro has been de-politicized. She writes, "I am remembered as a hairdo. It is humiliating because it reduces a politics of liberation to a politics of fashion" (1998, p. 274).

Black women's hair is often featured as topics within popular culture. Most recently Chris Rock's documentary, *Good Hair* (2009) received a high level of attention on televisions shows, web sites, and blogs. Although hesitant at the fact that Rock was a man tackling these very personal issues as it related exclusively to black women's hair. I eagerly anticipated the release of this documentary; after all, Rock was a black man, and therefore I assumed his blackness provided him with some understanding of these issues. In NYDailyNews.com he stated, "'Just from growing up in Brooklyn and seeing my mother and aunt get their hair done, I knew a little bit about black women's hair'" (2009, p.1). However, Rock did not adequately address black women's hair politics in the film.

Based on the title, *Good Hair* I assumed that Rock would offer a more political critique on the "good hair/bad hair" dichotomy maybe even asserting that all black hair is "good hair" and suggesting that we relinquish these terms within the black community. The documentary opened with his deep concern regarding the negative perceptions his two young girls internalized about their natural hair. As he continued he discussed black hair care as a booming business and the ways in which black women worked to achieve "good hair" at any cost. He failed to provide a balanced view and excluded the perspective of women with natural hair.

Shortly after the release of this film while sitting in a restaurant with a friend, a woman of color came up to me, touched my hair and said, "your hair is so beautiful, it looks just like yarn, is it yours." This woman was culturally insensitive and normalized ideas associated with white power in her attempt to violate my body and personal space. As I close this essay I return to India Arie in her song *I am not my hair* (2006),

> Good hair means curls and waves
> Bad hair means you look like a slave
> At the turn of the century
> It's time for us to redefine who we be . . .

I am not my hair, I am not this skin
I am not your expectation, no
I am not my hair, I am not this skin
I am the soul that lives within

Overall, I agree with her that we must redefine beauty standards within the black community; however, her song is very utopian. The real life implications of not conforming to a European aesthetic often times can result in scorn, ridicule, isolation, and mistreatment within the workplace and the broader society. A history of white supremacy has deeply influenced many communities of color to internalize racism, and aspects of self-hatred. We must work to eradicate these practices in units, departments, and programs in higher education that foster academic achievement and student success as it relates to communities of color. Contrary, to India Arie my lived experience dictates that "I am my hair" and that it profoundly impacts my life chances when I decide to be a Black woman with natural hair in White academia.

References

Arie, I. (2006). I am not my hair. *Testimony: Vol.1, Life and relationship,* Motown Records.

Banks, I. (2000). *Hair matters: Beauty, power, and Black women's consciousness.* New York: New York University.

Byrd, A. D. and Tharps, L.L. (2001). *Hair story: Untangling the roots of black hair in America.* New York, St. Martin's.

Collins, P. H. (1996). What's in a name? Womanism, Black feminism, and beyond. *The Black Scholar* 26 (1), 12.

_____. (2000). *Black Feminist Thought: Knowledge, Consciousness, and the Politics of Empowerment.* (2nd ed.) New York: Routledge.

Cleage, P. (1994). *Deals With the Devil and Other Reasons to Riot.* New York:Ballantine Books.

Combahee River Collective. (1995). A Black feminist statement. In B. G. Shefthall (Ed.), *Words of fire: An anthology of African—American feminist thought* (pp.243). New York: New Press.

Davis, A. (1998). Afro images: Politics, fashion, and nostalgia. In James J. (Ed.), *TheAngela Y. Davis Reader.* (pp.274). Malden: Blackwell Publishers.

Giovabelli, D. and Ostertag, S. (2009). Controlling the body: Media representations, body size, and self-discipline. In E. Rothblum and S. Solovoy
(Eds.), *The fat studies reader* (p. 290). New York: New York University.

Harris, J. (2001). The culture of hair sculpture. In J. Harris and P. Johnson
(Eds.),*Tenderheaded: A comb-bending collection hair stories.* (p. 153).
New York: Pocket Book.

hooks, b. (1992). *Black looks: Race and representation.* Boston: South End
Press.

Kaba, M. (2001). When Black hair tangles with white power. In J. Harris and
P. Johnson (Eds.), *Tenderheaded: A comb-bending collection hair stories*
(pp. 104-105). New York: Pocket Book.

Karenga, M. (2002). *Introduction to Black Studies,* (3rd ed.) Los Angeles: University of Sankore.

Norment, N. (2007). *The African American studies reader,* (2nd ed.). Durham:
Carolina Academic.

Osterhout, J. (2009). Chris Rock's New York: As his documentary 'good hair' is
set to open, a tour of his hometown. In *NYDailyNews.com*.

Rock, C. (2009). *Good Hair.* Dir. Jeff Stilson. Lionsgate Entertainment.

Rooks, N. M. (1996). *Hair raising: Beauty, culture, and African American
women.* New Brunswick: Rutgers University.

Part II

Black Male Perspectives

Chapter Six

The Black Intellectual, Reflective, Resistant and Reconstructive: Defining Ourselves in the Predominantly White Academy

❀

Michael E. Dantley

This chapter uses an autobiographical lens to chronicle the life of one African American man in the academy. It offers practical ways for African American scholars to resist hegemonic policies, practices, and perceptions that undergird many of the rituals in predominantly white institutions of higher education. Further, this work grounds life for African Americans in academe employing Cornel West's conceptual frame that explicates the dilemma of the Black intellectual. The chapter ends with promoting a Black-created paradigm about academic life that is grounded in a position of resistance and reform of the white status quo.

My work as an African American man in the academy, particularly as a faculty member in a predominantly white institution, has been exhilarating, sometimes disheartening, intellectually stimulating, while at other times devoid of rhyme, reason or any modicum of rationality. I approach this assignment of articulating the substance of my journey in academe from a perspective of victory, resiliency, and a perseverance to see dreams and visions come to pass. I rejoice over the fact that my narrative, my story, my explication of the dynamics I have witnessed and traversed will be added to the chronicles of other Black professors who have had similar and also very nuanced experiences in the predominantly white academy. While I excitedly write this piece from an autobiographical position, I nonetheless ground my perspectives within the four categories of black intellectuals as outlined by West (1999) and other African American scholars. I first, however will articulate the narrative that circumscribes my experiences as a Black man in academe.

As long as I can remember education has always been a major focus of my life. Being a first generation college student, meandering through the very unfamiliar terrain of the University of Pennsylvania, the collegiate experience for me as an undergraduate student, was not only challenging but inspiring and daunting and somewhat intimidating as well. I attended Penn in the early seventies, when the country was in such positive disarray. It was a season of warranted insurrection and much needed subversion in various corners of society. The fringes had come to overtake the core. The hegemony of the U.S. culture was under critique and castigation. I deeply resonated with the revolutionary fervor that was sweeping the east coast and was really happy to join in a discourse on Penn's campus that centered on resistance and reconstruction. It was also in that revolutionary time frame that I was being prepared to teach middle school English and history while in the back of my mind remained the idea that I would someday become a college professor. This was a dream I had somehow concocted while in high school sans the full understanding of what such a position entailed.

I arrived at the academy as a professor almost immediately following the receipt of my doctorate, after having had a great career in an urban school district and as a result of the university's committed efforts to increase the number of Black professors in the institution. That year thirteen of us became tenure-track members of the faculty, the largest number of Black faculty ever contracted at one time in the history of the university. Such a feat has not ever been repeated; let me hasten to add.

It is important to recognize that the university characterized as a predominantly white institution has within it certain socially constructed norms, rituals, and policies that are purposed to ensure the perpetuity of its culture. So inherent in the very fabric of this system are mechanisms destined to propagate a white, Euro-centric mind set with its host of privileges and marginalizing proclivities. There is no predisposed penchant to celebrate otherness. There is no innate compunction to welcome racial and ethnic diversity. In fact, moves like the one my university took in employing such a large number of Black faculty at one time had to have been accomplished amid contrivances of deliberate and determined resistance, attempts of prevention, and/or well-thought out strategies to limit the impact of such an importation. So it immediately became inevitable that the cohort of new Black faculty members would coalesce in order to forge a formidable resistance and subversion to the systemic ways that the majority population rendered its angst. Allow me to hasten to add that the dominant culture at a predominantly white institution is not monolithic. Many of my white colleagues welcomed our addition to the faculty.

I recall my first office at the university being situated between the offices of two of the leading scholars in critical theory and pedagogy. This was my first encounter with this progressive theoretical frame. Coming to engage the tenets of critical pedagogy through conversations with these two white scholars and reading some of their work that I had not had the privilege to read while in my doctoral program, assisted me to name the multiple social injustices I had lived through as a public school administrator. Both of these scholars offered to read the rough drafts of my work or to co-author an article with me. One possessed so much academic cache that he invited me to write a book review that he assured me would be published in one of the journals on which he sat as an editorial board member. I was amazed that he made the offer with such confidence but I followed through thankful for his largesse and the book review was published. I had not yet performed a critical analysis on the whole publishing process but it did not take me long to discern that beyond writing pieces of intellectual substance, to be published demanded profitable networking and the political savvy to know the ideological bent of a journal as well as the celebrated authors whose work consistently appeared in the journal. My first encounter with publishing quickly taught me the efficacy of being in the right context while elucidating the right content. It was quite an eye-opening lesson I had learned. This was an essential academic lesson that white colleagues taught me.

Simultaneously, some of my Black colleagues eschewed any Black collaborative allegiance and chose to travel the circuitous terrain of the university as an isolate. Even those Black faculty members who had been at my institution prior to our arrival, en masse, as my white colleagues, were not monolithic in their perspectives concerning their experiences. Some of the veteran, Black professors were keenly aware of the racist practices both overt and covert that were embedded deeply into the very fabric of my university. They clearly articulated the marginalizing practices and warned us neophytes to steer clear of the political land mines they believed had been particularly set for us. To some, these voices of warning seemed to resound with a deep paranoia. To others they were telling it like it is. Many of us appreciated and gleaned from the candor of many of the groundbreaking faculty of color. Other faculty assured us that there was no racism on the campus; that they had never experienced disenfranchisement and those who testified that they had simply brought it on themselves. They believed the victims to have been the sufferers of a self-induced victimization because they refused to assimilate to the culture and would not bring themselves to appreciate the back-breaking accommodations the university was attempting to provide to ensure our comfort and fit. It was in this kind of stark binary that most of us found ourselves.

It is vitally important to more fully engage this binary notion. As I believe that this binary is contextualized in what Marable (2006) calls the African American intellectual tradition that has historically, he maintained, been positioned in three principles and practices. He offers that the first principle of this intellectual tradition is descriptive. This means that the work of Black intellectuals presents, "the reality of black life and experience from the point of view of black people themselves" (p. 57). The second principle or practice Marable calls corrective. By corrective, Marable meant that the Black intellectual tradition marshaled its efforts to challenge and critique the pervasive presence of both racism and the inculcation of racist stereotypes that fed reprehensible disenfranchising behaviors and perceptions. Finally, Marable offered the third part of this intellectual tradition as being prescriptive. He defines prescriptive as, "an intellectual orientation that consistently connected scholarship with collective struggle, social analysis, with social transformation" (p. 58).

There were those of us who grounded our intellectual labors in these three principles unknowingly. We did not subscribe to those who achieved Marable's castigation as the black intellectual elite crowned academicians after the civil rights era that distanced themselves from describing, correcting, and prescribing the realities of Black life through their intellectual work. For me, my scholarship had to possess a teleological grounding whose aim was a radical reconstruction of the institutions that were to harbor democratic practices particularly in the culture of educational systems in the United States. I am not suggesting that scholarship alone can deftly serve as the catalyst for societal transformation as may have been the mindset of Du Bois as the Harvard professor, Tommie Shelby (2005) alludes to. Shelby writes that Du Bois required that educated persons must continually remain cognizant of epistemological trends in order to bring about revolutionary social change. To Du Bois, the credentialed thinkers were under obligation to serve as leaders within the Black community with a diurnal view towards liberation and societal transformation. It is from this perspective that Shelby pens,

> This suggests that Du Bois came later in life to think of the black intelligentsia, narrowly construed, as the appropriate leaders of black folk, for only they will have the requisite knowledge and worldly experience to assess the current condition of African Americans and to guide their efforts at self-development in the postindustrial era of global capitalism. (p.93)

For me, my intellectual creativity had to fulfill an axiological calling or an avocation that positioned my work in the hands of other scholars who would be catapulted into a space of revolution and democratic transformation of places called schools. I will go in greater depth on this issue of calling later but suffice it to say that I have always believed that my work was to be subsumed in a progressive, political agenda. One would be unable to read my work and not become agitated to either respond with the motivation to bring about positive democratic change or to become put off by the inherent call to action and accountability so deeply imbedded in my scholarship. This is a very contested notion particularly among Black scholars.

I have taken the approach of writing from a critical, spiritual theoretical frame to prospective school leaders and those who prepare them in institutions of higher education. Unashamedly, I confess that writing to other scholars and students is my niche. I completely understand the notions of our scholarship reaching the masses and those without the benefit of degrees and academic credentials. The late Manning Marable (2006) cited the work of Edward Said who proposed that the intellectuals' responsibility was to articulate a message or a philosophy to a public. In a 1993 lecture as cited by Marable, Said remarked that the intellectuals place is,

> publicly to raise embarrassing questions, to confront orthodoxy and dogma (rather than to produce them) to be someone who cannot easily be co-opted by governments or corporations, and whose raison d'etre is to represent those people and issues that are routinely forgotten or swept under the rug. (p.111)

I wholeheartedly agree with Marable's promotion of Edward Said's position. However, I have established as my field to ask those embarrassing and contentious questions in the very place where traditionally we have been trained to think, to wrestle with ideas and concepts and to create solutions for the formidable problems and enigmas the society faces. I trust that my critical position asks the field of education to grapple with its ways of routinely and systematically forgetting certain segments of the population and to sweep them under the rug in order to propagate its own capitalist-supporting agenda. Over the years, I have not wavered in my calling into question the orthodoxy promoted in the educational system. I have not rested from offering a critical theoretical frame to how schools operate in the hopes of seeing the field of education serve as one of the instruments to forge a substantive agenda of resistance whose result would be a radical reconstruction of our society.

To write from such a political and ideological grounding demanded coalescing with others of similar ilk and calling who could undergird my efforts with encouragement, alternative and yet affirming conceptual and theoretical dispositions and critical listening ears willing to discern the gaps in my thinking and where my intellectual arguments needed to be strengthened. And so the establishment of a special kind of alliance became a necessity.

The Creation of the Safe Space

Those of us who did build camaraderie believed that we were in not only a friendship but also a mentoring and accountability coterie. It was helpful to have other Black folk with whom to commiserate. There were many times as we interfaced with students, other faculty and departmental administrators that we were compelled to inquire of one another, "Am I crazy?" We understood the pervasive nature of racism, however we were somewhat reluctant to label every negative reaction we received as racist. So it was within the intimacy of the small, lunchtime group that we were free to be transparent and to ask the questions that could only be voiced within the confines of a safe space. It is virtually impossible to underestimate the monumental value of a safe space. Were I to offer specific characteristics of a safe space I would list that such a venue has three major constituents. First, a safe space is *affirming*. It is a place where the multiple strengths and contributions we had within us to enhance the institution were auto and externally explicated. It was in this space where colleagues who had taken the time to become acquainted with our strengths, our area(s) of research and our teaching and service contributions dissipated self-doubt. The acclaim that we may have been short on from the university community, we received in the safe space. It was impossible to sustain self-doubt for any extended length of time.

Before discussing the second component of the safe space, it is imperative to give a well-deserved nod to the potentially paralyzing notion of self-doubt. I cannot project onto all Black academicians but for me I have lived in the valley of self-doubt far too long. There have been times when the dominant powers in the academy made me wonder if I was really prepared intellectually to deal with the rigors inherent in an academic life. Part of this seriously pathological irrationality was the way I was raised. My parents propagated a mind -set that offered that I had to be better than my white counterparts. I had to make better grades, work harder to make those grades, go to what were perceived to be better schools to simply be all round better than they were in everything that I did. The pressure to perform is a constant, nagging, and exceptionally annoying part of my academic life. However, being able to talk about it, being able to be transparent about its debilitating presence in the safe space was and continues to be actually liberating because it has allowed me to name my world, to own my own sense of malaise and to be able to free myself from it.

The second characteristic of the safe space is that it complemented affirmation with *accountability*. Out of a motivation of caring and a deep desire to see each of us successful in the institution, the safe space also provided honest feedback and very often a swift kick to either begin the next writing assignment, to complete the one in progress, to revise and resubmit or to send the rejected piece to the next journal. Candor wrapped in concern ran rampant in the safe space, often dressed in humor but genuine sincerity nonetheless. If one of us, over an extended period of time, failed to articulate how we were implementing the next phases of our research agenda the members of the safe space would raise the question regarding our scholarly endeavors or lack thereof. There really was no escaping the call to produce in all of the traditional areas of collegiate responsibility, teaching, scholarship, and service.

The third component of the safe space was *ascription*. Ascription is all about recognizing the qualities or actions specifically germane to someone or something. What ascription looked like in the safe space were the unvarnished, demythologized truths about the university system clearly articulated by each of us there. We would talk about the politicization of the tenure and promotion process. We'd discuss the essential networking that was so advantageous to get our work published. No one was left unscathed by the call and expectation to produce that emanated within the safe space.

Within this context of ascription was always the tension between unraveling the truth about the academic operation and the exercise of healthy paranoia that seemed to be of significant benefit for a scholar of color. There were grounded in the ascription portion of the safe space both the horrendous testimonies of colleagues who failed to attain tenure and promotion because they had totally trusted the system as well as the chronicles of those professors of color who had blazed the trails and had received the coveted award that legitimated academics' labor. I must admit, however, that no Black person's narrative about having achieved tenure and promotion lauded the process as a straight forward and fair one but often lamented the political acumen that was essential to fiord the often inconsistent and surprise-ridden waters. There was the latent power discourse that was pervasive whenever we talked about our work in the academy. We were constantly aware that injustice was an inherent part of the fabric of higher education and yet we each knew that we were called to this work with all of the issues that attended to being in the academy. So though ascription was necessary, affirmation and accountability kept us from becoming so jaded that we would become paralyzed and unprofitable. This was a tension with which each of us regularly contended.

So in this safe space there was laughter and relief but they were laced with injunctions, commissions, and imperatives to get the work done. Insouciance was never displayed in the safe space. One of my colleagues constantly advised us to "take care of ourselves first". My not being familiar with academic life left me to think that my friend meant to provide for our emotional, spiritual, and physical well-being first. Indeed, what he meant was to take care of ourselves, to secure our wobbly place in the academy by writing something everyday, if only one sentence. Undoubtedly, what he knew was that the disciplined regimen of consistent writing would be one way to help us to be emotionally, spiritually, and physically well.

While this has been my personal history as an academic, I am pleased to share that I have achieved tenure and promotion, I am a full professor and now serve as an associate provost and associate vice president for academic affairs. What I would choose to do next in this piece is to locate my personal experiences in the intellectual life in a broader theoretical context. Doing so may provide more generalizability to my testimony as well as to provide a conceptual framework for the lives we lead as Black academics. To assist in this theoretical grounding I will subscribe to West's (1999) essay on the dilemma of the Black intellectual.

Cornel West and the Dilemma of the Black Intellectual

Cornel West argues that the life of a Black intellectual is caught between a general American culture that dismisses and denigrates Black academic work, that minimizes and is most often suspect of the Black academics' intellectual labors and what West regards as a lack of concern and celebration in the Black community for the work Black intellectuals perform. If one contextualizes the Black academic in such a setting, it is easy to see why West contended that the life of a Black intellectual was a lonely one. In fact, West maintained that the Black person, "who takes seriously the life of the mind inhabits an isolated and insulated world" (p. 302). That, West avers, is the crux of the dilemma of the Black intellectual. It is as if the academic is bereft of a place that celebrates and cajoles him/her to continue the work because what the Black academician does is valued and honored.

Though West paints a rather bleak picture for the Black intellectual, one that depicts him/her as having submitted to a "self-imposed marginality" (p.302), I am convinced that the experience of isolationism that may be lived out by some Black scholars comes as a result of doing one's intellectual work with no communal or altruistic purpose. When scholarship is done simply for publishing purposes that leads to a scholar's personal aggrandizement and not for a larger more selfless purpose, then the life of the scholar is doomed to be a solitary one. West offers that for too many Black intellectuals our work is not readily consumed or enjoyed by our own community. Such an assertion assumes a particular nature of scholarship that I am not sure it needs to enjoy. I strongly believe that the enjoyment of scholarship is best manifested as the consumer engages the work, has one or several aha moments and then embraces the arduous task of strategizing to implement or execute what he/she has gleaned from the work. Perhaps this is way too pragmatic for those who disdain a rather utilitarian perspective regarding scholarship but it comfortably rests within my penchant for joining intellectual work with an agenda of reflection, resistance and reconstruction. To separate scholarship from a revolutionary agenda, in my mind, leaves it lifeless and languishing without purpose. So my goal has always been to wed my work with a civil rights, social justice agenda so that actions of transformation and much needed reform emanate from the words I write and speak.

Over time students have come to recognize that my niche is the amalgamation of critical theory, leadership, spirituality, and social justice and so they choose the classes I teach because those ideological frames contour my pedagogical practices. Beyond espousing a particular theoretical position, it is much more profitable, in my opinion, to promote thinking and actions that bring about societal change and over the years students and colleagues have come to expect as well as mostly celebrate the nature of my work. So the stark isolation of which West speaks has not been my experience.

What I have found and continue to discover is that scholars and students alike find their voices through my work, not because my scholarship is so earthshaking but because I have been able to explicate notions that deeply resonate with others because they have felt that there is a connection or nexus among their spirituality, leadership and their deep sense of urgency to bring about societal transformation. Perhaps for the first time, the consumers of my work have found the permission to express these linkages in a way that allows them to be their genuine selves in the academy. That has been so helpful in founding alliances and building substantive relationships throughout academe.

Before leaving this notion of isolation, it is important to share additionally how I have been able to contend against this solitary dynamic West purports. Being in a predominantly white institution, it has been increasingly important that I reach out to probationary faculty and students, particularly Black faculty and students to encourage and edify them as they journey through the labyrinth that so marks life in the academy. Isolationism is minimized when we prioritize the mentoring of other Black scholars. It is as if those of us who were novices now have an obligation to share our wisdom particularly with up-and-coming Black intellectuals. This includes joint writing projects, being ex-officio members of dissertation committees, providing guidance during the promotion and tenure process and establishing a safe space for them as one was created for us.

Academic work can be so individualistic that coming outside of the silo can be almost anathema to the Black intellectual especially as the responsibilities for scholarship production are almost reified by the academic world's hegemony. But it is essential that Black academics embrace the call to build affirming relationships with other

Black academics. What is also essential is for us to engage one or several of four categories Cornel West outlines to contextualize the Black intellectual. Doing so provides a strong theoretical grounding for our work as well as a conceptual lens through which we view the academic experience. I found that adopting two of these frames assisted me to more accurately articulate the theoretical positioning of my scholarship, teaching, and service responsibilities.

Four Conceptual Frames of Black Intellectuals

West offers four ways to identify the work of Black intellectuals. They are the bourgeois model or the Black intellectual as humanist, the Marxist model or the Black intellectual as revolutionary, the Foucaultian model-the Black intellectual as the postmodern skeptic, and finally, the insurgency model or the Black intellectual as critical, organic catalyst. Two of these models over time have genuinely resonated with me and have helped me to be more definitive as well as deliberate about my work. Such definition has been vital because when a Black scholar writes about Black issues it has been traditionally easy for such scholarship to be dismissed by the dominant, academic elite as a catharsis for relieving Black folk of our anger as opposed to genuine intellectual inquiry. But I firmly agree with West, who asserted, "There is always the need to assert and defend the humanity of black people, including their ability and capacity to reason logically, think coherently, and write lucidly" (p.307).

Two of these categories of Black intellectuals really resonate with me and fairly accurately describe my life as an academic. The first is the Marxist or the Black intellectual as revolutionary. West argues, "This adoption satisfies certain basic needs of the black intelligentsia: the need for social relevance, political engagement and organizational involvement. The Marxist model also provides entry into the least xenophobic white intellectual subculture available to black intellectuals. The Marxist model privileges the activity of black intellectuals and promotes their prophetic role" (pp. 309-310). I strongly agree that my work has to be in a context that welcomes social and political engagement as well as organizational involvement. In the nascent days of my research and scholarship, choosing to write from a critical theoretical position about educational leadership, especially the educational leadership of Black, school-aged children was a great risk. I had to genuinely believe a number of presuppositions. First, I had to acknowledge that writing from this perspective could spell career disaster for me but that scholarship emanating precisely from this point of view was absolutely necessary and fulfilled the calling on my academic life. Second, I had to believe that creating scholarship that forced a counter-hegemonic discourse was an endeavor I had no problem igniting. So that if negative consequences were birthed from my writing that I would bear up under them. Third, I had to be clear in my commitment that beyond my work being published in leading journals in my field or well beyond being accepted in the academy and celebrated for my work as a scholar, I had to be prepared for the possible castigation that could arise from my intellectual labor. So acceptance, validation and legitimation by those who wield the power in the academy may have resulted in some fundamental level of comfort was not essential especially if it came with silencing my position on leadership and social justice.

I strongly believe that the revolutionary model manifests what West describes when he wrote, "On the one hand, the Marxist model is liberating for black intellectuals in that it promotes critical consciousness and attitudes toward the dominant bourgeois paradigms and research programs" (p.310). West, however, offers an oppositional position regarding the Marxist model when he posited, "On the other hand, the Marxist model is debilitating for black intellectuals because the cathartic needs it satisfies tend to stifle the further development of black critical consciousness and attitudes" (p.310). What I believe to be essential is that the whole notion of self-aggrandizement that West offers as a caution to Black scholars who contextualize their work in a Marxist paradigm must have around them those who will level the poignant inquiries of what's next? How do you operationalize solutions after the essential critique? How do you ensure that becoming part of the bourgeois intelligentsia by being a renowned scholar does not impede your revolutionary fervor? How do you prevent yourself from becoming co-opted by the machinations of academe? These are the brutally difficult questions I either had to ask myself or have asked of me by others.

The Black Intellectual as Postmodern Skeptic

I believe that being a Black professor in a predominantly white institution lends to considering the tenets of this Foucaultian model though I don't fully subscribe to it. Indeed, this model compels all scholars to consider the complexities of epistemological positions and even if such positions need to be established in the first place. It definitely situates notions of power in a contested terrain, as they should be, and as West argues, "compels intellectuals to rethink and redefine their self-image and function in our contemporary situation"(p.311). Many times I have wondered, especially as an institutional administrator, how I must personally juxtapose and often resolve the tensions between my ideological position and the often-antithetical administrative responsibilities that are inherent in this leadership role I now hold. I have never kidded myself that there abides in my holding a titular leadership position the commensurate power to actually bring about substantive changes in the way the institution operates. Parenthetically, this may very well be a self-inflicted stultifying mind-set that limits even my individual attempts to make things happen. But I am not ignorant concerning the hindering devices of racism and racist strategies and tactics that are inherent in these institutions. The revolutionary fervor I have when functioning as a professor is tempered while I carry out administrative responsibilities. The bifurcation is troublesome at best and one that I have to bring to resolution.

I clearly understand the Foucaultian notion of being "othered" and the residuals that attend to such a marginalized space. Even as I write this, however, I am incensed by the debilitating perspective my embracing of this positioning brings. The postmodern skeptic model calls into question dominant discourses, discursive practices, and familiar as well as celebrated tropes of life in the academy. With such deconstruction then, comes the interrogation of what has been accepted as truth as well as the inquisition of regimes of truth that have historically undergirded the values and functions of higher education. Where I am is actually living out West's conclusions regarding postmodern skepticism. I am embracing "an intense and incessant interrogation of power-laden discourses in the service of neither restoration, reformation, and revolution but rather revolt. And the kind of revolt enacted by intellectuals consists of the disrupting and dismantling of prevailing 'regimes of truth'—including their repressive effects-of present-day societies" (p.312).

I am constantly laboring in what, up until now, I have deemed to be a contested space between returning to the faculty and remaining as a university administrator. What this battle has allowed me to do however, is to dismantle the regime of truth that reifies being one or the other, that requires that I make a choice between two binary positions rather than strategizing to determine how being planted in both spaces allows me to voice critique and substantive change in an antiphonal fashion. I have reflected on how can I genuinely activate in administrative practice what I write and lecture about so that my life is genuine and authentic as opposed to constantly warring within myself. I believe seeing my work as the critical organic catalyst or the implementation of the insurgency model allows that to happen.

The Black Intellectual as Critical Organic Catalyst

Inherent in this model is the liberating opportunity for the Black intellectual to establish a new truth, one that is grounded experientially but also builds on the historicity of Black experiences while simultaneously constructing a counter-narrative within which to ground our work. In my mind, this is a very spiritual endeavor because it calls for the Black intellectual to create a new space carved from one of hostility and derision. It compels the Black intellectual to recognize while at the same time dismantling and demystifying positions and hierarchies of truth that have been crafted about our position in the academy and the fortitude to articulate our own dynamics, our own dimensions, and our own destinations in higher education. It is spiritual because such a move demands that we have the ability to envision a new reality, to actually bring forth institutions and practices that don't currently exist and the pervasive structure will not tolerate. But we see it as doable anyway.

I would like to propose that this insurgency model begins with Black intellectuals grappling with the exigencies inherent in critical self-reflection. It is so important that we come to grips with locating the epicenter of our motivation for being in the academy and in a predominantly white institution in particular. I strongly believe that a Black scholar must be specifically called to work in a white institution. That calling entails demystifying the racist context of most institutions but concomitantly envisioning a place where Black students and faculty may flourish, nonetheless.

The insurgency model demands an almost dismissive posture to be established by Black intellectuals where the hegemonic notions of academe and the intrinsic racist ideas and conceptualizations are concerned. This new idea of Blacks in the academy must emanate not merely from a space of resistance and reconstruction but one that is not forgetful of the past but instead is determined to construct an identity sans the identity that has traditionally and historically been crafted for us as intellectuals. Indeed, what this means is for those of us in institutions of higher education to name our world or worlds comprehensively. Such an endeavor celebrates the multiple experiences and perspectives we would bring to this naming process. It would also include an effort stoppage in contending with the figments of a racist imagination. An insurgency model includes the spiritual endeavor of creating our own space that does not have its life breathed into it as a result of countering any other prevailing ideology. As opposed to being on the defensive, we as able Black scholars would clearly articulate what it means to be a Black scholar and to establish an agenda that promotes and celebrates our intellectual labor. Such a move demands a collaborative effort on the part of Black intellectuals to name for us the essential nature and nuances of our position (s) in the academy. Serving as critical organic catalysts demands reflecting and creating a new or multiple realities. It is not an ahistorical move but one that requires a press into the future, a press to preserve the rich intellectual history that has always existed in the culture of Black folk. West's (1999) comments about the insurgency model capture my perspectives regarding our work in the academy. He says,

> The central task of postmodern black intellectuals is to stimulate, hasten, and enable alternative perceptions and practices by dislodging prevailing discourses and powers. This can be done only by intense intellectual work and engaged insurgent praxis. (p.313)

There is such a complex dynamic involved in casting the new reality as called for by this insurgency model. For it entails having an exogamous relationship with the multiple institutional machinations that are particularly designed to perpetuate an exclusionist, xenophobic existence; that almost reifies a white, Euro-centric conception of academic life. But if this organic catalyst frame is to work, we must reckon as paramount, our creating our own academic space that can thrive in a predominantly white space. This could mean asking our white colleagues to collaborate with us but definitely not to serve as the measuring rods of intellectual success or the definers of academic work. We no longer celebrate the primacy of the dominant hegemony but understand that it does exist but not to the exclusion of a way of perceiving intellectual work from the plethora of Black perspectives. This will require extensive communal intellectual work that eschews notions of individual heroes and champions but the naming of our space in the academy would emanate from intense intellectual engagements that grapple forthrightly with our dreams and visions for ourselves. This means that we would unabashedly call those things that are not a part of our realities as though they were and to coalesce with other Black intellectuals in the mental and spiritual labor of seeing these created realities manifested.

In conclusion, I have much hope as we continue to contribute in substantive ways to intellectual work. The labor is intense and demands that we, with courage and spiritual endowment, take the steps to create an intellectual space that enriches, disrupts, creates, edifies, challenges, and pushes us to more enriched academic spaces. This work, I believe, must not simply be for self-aggrandizement but must have an axiological and teleological bent-to see the lives of Black folk lived in a more democratic and fulfilling and purposeful context. The work of Black intellectuals is one of a variety of ways this vision can be achieved.

References

Marable, M. (2006). *Living black history: How reimagining the African American past can remake America's facial future.* New York: Basic Civitas Books

Shelby, T. (2005). *We who are dark: The philosophical foundations of black solidarity.* Cambridge: Harvard University.

West, C. (1999). *The Cornel West reader.* New York: Basic Civitas Books.

Chapter Seven

Philosophical Racism, Mobbing, and Other Infractions on Black Male Faculty in Majority White Space: With Reference to Africana Studies

Mark Christian

Introduction

Employing a semi-autoethnographic approach (1), this chapter argues that there is a nuanced, diverse, yet uniform reality in being a Black male faculty member in the predominately US White university (PWU) setting. (2) Of course there will always be specific and unique experiences among Black male faculty; depending on, for example: sexual orientation, class background, institutional affiliation and geographical region, one's field or discipline, and one's school of thought in terms of philosophical grounding. All these variables, and more, can determine one's day-to-day existence in the PWU setting. Nevertheless, given the historical context of racialized phenomena, there is still something tangible and universal about the emotional and intellectual abuse in the racialized university workplace. Whether it be in terms of isolation, marginalization or outright mobbing, it deserves immediate ethical attention and intervention from high-level administrators. The facts are obvious, Black folks are conspicuous by their absence in both tenured faculty positions and at the administrative high end of power and influence in PWUs. Finally, this chapter fleshes out the idea that philosophical racism and the concomitant hierarchy of knowledge has a negative impact on those Black faculty connected and qualified in the field/ discipline of Africana/Black Studies.

Writing at the turn of the twentieth century, a famous sociologist, W. I. Thomas (1907) wrote,

> The world of modern intellectual life is in reality a white man's world. Few women and perhaps no blacks have ever entered this world in the fullest sense. To enter it in the fullest sense would be to be in it at every moment from the time of birth to the time of death, and to absorb it unconsciously and consciously, as the child absorbs language. When something like this happens, we shall be in a position to judge of the mental efficiency of woman and the lower races... (p.469)

The above citation from W. I. Thomas may now seem dated to some, yet the noted sociologist was on point, even if the tone of his writing is patronizing, sexist, and indeed racist. At the turn of the twentieth century it remained palpable that contemporary mainstream intellectual life was essentially White male dominated. As we fast-forward and consider the second decade of the twenty-first century one could, even comfortably perhaps, sustain the position that the Thomas perspective continues to hold validity. Indeed, one only has to consider the current dilemma and relative absence of Black faculty in PWUs across the US to note the longevity of this intellectual exclusion from the mainstream academic life. In point of fact, one hundred years after Thomas had pointed out an obvious social fact, the *Journal of Blacks in Higher Education* in the November 19, 2007 issue noted the long term effects of such racialized exclusion in mainstream education,

> Nationwide, just over 5 percent of all full-time faculty
> members at colleges and universities in the United States
> are black. The percentage has increased slightly over the
> past decade [2000s]. But the percentage of black faculty at
> almost all the nation's high- ranking universities is sig-
> nificantly below the national average of 5.2 percent. (3)

Considering the existing social statistical data, there is a low participation and presence of Black faculty in higher education across the
board: male and female, junior in career to senior status. Yet perception often masks reality as many commentators suggest we are now
in an era that is deemed a "post-racial" America. The often noted
progress for citing this post-racial era is apparently manifested via
the election of President Barack Obama in November 2008. Moreover, it is contended that racial inequality is something that hurts
Whites just as much as it may hurt people of color. Interestingly,
those that spout such erroneous arguments rarely tackle the macro
social statistics concerning the overall disempowerment of Black
males in US society. Crucially, the present White backlash toward
any aspect of societal progress for people of color is indisputable.

Indeed, a recent academic journal article (Norton and Sommers
2011), which gained traction and debate in the *New York Times* (4),
contends that Whites' perception of racism is akin to a zero-sum
game. In other words, any imagined or real decrease in institutionalized racism against Blacks over the past six decades is perceived as
bias against Whites (p. 215). The fact that many Whites perceive any
gain in society for people of color as a loss to them is not a new theme.
There has most often been a White backlash whenever African
Americans have gained in US society. However, contemporary forms
of White racism tend to be more covert than overt, more subtle than
brutal (Anderson 2010).

The erroneous idea of African Americans gaining at the
expense of Whites has endured for decades, just as the mispercep-
tion of affirmative action policy has created a labyrinth of myths to
enable stereotypes to act as truth (Pincus 2003; Katznelson 2005).
Fred Pincus noted in his study that there are far greater obstacles
in the way of White men, for example, than the myth of affirmative
action policies; as he writes,

I have argued that affirmative action has a minimal negative impact on white males. Globalization, downsizing, corporate greed, and cutbacks in government services have a much more profound negative impact on white males and on the rest of the population. The majority of white men would be much better off working alongside people of color and women to improve their positions... [in relation to] the small number of wealthy and powerful people, mostly white men, who have disproportionate control over our society...(pp.145-146)

It is a social fact that there is no major threat to White males via affirmative action policy but the myth continues to perpetuate (Anderson 2010; Pincus 2003). In fact, one could argue that affirmative action is almost dead in the water with the disheartening statistical data related to Black communities, and African American men in particular. The staggering incarceration rates of Black men alone engenders thoughts of an unfair criminal justice system. Michelle Alexander opens up her powerful book, *The New Jim Crow: Mass Incarceration in the Age of Colorblindness* (2010), with the story of a contemporary African American male,

Jarvious Cotton cannot vote. Like his father, grandfather, great-grandfather, and great-great-grandfather, he has been denied the right to participate in our electoral democracy. Cotton's family tree tells the story of several generations of black men who were born in the United States but who were denied the most basic freedom that democracy promises—the freedom to vote for those who will make the rules and laws that govern one's life. Cotton's great-great-grandfather could not vote as a slave. His great-grandfather was beaten to death by the Ku Klux Klan for attempting to vote. His grandfather was prevented from voting by Klan intimidation. His father was barred from voting by poll taxes and literacy tests. Today, Jarvious Cotton cannot vote because he, like many black men in the United States, has been labeled a felon and is currently on parole. (p. 1)

Echoing Michelle Alexander (2010) and the unutterably sad history of African American disenfranchisement depicted in her above example, Bob Herbet, writing for the *New York Times* (August 20, 2010) stated,

> That the black community has not been mobilized en masse to turn this crisis around is a screaming shame. Black men, according to the Bureau of Justice Statistics, have nearly a one-third chance of being incarcerated at some point in their lives. By the time they hit their mid-30s, a solid majority of black men without a high school diploma have spent time in prison. (5)

What this brief macro meandering into the broader society offers is an insight into the difficult place in contemporary society that the Black male holds. Of course, millions of African Americans do not face prison, and there is still opportunity to follow, and there is still room for individual success against the odds. There exists, too, a marginalized but consistent Black intellectual community committed to self-determination (Asante & Karenga 2006). However, and this is important for the reader at the outset, any African American male that makes it through graduate school and gains a PhD to teach and research at the university level is in essence a "great achiever" in the present day. To put it another way, the Black male faculty member in the PWU is akin to a "special species" that is rare, hard to create, and in danger of becoming extinct due to the pipeline of Black males in society being clogged up with elevated rates of non-high school graduation, incarceration, intracultural homicide, and overall inadequate family structure to strengthen the possibilities of success in education.

At bottom, this chapter is concerned with the often difficult terrain of the PWU for Black male intellectuals; and the focus on Black males is because other chapters in this book are specific to the experience of Black female faculty. Moreover, it is focused on shedding light on a complex experience of Black male faculty that endeavor to teach and research philosophically grounded in the field of Africana/Black Studies while operating in predominately White space.

Black Intellectual Self-Determination in the Face of White Privilege

The Black male scholar who strives to "sing his own songs" in the PWU can face tremendous setbacks and viciousness from those who endeavor to maintain the status quo. It is such a burden on one's time to face a myriad of passive aggressive resistance to Black empowerment, frequently by well-meaning Whites (Trepagnier 2006). Because at the end of the day the majority of Black male scholars are dealing with the realities of trying to forge a space in places where Black faces have been rare and/or unwanted. Sometimes the truth is harsh, demanding, and yet liberating (Said 1994). To survive in terms of having a self-determinist intellectual attitude is to side with those whom have struggled to actually create the space one occupies in the PWU. Some tend to forget that Black presence at PWUs is due to the struggle of past generations who opened up opportunity for the current generation of scholars to participate. Nevertheless, the journey to intellectual self-determination is far from over as the present generation is only the second to walk the corridors of PWUs. We ought not to forget this fact, which means we actually remain in the embryonic stages in terms of gaining racialized parity within PWUs.

In regard to the time spent fighting racism, a noted White American sociologist, Joe Feagin, who is known for his comprehension of White male privilege in the PWU and beyond, interviewed a distinguished and senior Black male professor for a study, who then explained to Feagin (2010) what it was like to deal with energy-sapping racism in the PWU setting,

> If you can think of the mind as having one hundred ergs of energy, and the average man uses 50 percent of this energy dealing with the everyday problems of the world... then he has 50 percent more to do creative kinds of things that he wants to do. Now that's a white person. Now a black person also has one hundred ergs; he uses fifty percent the same way as white man does, dealing with what the white man has [to deal with], so he has 50 percent left. But he uses 25 percent fighting being black, [with] all the problems being black and what it means. (p.189)

Joe Feagin goes on to explain that "by virtue of an accident of birth," African Americans will ordinarily use up large quantities of energy and time defending oneself and one's family from various forms of racism; whether at the workplace or in society (buying a home, getting a mortgage, defending their children in negative school experiences, to getting a table at a restaurant; these are only a few examples), confronting being Black on a day-to-day level is energy-sapping and difficult. Yet when it involves a serious matter in the workplace it can lead to severe stress, leading to depression and/ or other debilitating illnesses (Namie & Namie, 2003, p. 56). Feagin contends that in general the White person does not have to deal with such emotionally draining experiences, and he calls this being a form of *white privilege*. It is the unacknowledged aspect of living as a White person: you are given the benefit of the doubt, or more lenient punishment if one does step out of line in society, and generally more scope to get ahead in life (Jensen 2003).

Given that academia is not divorced from the broader society there should be no surprise that Black professors face struggles not met by White professors (Baszile 2003; Christian 2010b; Feagin 2010; Lemelle 2009, Stanley 2006; Turner & Myers; Warde 2009). When Black professors navigate a PWU it is usually with extreme caution, not wanting to put a foot wrong while adapting to a culture that ordinarily is not particularly friendly (Moore, Alexander & Lemelle 2010). The hostile environment is not one usually of overt physical violence. It is a milieu more akin to a complex interconnection of passive aggression. However, if you are a "good man" in the eyes of the majority, and play by the(ir) rules life can be less professionally stressful. A difficult task for a Black male professor is to comprehend that to survive in a PWU means to learn quickly to put White faculty at ease. This is incredibly frustrating, but it is at the heart of such experience. For if the Black male professor can learn to ignore White privilege and how it operates, it is possible to avoid being targeted for discrimination. The key thing is to learn to evade destabilizing White power while being true to oneself as a scholar. This can be extremely difficult and hypocritical if one occupies a position in Africana/Black Studies and your role is to teach the truth about the Black experience. Yet when there is no genuine support for the field/ discipline in the PWU—which is very often the case (Christian 2004, 2006a, 2007), one is always treading on thin-ice in every day activity.

This, in a sense, is the conundrum of the Black male professor, how to keep one's head up without drowning in a rather monocultural setting that was not created for him (Thomas 1907).

Anthony Lemelle (2009) explains the origins of institutionalized education in the US and how exclusion of select groups was evident at the outset and continues to have a cultural impact in the present context, ironically in the age of diversity policy,

> A group of privileged men developed private and public U.S. education. Their political group was concerned about exclusion of selected groups. This is political in the sense that they denied citizenship rights to certain groups, for example, they denied suffrage to women. Moreover, they denied educational opportunities to certain classes, or, they promoted a "separate but equal" enrollment in school policy... (p.100)

This knowledge is not particularly new, but what stands out is how cultural hegemony manifests in a contemporary sense and stifles those that teach and speak to Black concerns (Mills, 1998). The fact is we do not have similar social backgrounds due to the racialized social world. To expect Black professors to exist in a colorblind world is quite frankly ludicrous and myopic. People of color in PWUs operate as the "other" in a cultural organization that is culturally designed to maintain the power of those that hold power in society. We are not so much "separate but equal" in these environments; rather, we are "integrated but unequal" and any legitimate survey will testify that this is quotidian in operation (Lemelle, 2009). What is more, if one is aware of this situation, it means one is occupying a conflictual or counter-hegemonic seat at the mainstream academic table. Yet not all people of color are "aware" of their implicit, and to a large extent engineered, subordinate academic status. Some actually attempt assimilation or feign it to the degree of "acting White" to the extent of "hating blackness" and everything associated. The reasons for this are manifold: miseducation, self-hatred, self-denial, sheer ignorance, or as a personal survival tactic (wearing a mask). In explaining the complexity of Black male psychology in particular, Leon Caldwell (2000) explained,

> Black male psychology is at best a complex amalgamation of misinterpretations and at worst a labyrinth of uncertain identities. Historically the psychology of Black males... has involved the study of the mind as interpreted with European definitions of intelligence, personality, function, and other constructs. These definitions have unequivocally diminished the humanity of Black men; White racial supremacy must be validated in order to perpetuate oppressive social, educational, and economic systems. The White supremacist definition of *Black psychology* has been so pervasive in these systems that even most African Americans cannot produce an authentic of self without referencing White cultural norms. (p.131)

Indeed, to add to Caldwell's (2000) frame of reference, to be a Black male professor in contemporary society and based at a PWU is difficult enough for an economist, a botanist, or a computer scientist; but to be a Black male professor expressing his self-determination (independence of epistemological thought) via Africana/Black Studies is exceptionally difficult. Indeed, one faces conflict with both the status quo and those persons of color doing all they can to assimilate into the dominant cultural apparatus. In this scenario one's allies can often be White marginalized academics such as gay women. There are also Whites who understand the unfairness in the system and endeavor to help you navigate through the environmental hostility (Feagin 2010, Jensen 2005). Yet allies are few and rare, if you are able to secure White allies in this context it is a very fortunate situation to have in your career.

Considering Philosophical Racism in PWUs

A definition for philosophy reads: *the use of reason in understanding such things as the nature of reality and existence, the use and limits of knowledge and the principles that govern and influence moral judgment.* (6) A common definition for racism reads: *a) a belief that race is the primary determinant of human traits and capacities and that racial differences produce an inherent superiority of a particular race; and b) racial prejudice or discrimination.* (7) If we connect the two concepts we have *Philosophical Racism,* in which I define as: *the use of knowledge in a hierarchical fashion that produces unequal status and privileges in predominately White colleges and universities.* The combination of these terms were used back to front for a powerful book published in 1999 entitled *Racism & Philosophy,* edited by Susan Babbitt and Sue Campbell. However, their major concern was to look at the discipline of philosophy within the context of racism and to have contemporary philosophers acknowledge it as a fundamental problem to be discussed in philosophical theory. Babbitt and Campbell (1999) frame the outset of their study in this manner,

> Racism must be of concern to all philosophers in all areas of philosophy. Racism is not just a topic for ethics and political philosophy. The existence of systemic racism—its consequences for the structures of the societies in which philosophy is done, as well as for how philosophy has been done and by whom—has deep implications for epistemology, metaphysics, philosophy of mind, and philosophical methodology. (p.1)

After nearly twenty five years of being in higher education, in liberal arts and social science, as an undergraduate and graduate student, to university professor, I believe it is not wise to label one's negative experiences as simply individual acts of racism at the hands of White faculty and administrators *per se.* Indeed it is far more complex than that, and a more suitable term to employ could be the concept of *philosophical racism.* As this then allows us to move beyond the simple dichotomy of Black and White to a more nuanced comprehension of inequitable treatment. Also, philosophical racism allows one to have both Black and White faculty allies, or conversely, enemies. To put it another way, if an administrator in the university or college actually believes in and practices a hierarchy of knowledge then she could be deemed *philosophically racist,* and this can mean a person of color actually holding such a belief, as well as a White faculty/administrator functioning in academia. This takes away much of the complexity derived from being a Black male professor at a PWU. For one can have White allies as well as enemies, as is the case with fellow faculty members deemed people of color. This point has to be firmly established, as it has been my experience to have both White faculty allies and Black faculty enemies, and vice versa. Crucially, we are focusing on the philosophy and practice of all individuals regardless of color and ethnic affiliation.

Currently, I occupy a mid-career faculty experience in Africana/Black studies and sociology, having taught in universities in the US and UK since 1992. In this sense, I believe there is a fundamental hierarchy of knowledge found across academic disciplines. For example, it is well known and largely taken-for-granted that if you are an economics professor you will earn more than most faculty in the liberal arts or social sciences. Indeed anyone connected to the business sector as faculty in academia will ordinarily earn more than faculty in other fields/disciplines. Therefore, transcending racialized and gender hierarchies, there is an inherent bias within the academic world toward certain areas of knowledge in comparison to others, this is common knowledge in some philosophical circles (Mills 1998).

However, and maybe due to there being an unacknowledged acceptance of knowledge-based inequity, scholars that teach and research in "racialized matters" often find their salaries and credibility lower than that of others in the *same* disciplines as themselves. Therefore what is at play can be deemed a sub-strata of hierarchical subject matter whereby what you teach and research can determine your experience in terms of salary rewards, promotion, and general advancement in the university system. It is a tricky and inequitable reality that few high level administrations care to take into account to remedy. It is advanced here that more has to be done if equal opportunity policy is to have any meaningful effect and substance in PWUs.

Philosophical racism works in a way that can be covert and naked to the eye, and even the mind. It can operate behind closed doors, out of the way, hidden in policy that wipes away, for example, an Africana/Black Studies department or program; does not renew a line for a Black scholar who has retired; it can be used inadvertently to impede one person over another. It is hard to prove any form of discrimination has took place. Yet, if one studies an institute, how funds are distributed, how scholars are hired, supported, and retained in PWUs it usually falls short in its commitment to issues relating to, for instance, Africana Studies/Black Studies (Christian 2006a, 2007, 2010b).

Philosophical racism can therefore be related to the implementation of policies that fail to acknowledge the importance of a diverse curriculum that embodies cultural diversity. Philosophical racism is the act of a dean not acknowledging the accomplishments of a Black faculty member who happens to research and promote equality of all peoples in her work, while the same dean publically extols her fellow White faculty who produce far less in terms of scholarship. Philosophical racism is when a Black male professor out-writes all around him, out-publishes all around him, yet fails to win year by year, after being nominated for the "Researcher of the Year award," while other White colleagues far less productive step up to receive it, year after year. Philosophical racism is in the act of a Black male professor being ignored for scholarly recognition that is thoroughly deserving yet not forthcoming. Philosophical racism tells us subliminally that "White is right and balanced in academic thought" and that "Black or Brown is biased and/or political in academic thought." Philosophical racism can be followed unwittingly by people of color faculty as they reject alternative, counter-hegemonic, perspectives for those that enhance the status quo and do not challenge racism in the workplace. To put it bluntly, philosophical racism is a form of "White supremacy without racists" (Bonilla-Silva, 2001). It is mostly covert in action but ubiquitous within the PWU where knowledge is still hierarchical and skewed toward a Eurocentric frame of reference (Mills 1998).

Charles Gallagher (2007) explains further the broader macro aspect of philosophical racism, the White privilege that is inherent in a covert hierarchy of knowledge. His analysis dissects the concept of "White" to show how fallacious the term is in a biological scientific sense, but salient in terms of being a normalized social construct. Gallagher puts it this way,

> ...Institutions and social practices redistribute resources along racial lines in ways that are often made invisible or justified through racist ideology. For hundreds of years religion and science justified white supremacy on epistemological and moral grounds. These institutions were, and in many ways continue to be, racial projects because they maintain, reproduce, and normalize white privilege... (p.13)

Gallagher is correct in his assessment that white supremacy has been sanctioned over hundreds of years, and via institutional practices that endeavor to maintain its power (Bonilla-Silva 2001; Feagin

2010). Many fail to see the connection of the past to the present, preferring to view the world as "post-racial" rather than looking at the reality of the continued disempowerment that abounds in society for people of color. To suggest that society has moved on from being racist and discriminatory is illusory. It is going to take further concerted effort before we break free totally from the racialized past. Philosophical racism is in a way less overt, but the outcome is pretty much the same, a lack of resources and opportunity offered toward initiatives that will actually remedy the myriad of racialized inequities found at PWUs.(8)

Mobbing and Bullying in the Age of Diversity

While under the usual pressure faced by a Black male professor at a PWU, I stumbled on research in the workplace relating to bullying and mobbing. It was an epiphany as this workplace literature had somehow passed me by. Although I knew something was taking place to isolate my contributions to the university, I did not know how to explain it to anyone. That is until I began to read the mobbing and bullying literature as it relates to academia (Namie & Namie 2003; Twale & De Luca 2008). Arguably, it is the noted Canadian sociologist, Professor Kenneth Westhues (2004, 2006, 2008) who has studied mobbing and bullying in academia most profoundly. His contributions to this area of knowledge provide a framework for understanding how one can be isolated by pettiness and professional envy in a university or college setting. His work is universal covering all academic situations, but he does acknowledge that racism and sexism can be key reasons behind the mobbing of a faculty member. Most professors do not suffer the severe experiences that Westhues offered as case studies. Nevertheless, he provided five key reasons for why a professor could be mobbed, or for what may increase the vulnerability of it happening to someone, they are:

- Foreign birth and upbringing, especially signaled by a foreign accent
- Being different from colleagues in an elemental way (by sex, for instance, sexual orientation, skin color, ethnicity, class origin, or credentials)

- Belonging to a discipline with ambiguous standards and objectives, especially those (like music or literature) most affected by postmodern scholarship
- Working under a dean or other administrator in whom, as Nietzsche put it, "the impulse to punish is powerful"
- An actual or contrived financial crunch in one's academic unit (according to an African proverb, when the watering hole gets smaller the animals get meaner) (p.19)

In reading this short article on mobbing in academia by Professor Westhues it suddenly dawned on me that that I could relate perfectly to his first five points: 1) I was born and raised in Liverpool, England; 2) I am of Black British heritage; 3) I belong to a field/discipline that is contested and maligned in mainstream quarters due to its counter-hegemonic historical roots (Africana/Black Studies); 4) the dean that hired me left in my first two years and after a one year interim they hired a person akin to an oligarch who favored the few and undermined the many. I was situated in the "many" group, but on top of that he had a professional dislike for my research and being that was obvious in all his social interaction with me during his tenure. Nevertheless, I survived professionally through sheer productivity to become a full professor; and 5) all institutions are under financial strain to cut back, while Africana/Black Studies is one area that suffers most at PWUs (Christian 2006a, 2007).

Professor Westhues (2006) also states that being a high-achiever as a professor can actually hurt you not improve one's situation. Often the "target" of a mobbing is worn down emotionally by the constant shunning, gossip, ridicule, and bureaucratic hassles. Westhues uses the German word Todschweigen (death by silence) to describe the initial phases in the mobbing of a target that can occur in his or her workplace environment. The statistical data according to Westhues (2006) indicates that most targets eventually end up leaving the institution. A case in point is Lemelle (2009) who under insidious bullying/mobbing left his position for another university. When I recall colleagues' experience who had to leave my university, three out of four of them left due to being either bullied (one on one) or mobbed (numerous individuals all playing a role in his/her workplace isolation). Moreover, if I am to be honest, there is no doubt that I have experienced being mobbed in my academic career. However, I must be one of the few that survived to succeed at the institution where it took place, and left only to take up a better position in a more diverse and cosmopolitan city.

Keep in mind that mobbing in academia does not have to be racially exclusive. As contended throughout this chapter, being either attacked under philosophical racism or mobbed can mean there being people of color involved in the insidious assault. Usually, the person of color is seeking personal gain from the discrimination meted out to a fellow person of color. It is complex, yet simple too. Most professors in PWUs work to gain tenure by doing their work diligently, but in that there are "games" one often has to play to succeed. Such games include: being deferential to all senior scholars, and tip-toeing through the labyrinth of departmental and/or program politics. One major impediment to Black male faculty is the sheer lack of mentors who can act as guides to faculty of color. Too often there is no one who can share with you their experience and to guide you through the tenure process. As Warde (2009) explains,

> ...African American male tenure-track professors in institutions of higher education often lack effective mentoring, which might be due to the fact that mentors typically choose protégés who share the same ethnic, religious, academic, and/or social backgrounds... As a consequence, African American male tenure-track professors typically have a more difficult time than their White counterparts in gaining access to the professional and social networks that are so vital to advancement in the professoriate and earning of tenure... (p.498)

Clearly a key factor in the isolation of so many Black male faculty in academia is due to the lack of mentors. There is little in the way of social networking that aids the so-called minority professor. Moreover, with the growing problem of faculty incivility (Twale and De Luca 2008), coupled with the stagnant education pipeline for new Black male cohorts coming through to compete for professorship appointments (Warde 2009), the future looks pretty bleak indeed for indigenous African Americans particularly. The word "crisis" is often used without enough thought, but in terms of the current and future prognosis of there being fewer Black male faculty it is a definite crisis situation.

In addition, existing Black male and female faculty have to deal with insidious forms of racism, what Anderson (2010) deems in her book *Benign Bigotry* as subtle forms of prejudice and psychological mind games. In other words, the present situation needs attention and the future for Black faculty looks even bleaker. That is unless social engineering can be put to use to improve the high school graduation rates of Black males and improve their opportunities for entrance into universities and colleges. Without such concentrated measures, we cannot expect much in regard to the current low numbers of Black male faculty increasing in the long term. Moreover, with the existing lack of mentoring via Black male senior faculty to junior being apparent, the situation is unlikely to improve in the foreseeable future.

However, mentoring much like anything else does not necessarily have to have a Black face. In point of fact, I would not have survived my first appointment as an assistant professor through to full professor without the mentorship of a gay White female colleague. The fact that she is gay is probably a strong reason why she felt an affinity with me, although this was not the only reason. Indeed we both enjoyed discussing foreign movies and issues relating to social stratification. The point is, as a Black male faculty member at a PWU I needed some guidance and it came from a White female. This situation is not unique, Warde (2009) shares the view of a Black male tenured and senior professor in his study on the topic of gaining tenure and mentoring,

> I was very lucky to have my mentor, who was White and an esteemed senior faculty member in the department. For example, when I would do a presentation or talk and nobody else in the department would turn up he would be there, which was great support for me. The most helpful thing he did for me, though, was to use his contacts to get me a meeting with a representative from one of most prestigious publishers in the field. From this meeting I got a book deal without having to go through the process of submitting proposals. Without this mentorship my career

might have been very different; so yes, his mentorship was
critical to me getting tenure. (p.500)

Although my mentor did not provide me with ways to get published
or how to teach, she was a great resource for me in terms of navigating the university system. Moreover, she was someone I could
actually trust and be honest with about the things going on in my
career. This may sound odd, but her advice was most often for me to
stay focused, to stay on track, and to "suck it up" while keeping my
eyes on the prize of tenure. It was sobering advice at times, given my
passion for social justice and fair play, but actually in the long term
it was good advice for achieving the goal of tenure. She was also
instrumental in sticking by me through some very difficult professional situations that I eventually overcame. To be honest, it would
have been extremely tricky to have succeeded without the help and
guidance of her. To admit this as an African centered scholar is to
show that we comprehend clearly that there are allies and enemies
of all colors and cultural backgrounds.

It took me a long time to digest my situation, as a Black male
teaching Africana/Black Studies and the sociology of "race" at a
PWU, and my mentor being a gay White female professor. Again, it
has profoundly changed my thinking on who allies and enemies are
in academia, and ushered in my thinking on philosophical racism
and epistemological arrogance rather than a "Whites stopping
Blacks getting ahead" thought process, as the latter is too narrow,
too limiting in understanding how contemporary institutional
discrimination operates. Crucially, without the assistance of progressive Whites people of color have little chance in succeeding at
a PWU. This is due to a sheer lack of power and numbers among
people of color. Therefore people of color should have a willingness
to work with people of good faith, regardless of their racialized and
cultural background. More importantly, to keep in mind the fact
that one cannot assume that a person of color faculty member is
going to support one's road to success. On the contrary, he or she
may deem another person of color as a threat to his or her existence
and limited privileges at the PWU, divide and rule is as pertinent to
academia as it was during the days of enslavement and colonialism.

Africana/Black Studies and Black Male Professors in PWUs

Although I have spoken to the issue of Africana/Black Studies (often used interchangeably with: African and African American Studies or African American Studies; this list is long) facing problems in the US university system via administrations that do not fully support departments or programs, and that there is a lack of qualified leaders in the field/discipline (Christian 2004, 2006a, 2007, 2010a; Christian and Evans 2010), there is more to be considered regarding the individual experiences of those Black professors who teach in departments and programs. Indeed, there is so much to explain that it goes beyond the confines of this chapter. Nevertheless, there needs to be an acknowledgement that philosophical racism is inextricably interwoven into the experience of the Africana/Black Studies professor's day-to-day existence in a PWU. Under constant pressure from within the institution that merely pays lip service to establishing a vibrant department or program, this is not the same as being a professor connected to one of the traditional disciplines. And being a joint-appointee in a traditional discipline and Africana/Black Studies is fraught with even greater difficulty (Christian and Evans 2010, p. 237-238).

With the ubiquitous philosophical racism that manifests in PWUs, it should not be of surprise that some scholars have called this a form of intellectual warfare (Carruthers 1999). That is, in terms of having to fight for one's right to the life of the mind that is free from the constraints of Eurocentric paradigms (Asante & Karenga 2006; Karenga 2010). Davidson & Davidson (2010) sum up the role of Africana/Black Studies in this way,

> ...The story of [Africana/Black Studies]...has always been about finding a place to stand—securing a footing in the academy, finding a clearing (opening) for pedagogy, and being integral to the process of discovering, transmitting, and creating knowledge without the Black focus being assimilated, diluted or commodified by that (typically) White power structure in the academy.(p.282)

The problematic reality of incarcerated Black minds was not limited to pedagogy, but also to the reality of one's research output. Philosophical racism encroaches on the Black scholar's publication possibilities and it was (still is) difficult to get published in mainstream predominately White journals. Yet the creation of Black journals largely in the 1960s was met with skepticism by White faculty with the power to determine what is "quality" in one's publication record. Talmadge Anderson (2007), the founding editor of the *Western Journal of Black Studies* explained the necessity of Black journals in historical context,

> Traditional white scholarly journals would not generally accept for publication articles on Black life and history by African American writers. If a work by an African American author was accepted, it could not contradict prevailing white scholarly assumptions or be racially sensitive regardless of its research quality or theoretical profundity. For the most part, a form of "domestic intellectual imperialism" prevailed to scholarship of African American life, culture, and history. (p. ix)

Presently this contested history of Black professoriate experience in predominately White institutions of higher learning is still alive and kicking. To suggest that it is not an issue is to be rather naive about the situation. It is probably more evident in relation to Africana/Black Studies departments and programs and their relationship to the broader PWU administrations. However, Black male professors who are affiliates from traditional departments to Africana/Black Studies will usually encounter the problems of philosophical racism in their day-to-day existence at PWUs.

Over the last thirty years there has been a prolific surge in the contributions of Black scholarly research within the confines of PWUs (Aldridge & Young 2003; Aldridge & James 2007; Anderson & James 2007; Christian 2006a, 2006b, 2007; Christian & Evans 2010; Conyers 1997; Hudson-Weems, 2007; Karenga 2010, Marable 2000; Norment 2001). In this sense there is no denying the creative impulse of Black scholars to "sing their own songs" and produce writings that speak to the collective, myriad, complex, realities of Black folks. This is something to be celebrated. Yet too often the scholarship is ignored by mainstream White scholars and many Black scholars who prefer only to employ a Eurocentric paradigm, even those connected to the field/discipline of Africana/Black Studies. Indeed I am confident that very few White scholars in particular know of the works cited above. I state this with confidence because I read the books of White liberal scholars and rarely do they acknowledge the books in the field of Africana/Black Studies written exclusively by Black professors. Most often they refer to other White liberal scholars, and they may cite the works of *famous* Black writers such as James Baldwin or Toni Morrison. Rarely, however, do you see referenced the works above, which are profoundly related to the notions and practice of Black intellectual self-determination.

The Black male professor who is grounded in the scholarship created by Black scholars and who writes from an empowerment approach in the field/discipline, and for Black people in general, can be isolated in the PWU for simply following such an intellectual course. There is nothing racist about Black professors wanting to write from their perspective, wanting to create new paradigms of knowledge that engender novel ways to approach the life of the mind from what they themselves experience. Indeed it makes no sense to write and think outside one's cultural heritage. It does a disservice to the art of self determination and intellectual freedom. In a real sense, Black male scholars who write to please mainstream cultural norms are actually being antithetical to what the liberal arts stands for—freedom of thought and expression. Too often, however, due to the philosophical racism that abounds in PWUs, many Black scholars feel it is necessary to cite exclusively White knowledge in order to get ahead in the specific university environment. This is nothing new, it is a form of philosophical racism that acts as an invisible coercive force on the mind of the Black professor functioning in the PWU. To be sure, it is an unpardonable tragedy to witness such psychological and career-related fear in Black academics that should only have the freedom of expression to care about. On the deeper reaches of our consciences there is something rather unsavory occurring that can be deemed an Orwellian academic world controlled by insidious "thought policing" and conceptual incarceration. How does such a scenario bode for freedom of expression? After all, the essence of the liberal arts world is to delve deeply into the human condition without fear of what harm can be done to a scholar's career in the university system. Freedom to take a stand against the prevailing status quo is something that brought down despotic governments and tyrants. If we lose the spirit of challenging existing social conditions it will be the death knell to genuine democracy and individual freedom. This is something that should not be countenanced, and in a real sense Black faculty and other people of color represent the repositories for freedom of expression. Measure their collective experience in a PWU and one measures how well that university is doing in terms of faculty of color empowerment.

Conclusion

When all is said and done, people of color have a rightful place in the PWU. A place that has been earned, fought for, and there is no going back in a world that is shrinking day by day due to advanced technology. In this sense, a modern university ought to have the look of a global and cosmopolitan institution that is free of racism, sexism and any other ism. Yet administrations at PWUs need to be more bold in their promise of diversity. It should not be a mere policy that is highlighted in the university mission statement. Diversity in a real sense allows for all cultures, all ideas, and all perspectives to breathe. There should be no faculty member who is bullied or mobbed because the person has a passion for Black empowerment or racial justice. No one should have to endure being stigmatized and ostracized for being a Black scholar who thinks and writes for the benefit first of his people and secondly for the benefit of all. Society tells us every day that there is a lot of work to do before racism is defeated. It resides in the workplace of all institutions, not only in higher education. Chesler, Lewis, and Crowfoot (2005) are correct when they suggest,

> The institutionalization of discrimination toward some and corollary privileges for others are present in the organizational structure and processes of colleges [and universities], and managerial and instructional behavior of boards, administrations, faculty, staff, and students. They occur in every dimension of the educational organization and help maintain the status quo. (p. 293)

145

In terms of Black male faculty, it is a difficult challenge to compete with the mounting challenges outlined above. Other writers have found major disparities between White faculty and African Americans in terms of salaries and job satisfaction via a study of Midwestern PWUs (Allen et al. 2000). Yet regardless of the many obstacles that exist across the breadth of universities and colleges, there is evidence of successful examples of Black male academics (Jones, 2000). Indeed, the majority of the writers in this volume hold tenure and have followed successful career paths in their chosen fields. This is something that cannot be denied, but the road to success is uneven and laden with traps and unfair situations. Quite frankly they succeed in spite of the impediments, as there is not one Black professor I have met and talked to that does not have at least one horror story to reveal. Most of us "suck it up" and keep moving, keep focused, to win against the odds. If one does succeed in gaining tenure and/or promotion it is a tremendous achievement, and most come through such a process definitely against the odds.

A famous African American scholar, a pioneering scholar who has published over seventy-books to date, was once asked, "what is your recipe for success?" He replied, "work harder than anyone else around you." Very simple. It is something I took on board, and *still*, because of such a work ethic, a Black male professor can encounter other problems, such as: professional envy, mobbing, isolation, and unfair salary increases that do not reflect one's productivity.

What is at the bottom of all this murky professional waters? Of course, it is philosophical racism. The socially engineered hierarchy of knowledge that puts White scholarship and faculty above all else. It may well be covert in operation as no one wants to be labeled a racist in present day society. So those that would have once performed racist acts openly now find other ways to conceal the professional harm they do to those of us who come from outside and do not easily conform to the White cultural paradigm. Whereas there should be a celebration of cultural diversity, many White academics find it annoying and do all they can to avoid participating in programs designed to improve diversity in the given PWU. What is needed is a commitment from the top down to eradicate this inequitable treatment. Equal opportunity policy statements are obviously not enough as the few faculty of color that do exist are getting fewer in number each passing year, each passing decade.

A major problem with promoting cultural diversity is that most Whites do not feel there is a problem to fix (Chelser, Lewis, Crowfoot 2005). In fact, as presented earlier, Whites feel that they are actually losing when Blacks get ahead in society (Norton & Sommers 2011). Even well-meaning Whites perpetuate the racialized divide with their unconscious racism (Trepagnier 2006). Until there is a recognition by high-level administrators in colleges and universities that a problem exists the status quo will continue to perpetuate an uneven, unfair, and unsavory experience for people of color. Yes, most of us continue to succeed, in spite of the insidious forms of racism and discrimination. There are those among us too afraid to write a chapter like this one that speaks truth to power. They want to "get promoted first" before they would dare such an exposure of the self to the perils of the PWU they exist in. Others want to be viewed as "raceless" and ignore all the acts of implicit intellectual inferiority from the majority cultural apparatus. They endeavor to assimilate, to attack anything deemed "radical Blackness" in order to prove their worth to the majority culture. Most often, and sadly, this mode of behavior does gain reward. After all, Uncle Tom was always rewarded on the plantation for having servile manners. However, sometimes even obsequiousness does not work on behalf of the Black male professor.

Mobbing and bullying is a growing and ugly part of higher education (Namie & Namie 2003; Twale & De Luca 2008; Westhues 2006). Administrators tend to ignore such incidents and hope that such situations do not exacerbate. Being isolated in PWUs is something common to Black male professors, especially those that happen to be successful in African/Black Studies. Indeed, the more the Black male professor is connected to the history and culture of peoples of African heritage, the more likely he is to countenance a mobbing in academia. Because of this situation increasing due to the higher numbers of Black scholars graduating with PhDs in the field of Africana/Black Studies (Christian & Evans 2010), it is recommended here that university and college administrators should respond to such claims of bullying and mobbing in academia seriously. Too often the "target" of such behavior is ignored and/or hurt more professionally for standing up for him/herself (Namie & Namie 2003). However, the best form of self-defense for a "targeted" academic is to be successful. That is, to publish often is the optimal decorum in showing that one has not been disempowered and beaten by the mobbing culture in the academic workplace. Indeed, this tactic is echoed via the famous African American male scholar, who has published over seventy books to date, and does not have to be named here due to such fame, who said: *work harder than anyone around you, and success will eventually be yours.* In the final analysis, philosophical racism, or any other form of discrimination has no place in modern academia, but it will take a tremendous amount of effort to rid PWUs of this ubiquitous phenomena.

Notes

1. Autoethnographers connect their research experience to the living body, unlike with many positivist approaches that appear to disconnect the researcher and writing from the actual research process. Auto-ethnography acknowledges the role of the researcher in the research process and draws from his/her participant observations and skills in the given social context (see Lemelle, 2009; Spry, 2006).

2. The focus here is on the US, but I have also considered the Black faculty experience in the UK in terms of Africana/Black Studies and predomi-nately White intellectual space (Christian 2010a, 2010b). Finally, the use of the terms Black and African American are interchangeable in this study.

3. *Journal of Blacks in Higher Education,* (November 19, 2007). http://www.jbhe.com/news_views/57_black_faculty_liberalarts.html [accessed May 19, 2011]

4. See *New York Times,* (5/23/2011) [accessed May 26, 2011], http://www.nytimes.com/roomfordebate/2011/05/22/is-anti-white-bias-a-problem?nl=todaysheadlines&emc=thab

5. Bob Herbert syndicated article, Too Long Ignored, for the *New York Times* (8/20/2010) [accessed May 19, 2011], http://www.nytimes.com/2010/08/21/opinion/21herbert.html

6. Definition of philosophy came from the online *Cambridge dictionary* [retrieved May 28, 2011], http://dictionary.cambridge.org/dictionary/british/philosophy

7. Definition of racism came from the online *Britannica encyclopedia* [retrieved May 28, 2011], http://www.britannica.com/facts/102/1634/ definition-of-racism

8. Further research is required in regard to the notion and practice of *philosophical racism.* I merely want to introduce the term here for consideration. More research and case studies should reveal how it operates in manifold ways.

References

Aldridge, D. P., & Young, C. (Eds.). (2003). *Out of the revolution: The development of Africana studies.* New York: Lexington books.

Aldridge, D. P., & James, E. L. (Eds.). (2007). *Africana studies: Philosophical perspectives and theoretical paradigms.* Pullman, Washington: Washington University.

Alexander, M. (2010). *The new Jim Crow: Mass incarceration in the age of colorblindness.* New York: The New Press.

Allen, W. R. et al. (2000). The Black academic: Faculty status among African Americans in U.S. higher education. *Journal of Negro Education.* 69(1/2), 112-127.

Anderson, K. J. (2010). *Benign bigotry: The psychology of subtle prejudice.* Cambridge: Cambridge University.

Anderson, T. & James, J. (2007). *Introduction to African American studies: Transdisciplinary approaches and implications.* Baltimore, MD: Black Classic.

Asante, M. K., & Karenga, M. (Eds.). (2006). *The Handbook of Black Studies.* Thousand Oaks, CA: Sage.

Babbitt, S. E. & Campbell, S. (Eds.). (1999). *Racism and philosophy.* Ithaca: Cornell University.

Baszile, D. T. (2003). Who does she think she is? Growing up nationalist and ending up teaching race in white space. *Journal of Curriculum Theorizing, 19*(3), 25-37.

Bonilla-Silva, E. (2001). *White supremacy & Racism in the post-civil rights era.* Boulder, CO: Rienner.

Bonilla-Silva, E. (2003). *Racism without racists: Color-blind racism and the persistence of racial inequality in the United States.* London: Rowman & Littlefield.

Caldwell, L. D. (2000). The psychology of Black men. In L. Jones. (Ed.). *Brothers of the academy: Up and coming Black scholars earning our way in higher education.* (pp. 131-138). Sterling, Virginia: Stylus.

Carruthers, J. H. (1999). *Intellectual warfare.* Chicago: Third World Press.

Chesler, M., Lewis, M., & Crowfoot, J. (2005). *Challenging racism in higher education: Promoting justice.* New York: Rowman & Littlefield.

Christian, M. (2004). Unmasking the mis-education and other impediments to the progressive Black studies scholar. *Africalogical Perspectives. 1*(1), 49-75.

Christian, M. (Guest Ed.). (2006a). The state of black studies in the academy (special issue). *Journal of Black Studies. 36*(5).

Christian, M. (2006b). Philosophy and practice for black studies: The case of researching white supremacy. In M. K. Asante & M. Karenga. (Eds.). *Handbook of black studies.* (pp. 76-88). Thousand Oaks, CA: Sage.

Christian, M. (2007). Notes on black studies: Its continuing necessity in the academy and beyond. *Journal of Black Studies. 37*(3), 53-70.

Christian, M. (2010a). Black studies in the UK and US: A comparative analysis. In J. R. Davidson. (Ed.). *African American Studies.* (pp.149-167). Edinburgh: University of Edinburgh.

Christian, M. (2010b). Notes on the dilemma of the Black scholar in predominately White universities: A personal perspective via postmodernist agency. In S. E. Moore, R. Alexander, Jr., & A. J. Lemelle, Jr. (Eds.), *Dilemmas of Black faculty at predominately white institutions in the United States.* (pp. 53-70). New York: Edwin Mellon.

Christian, M. & Evans, S. Y. (Guest Eds.). (2010). Africana studies at the graduate level: A twenty-first century perspective. *Western Journal of Black Studies. 34*(2).

Conyers, Jr., J. L. (Ed.). (1997). *Africana Studies, A disciplinary quest for both theory and method.* North Carolina: McFarland.

Davidson, J. R. (Ed.). *African American Studies.* Edinburgh, University of Edinburgh.

Davidson, J. R. & Davidson, T. (2010). African American studies: Vital, transformative, and sustainable. In J. R. Davidson. (Ed.). *African American Studies.* (pp. 281-308). Edinburgh: University of Edinburgh.

Feagin, J. R. (2010). *Racist America: roots, current realities, and future reparations, 2nd Edition.* New York: Routledge.

Gallagher, C. A. (2007). White. In H. Vera & J. R. Feagin. (Eds.). *Handbook of the sociology of racial and ethnic relations.* (pp. 1-14). New York: Springer.

Hudson-Weems, C. (Ed.). (2007). *Contemporary Africana theory and thought: A guide to Africana Studies.* Trenton, NJ: Africa World Press.

Jensen, R. (2003). White privilege shapes the US. In M. S. Kimmel & A. L. Ferber (Eds.), *Privilege: A reader.* (pp. 79-82). Boulder, CO: Westview.

Jensen, R. (2005). *The heart of whiteness: Confronting race, racism, and white privilege.* San Francisco: City Lights.

Jones, L. (Ed.). (2000). *Brothers of the academy: Up and coming Black scholars earning our way in higher education.* Sterling, Virginia: Stylus.

Karenga, M. (2010). *Introduction to Black studies, 4th Edition.* Los Angeles, CA: University of Sankore.

Katznelson, I. (2005). *When affirmative action was white: An untold history of racial inequality in twentieth century America.* New York: W.W. Norton.

Lemelle, Jr. A. J. (2009). Social and economic organization of the Black professoriate at predominately-white colleges and universities. *Journal of African American Studies. 14*(1), 106-127.

Marable, M. (Ed.). (2000). *Dispatches from the ebony tower: Intellectuals confront the African American experience.* New York: Columbia University.

Mills, C.W. (1998). *Blackness visible: Essays on philosophy and race.* Ithaca: Cornell University.

Moore, S. E., Alexander, Jr., R., Lemelle, Jr., A. J. (Eds.). (2010). *Dilemmas of Black faculty at predominately White institutions in the United States: Issues in the post-multicultural era.* New York: Edwin Mellen.

Namie, G., & Namie, R. (2003). *The bully at work: What you can do to stop the hurt and reclaim your dignity on the job.* Naperville, Illinois: Sourcebooks.

Norment, Jr., N. (2001). *The African American Studies Reader.* Durham, NC: Carolina Academic.

Norton, M. I., & Sommers, S. R. (2011). Whites see racism as a zero-sum game that they are now losing. *Perspectives on Psychological Science. 6*(3), 215-218.

Pincus, F. (2003). *Reverse discrimination: Dismantling the myth.* Boulder, CO: Lynne Rienner.

Said, E. W. (1994). *Representations of the intellectual.* New York: Vintage.

Spry, T. (2006). Performing autoethnography: An embodied methodological praxis. In S. N. Hesse-Biber & P. Leavy (Eds.). *Emergent methods in social research.* (pp. 183–211). Thousand Oaks: Sage.

Thomas, W. I. (1907). The mind of woman and the lower races. *American Journal of Sociology, 12*(4), 435-469.

Trepagnier, B. (2006). *Silent racism: How well-meaning white people perpetuate the racial divide.* New York: Paradigm.

Turner, C. S. V., & Myers, S. (2000). *Faculty of color in academe: Bittersweet success.* Boston: Allyn & Bacon.

Twale, D.J & De Luca, B.M. (2008). *Faculty incivility: The rise of the academic bully culture and what to do about it.* San Francisco, CA: Jossey-Bass.

Warde, B. (2009). The road to tenure: Narratives of African American male tenured professors. *Journal of African American Studies, 13*(1), 494-508.

Westhues, K. (2004). *The envy of excellence: Administrative mobbing of high-achieving professors.* New York: Edwin Mellen.

Westhues, K. (2006). The unkindly art of mobbing. *Academic affairs, Journal of Higher Education.* OCUFA, (Fall), 18-19.

Westhues, K. (Ed.). (2008). *The Anatomy of an academic mobbing: Two cases.* New York: Edwin Mellen.

Chapter Eight

Pitfalls and Struggles in Progress: Challenges in Negotiating Organizational Culture as an African American within a Predominately White College and University

✤

Martell Teasley

Introduction

While African-Americans comprise 12% of the U.S. population, they are approximately only 4% of the postsecondary faculty, and they constitute an even smaller fraction of faculty members in four-year colleges and universities with predominantly white students (Kulis, Chong, & Shaw, 1999). As such, there are several challenges that African American faculty members encounter at predominately white institutions of higher education, many of which are unintended and nonsystematic yet nevertheless problematic and stressful. Among the challenges are understanding organizational culture and informal networks, identifying appropriate methods of communication, combating racial marginalization, and finding appropriate mentorship. The author shares his experiences in each of these areas and suggests strategies for negotiating the dynamics of black faculty members at PWCU. Information on formal and informal mentorship, promoting cultural diversity, faculty relationships, and strategies for facilitating scholar productivity and professional growth are discussed. The benefits include rewarding collegial experiences and facilitating student achievement and personal growth though teaching, learning, and mentorship (Bank, 2006).

Paul Barrett's (2000) text *The Good Black* is a rags-to-riches account of an urban youth who works hard in school and other phases of life to achieve the American Dream. The protagonist in this true story learned from his mothers as a child the value of good school grades, hard work, and achievement as a way of making it in life. She gave him a simple philosophy that would personify his no excuses attitude towards race and achievement..."being human first, an American second and black third." After graduation from Harvard Law School and work as an associate at several law firms, he signs with a prestigious Washington, DC firm with aspirations of finally achieving full partnership. What he receives as the sole African American at this law firm was demeaning work, zero advancement, workplace insults, and in finality an ugly legal battle over his claim of workplace racial discrimination (for which he ultimately lost his case) that ultimately the ends his career. The lesson from *The Good Black* is a testament in how subtle forms of racism and unintended bias can impact one's career and psychological wellbeing, particularly for those who have decided that racial discrimination is an afterthought in a post-racial American society.

In predominantly white academic institutions or what is phrased as predominantly white colleges and universities (PWCU), the *good black* is one who forgoes the realities of cultural and organizational racism and works for self-achievement and the betterment of the institution. Despite brushes with borderline and unintended racial happenstances that become obvious patterns for those who experience them, the *good black* does not complain. Since they are often under the pressure of institutional promotion and tenure demands,

African American at PWCU certainly do not want the additional pressure that racial discourse generates and therefore may end up serving by default as the *good black*, where the realities of racism are obfuscated for political correct thinking and language. This is particularly true in the American South where the intersections among race, class, and good-old-boy and good-old-girl networks are all painfully present. In essence, the *good black* has to adopted a mindset similar to what Prashad (2002) refers to as the biggest racial challenge of the 21st Century—the challenge of the colorblind. Prashad maintains that since our society has shifted and that overt forms of racial bias are so demonstrably unacceptable, the last thing that anyone wants to be accused of is being a racist, because of its polarizing impact. The weight and gravity of, for example, telling racial jokes, blatant discriminatory practices, and open prejudice associates the offender with historical racial ills that have are now viewed as socially inappropriate and unacceptable. Individuals who engage in overt racial bias are ostracized and become polarizing figures. Therefore, new forms of political correctness, according to Prashad, have emerges creating an era where people do not want to openly discuss social issues related to race.

The story of the *good black* is a useful metaphor in describing the experiences of African Americans (including my own) at PWCU in negotiating spaces that are affected by race, but where radicalized experiences are rendered invalid and viewed as an unbiased product of normative workplace and organizational processes. Interesting are the ways in which many dominant groups at PWCU minimize racial discourse and see themselves as beyond the qualities of racism. Moreover, as *individual* faculty members and components of a given organizational culture, many whites do not view themselves as intentionally engaging in racial bias. Somehow they typecast themselves as the colorblind, and not only beyond the abhorrent actions of the overt racism, but likewise as colorblind when it comes to the experiences of non-dominate group members. "Because most people experience themselves as good, moral, and decent human beings, conscious awareness of their hidden biases, prejudices, and discriminatory behaviors threatens their self-images," (Sue 2009, p.5). What is more, many whites at PWCU fail to engage in the type of analysis that examines the realities of organizational cultural and its effects on minority faculty members, whether not included or isolated (Johnson 1991; Kashefi 2004).

The challenge of negotiating spaces within a PWCU as a black male requires awareness of your surroundings and the development of skills, strategies, and appropriate mentorship. In this essay I examine not only the reality of the *good back* as characterized by the challenges of dominant group cultural orientation and unintended bias, cultural marginalization, invisibility and invalidation, I exam some elements concerning the realities of organizational cultural within academia as well as methods evaluating and successfully negotiating PWCU. As part of my conversation I discuss some of the challenges that I have faced to include solution to confront these challenges. One salient method that I discuss for dealing with the attributes of academic organizational cultural at PWCU is the effective use of mentoring programs and practices. Faculty mentoring can be instrumental in bridging communication gaps and negotiating formal and informal dominate groups within academic settings and may serve a germane function in the success of black faculty within PWCU.

In navigating through the normal milieu of academia as an African American within a PWCU there have been many achievements, highlights and success stories. On the other hand, there have been shortcomings, challenges, and obstacles that have impeded progress and optimal professional development. There are many rewarding experiences as a faculty member, college instructor, and student mentor that I will discuss that may help other African Americans who are considering employment at a PWCU as a faculty member. Observing organizational cultural and developing pragmatic approaches to negotiating mainstream academic spaces is a skill that few Black Americans are schooled in at any level of their higher educational professional development. Thus, my contribution in this chapter is one of facilitating critical though towards how to develop strategies for negotiating the dynamics of PWCU and dominate group organizational culture.

I have been a faculty member since August 2002. At present I am still in my first academic appointment at a Research I Institution, in which I was successful in earning promotion and tenure as the first African American male in the history of the College of Social Work, and only the second to do so. The university has approximately 50,000 students on and off campus to include satellite campuses throughout the state. With approximately 11 percent of the student body enrolled at the University registering as African Americans, less than 5 percent of the entire faculty are African Americans in tenure earning positions. Currently, there are no African Americans in upper administration or serving as deans at the University.

The College of Social Work is a free standing academic unit at a southeastern university and is one of approximately thirty schools in the United States offering social work degree programs at all three levels: baccalaureate, master's, and doctoral. According to 2007 *U.S. World News Report*, the College is ranked in the top five of social work education programs with all three levels. Its mission is to provide quality educational services that prepare social workers to enhance human well-being and help meet the basic needs of diverse populations with particular attention to the empowerment of people who are vulnerable, oppressed, and/or living in poverty.

In terms of demographics at the College, in the fall semester 2008 there were approximately 400 students within the undergraduate program. Of these students, 30% were African Americans; 57% were Anglo-Americans; 9% were Hispanics; and 1% was listed as Asian American. There were 386 students enrolled in the college's graduate Master of Social Work programs in January 2008. Of these students, 61 (16%) are African Americans; 23 (6%) are Hispanic; and 291 (79%) identify as Anglo-Americans. Of the 29 students in doctoral education four (13%) are listed as African Americans; one (3%) is Hispanic; and 23 (79%) are Anglo-Americans.

Navigating Academic Organizational Culture

My experiences have been a part of the normative challenges that many new academicians face. However, there are both general and specific challenges that African American faculty members may encounter at PWCU, many of which are unintended and nonsystematic yet nevertheless problematic events that become noticeable as one accumulates certain experiences. In retrospect, several areas of my experience were helpful and provide a general framework for negotiating the organizational cultural and the realities of dealing with dominant group interest.

Organizational culture is defined as the shared values, beliefs, assumptions, perceptions, norms, artifacts, and patterns of behavior of an organization. It is the unseen and unobservable force that is always behind organizational activities (Harris 1994; Hatch 1993; Smart 2003). Harris contends that organizational culture encompasses both individual and group phenomena and influences individual sensemaking and decision-making. Organizational culture helps shape an individuals' orientation, understanding of events, and ultimately one's schema for cognitive processing and the interpretation behaviors within the context in which they occur. "Schemas refer to the cognitive structures in which an individual's knowledge is retained and organized" (Harris 1994, p. 309). Organizational schema is revealed within an organization's cultural manifestations and schema plays-out in patterns of practice through its structure and functions; information processing; templates for problem-solving; evaluation of experiences; and goal setting, planning, and execution (Harris 1994). Such patterns operate in an organization-specific schema that helps in the determination of *who is important, what is important, what has meaning, how individuals should respond* and *what implications to response are.*

Yet, although research on organizational culture has taken place since the 1970 (Hatch 1993), few studies have engaged in investigations on academia and there is basically a void of studies on individuals and organizational culture in academia (Harris 1994; Labianca, Gray, & Brass 2000). Harris explains that there is little research on how organizational culture affects individual cognitive processes and sense making. Even less research exist on how organizational culture and the structure and function of at predominantly white academic institutions affect black faculty members.

Most American organizational structures, including academia, are structured in ways that are based on European values characterized by "materialism, hierarchical control, bottom-line profits, and competition" (Warfield-Coppock 1995, p.30). Thus, the general organizational schema of a given academic unit is consistent with mainstream American values and practices. And as such, many academic units repeat the same patterns of practice found within the mainstream. For African American faculty members employed at a PWCU, research has demonstrated that this sometimes includes patterns of exclusion and marginalization. For example, using a national sample (N=230) Kulis (1992) examined barriers to equal participation and empowerment of black sociologists employed at PWCU at the departmental level. "Results indicate that the factors that promote better black faculty representation do not always provide African-Americans with other black colleagues, with substantial numerical influences within the department, or with equality in academic rank." (p.709)

To this end, and as a general component of selection criteria, African Americans entering PWCU should have a sense of how to assess the organizational cultural and climate of a potential academic unit. This should "include elements such as management style or philosophy, leadership style, administrative mode, power/authority, decision making, staff relations, work orientation, and productivity" expectations (Warfield-Coppock 1995, p. 32). Moreover, determining how conflict is resolved, and accessing both formal and informal modalities of communication are equally important. In the following sections, I comment on research in some of these areas as well as discuss some of the pitfalls and personal success strategies for negotiating the organization culture of PWCUs.

Understanding Informal Organizational Networks

Given this information, it is highly important that black faculty members in PWCU develop methods for assessing and negotiating informal organizational networks within their respective academic institutions. For sure, dominate groups use informal networks as a method of approaching and negotiating formal authority (Lemelle 2009). Informal networks are inherently part of campus culture and often set the tone for organizational cognitive and behavioral patterns (Smart 2003). Methods for joining informal networks come about in a variety of ways including similarities in research agendas, regional and ethnic ties, commitment to a particular ideology, and former institutional relations. Informal groups that many black faculty members encounter in PWCU are oftentimes those based on dominate group ties, which pans out to be ethnic ties among Anglo Americans. Unless Black American faulty member employed at PWCU tap into dominant group informal networks, it is unlikely that they will form their own, and if they do so, such a network may have little leverage in the organizational change process due to lack of a critical mass of constituents—organizations that use voting as the method for resolving competing contingencies, critical mass is important.

Quite often, administrators are part of informal networks and may gained their status in a particular academic unit partly though the use of informal networks. Administrators may use such networks as a means of information gathering, gaining allies among faculty members, and developing administrative decisions that impact faculty workload, careers, and resource procurement. Thus, when it is the case that there is linkage between organizational informal networks and the formal administrative structure of a given academic unit, such conditions mean that faculty members can face a two tier decision making structure: one formal and the other informal. For many African American faculty members this can mean the presence of additional barriers in gaining access to the decision-making process, placing them at a disadvantage in term of how decisions are made. Moreover, this can lead to a sense of ambiguity over the worth of one's input into the decision making process and frustration concerning the method in terms of how final decisions are made; it further dampens one's belief in the meritocracy of the decision making process (Sue 2009).

One sign of informal networks and their affects is going to committee meetings where decisions are perfunctorily discussed but have been deliberated within other venues, with the committee meeting servicing as a means of providing official sanctioning and legitimacy to informal decision making. Such a process can be detrimental to black faculty members who are not aware and/or left out of this informal process. In comparison to their white colleagues, it can hinder their research agenda, restrict their access to information, and hinder opportunities for professional growth and development.

Determining Communication Patterns

Many African Americans have a person-to-person way of problem-solving characterized by face-to-face interaction and communication (Warfield-Coppock 1995). However, in large PWCU communication is very impersonal with the frequent use of memorandums and emails for minor and major decision-making (Warfield-Coppock, 1995). In many situations, people are more willing to communicate via email than person-to-person for good reasons. Vast amounts of information are processed daily; individuals want to keep record of their communication process and email affords the most economic method of reaching multiple individuals/audiences at one time As such, Warfield-Coppock (1995) maintains that black people to need examine their environmental and personal fit within the structural and cultural norms of organizations; this includes its communication patterns. She further asserts that there is a need to systematically theorize and provide evidence of the organizational characteristics and cultural norms that can promote the needs of black people within mainstream organizations.

Micoagressions and Marginalization

In general, for Black American faculty members, the PWCU can be deemed a workplace laboratory for microaggressive behavior. As Sue (2009) informs,

> Microaggressions are defined as the everyday verbal, non-verbal, and environmental slights, snubs, or insults, whether intentional or unintentional, that communicate hostile, derogatory, or negative messages to target person based solely upon their marginalized group membership. (p.3)

According to Sue (2009) microaggression can take three basic forms: microassault, microinsult, and microinvalidation. As a researcher on microaggressions, Sue maintains that they take place often as unconscious factors by those who commit them. Here, I cited some of my perceived notions of microaggressions based on my experiences as a faculty member. One example is in walking though the hallway in conversation accompanied by another black male faculty member and being greeted with "there goes double-trouble," when encountering particular staff or faculty members— this has occurred numerous times, but never while in similar company with one of my Anglo-American male colleagues. There is also the notion of having students refer to black people as lazy, and having racist jokes told in my presence by faculty members. Once while sitting in my office with another African American colleague discussing some research, a colleague who is part of the dominate group culture stated, "What are you two doing, shucking and jiving?" When I confronted this individual and stated that African American do not like this traditionally stereotypical notion of their work ethnic, the individual informed me that this was just a typical term that can apply to anyone. Given the history of black people in America, I viewed this comment as highly insensitive and I was therefore skeptical of the individual's reply. Sue (2009) refers to such a situation as a microinsult – behavior or verbal "remarks or comments that convey rudeness and insensitivity and demean a person's racial heritage or identity" (p.8).

As a black male, it took a while to adjust to a classroom of prominently all white females who sometimes doubted my knowledge. I was cursed-out during my first semester by a student who did not like her grade on a paper. When I documented the event and reported this event to the faculty administrator, not only did I not feel supported, sometime later in the semester the administrator in question proposed and got approved the decision to delete the use for the incident reporting form that I used to write-up the situation.

As the owner of a foreign sports car, I was asked once by a colleague if I ever ran the car at a high speed. When I replied no, because I'm a black male and my lived experiences from "driving while black" are that engaging in speeding is not good when stopped by police, the individual stated that she would like to think that our country has moved beyond the "driving while black" phenomena. This "clash of realities" left me puzzled momentarily, because I viewed the person in question as a knowledgeable individual who is well informed on current events and consciously aware of national issues. While on the one hand the response gave me a sense of invalidation in the form of negating my reality and lived experiences, which were oftentimes at the end of a gun barrels for a minor traffic offense or for no offense at all—just blatant police harassment. Sue (2009) refers to this as a form of "microinvalidation—verbal comments or behaviors that exclude, negate, or nullify the psychological thoughts, feelings, or experiential reality of a person of color." (p.8)

Another former administrator at the College used my research data without my consent and gave a scholarly presentation without my knowledge. Nearly flooded while at a national conference and finding out that the presentation was taking place, the administrator later blatantly stated that I gave him the data, when in actuality, I did not.

On one occasion a colleague informed me that another African American colleague would receive a less than stellar third year promotion and tenure committee review because some faculty members felt that she was not being "collegial." The purpose was to send a message to the individual to be more visible at the College and too socialize more with other faculty members. Interestingly, the individual that informed me of the proposed less than stellar review (which did occur) did so prior to the review being conducted and was not eligible to be a standing member of the Promotion and Tenure Committee that conducted the review. Thus, the messenger gained this information via informal communication with other faculty members who were on the committee at the time. His stated *intent* in delivering the message was to do her a favor by informing me (as her friend) for the purpose of relaying the message. My reply to him was that this would not turn out as planned and that the individual in questions would not view a problematic third-year-review as anything but negative. And, this is what actually did occur as the individual in question then searched and found another academic position at another university, leaving the following year.

Although explained as well intended by the messenger, I viewed this situation as another form of microaggression by the majority. The problem with microaggressions, states Sue (2009), is that the most detrimental forms are "usually delivered by well-intentioned individuals who are unaware that they have engaged in harmful conduct toward a socially devalued group. These everyday occurrences may on the surface appear quite harmless, trivial, or be described as 'small slights,' but research indicates they have a powerful impact upon the psychological well-being of marginalized groups." (p.3) Yet, although such occurrences are psychologically stressful and anxiety provoking—and this situation did weigh on me heavily for sometime—, to overtly express their numerous occurrences may end up sounding like an ongoing saga—a soap opera of victimization that overshadows all other meaningful casual and intellectual conversations.

The point here is that for African Americans to ignore the realities of micoaggressions and individual marginalization within an academic unit is to take on the attributes of the *good black*; the consequences of this mindset is the development of a sense of unhealthy stress and psychological discomfort. "Most of the pain and detrimental impact of racism does not come from that of overt racists but from ordinary, normal, decent people who believe in life, liberty, and the pursuit of justice for all." (p.7) The lesson here is that African Americans entering PWCU should realize that academia has enough political and personal landmines for everyone irregularly of race, gender, or sexual orientation; yet, there is no empathy for victimhood in the publish and produce or perish environment of a Research I Institution. On the other hand, *blacks cannot ignore race in academia because it will not ignore them.* "Whether we like to acknowledge the fact or not, race is a central feature of American culture and society" (Rooks 2006, p. 9). Thus, in general, in order to avoid the so-called "good black" syndrome, African American faculty members at PWCU must find ways and methods to combat incidental stereotypical happenstances at the time of their occurrence and development strategic methods for negotiating the dynamics of a given academic institutions' organizational culture.

"To the extent that we talk about racial differences [in academia] at all, we prefer to speak about 'diversity,' or bring up race merely to dismiss its importance" (Rooks 2006, p.9). To this end, the challenge for many African Americans as faculty members at PWCU is to forge a dialogue that is inclusive of the black perspective and too engage in an open dialogue about issues of race and class as part of scholastic and intellectual discourse. For sure, the American integration project is not complete and the demographics of Black America in the academy are a testament to this fact. Thus, while the population of black students attending PWCU continues to grow, the struggle to education and development sufficient numbers of black academicians must continuously be undertaken.

Mentorship

Finding appropriate and meaningful mentorship is central to success for African Americans at PWCU and should be one of the criteria for selecting an academic unit. Academic mentorship can be both formal and informal. Formal mentors can be individuals assigned to new faculty members though official mechanisms. Such individuals should assure that new faculty members are abreast of need-to-know information, standard operating procedures, and strategies for successful negotiation of their academic units. The ideal formal mentor is one who has similar research interest and who can co-author one or two manuscripts for publication with the mentee in a reasonable time frame.

Both formal and informal mentors can help provide idiosyncratic information and facilitate career development. Informal mentors are those individuals who provide essential information within an unofficial capacity through causal conversation, emails, sharing of documents, or other mechanisms. Such individuals are those whom one may find helpful in understanding organizational dynamics, administrative functions, and successful integration within a particular academic unit, as well as throughout the greater university. The identification of informal mentors is often unannounced and obtained through serendipity. This may be an individual faculty member that one obtains a sense of camaraderie and personal friendship with, and finds that the newly formed relationship is informative and helpful toward career and professional development. African Americans within academic departments should identify such individuals as soon as possible, if possible. Key to the meaningfulness of this relationship is the objective evaluation of information provided by informal mentors for its timeliness and validity.

Thus, the relationship between mentor and mentee can serve not only the function of academic support and professional development, it may help bridge the impersonal environment of large PWCU and serve as an outlet for frequent communication and camaraderie. The warning here is that when mentoring only results in the development of interpersonal existentialism that is not accompanied by scholarly productivity, then such mentorship, while fruitful and essential to the African American ethos, is limited in scope.

Ways of measuring whether mentorship has been successful should partly be based on the mentee's individual goals and achievement of professional milestones. Some general attributes include the free flow of information; receivership of critical and constructive feedback; academic career counseling; production of quality manuscripts toward publication; a sense of being provided with guidance, knowledge and awareness of how to navigate the political and cultural climate of the institution; and finding that information provided is helpful and relatively true within a given context. Moreover, quality mentorship bridges communication gaps, reduces or eliminates unforeseen landmines towards the tenure earning process, and clearly defines institutional expectations so that mentees are clear on their profession expectations.

My own experience is that when there is no official mentoring mechanism, African Americans at PWCU can easily miss-out on idiosyncratic information that may be essential to success in the tenure earning process. This may occur even in the face of true outreach by faculty members. In academic environments where there is no formal mentoring process, then, informal mentoring and or planned institutional mechanisms may serve as outlets for information towards career building and tenure earning. When appropriate mentorship is not available at a given academic unit, it may be necessary to find both resources and intellectual stimulation outside of one's residential academic unit.

Events such as luncheons and other social gatherings can be instrumental sources of gaining informal information and ways of obtaining mentorship. The selection of a mentor should not be taken likely as it can be a highly political process within the organizational culture of a given academic unit—there are people that you may befriend that have workplace enemies. To this end, it is also important to assess the political climate of an academic unit and to assess faculty opinions of possible mentors. African Americans entering academia should develop a list of their own mentoring needs and find out if potential academic institutions, and individuals with those institutions, meet their specific criteria.

Research suggests that mentoring should be based on three based basic areas: *institutional socialization, academic productivity and development,* and *building a research agenda.* Institutional socialization includes discussions on faculty collegiality and expectations, orientation to University culture, strategic academic collaboration and planning, day-to-day advice, institutional and unit politics, exposure to example documents, and resource procurement among other entities. Academic productivity and development includes information on classroom instruction and pedagogical practice, teaching strategies, student and classroom dynamics, internal university opportunities, achievement and acquisition of knowledge, manuscript development, and the development of scholarly presentations should be coved by the mentoring group. Building a research agenda concerns the identification of funding opportunities and research mentorships. In this capacity, a given mentoring group should help a designated mentee strategize and cope with the demands of executing her or his research agenda. One way of doing this can be through the development of a checklist of criteria for assessing an academic unit for its ability to engage in formal academic mentoring.

Understanding the importance of faculty mentoring and given that there was no formal mentoring mechanism instituted by the College, I took the initiative and identified both formal and informal mentors. Both have been helpful in my transition into academia and in my negotiation of the organizational cultural at the College. For example, my formal mentor provided me with a $1,000 book purchase of my choice and also provided information that facilitated successful grant funding in the amount of $250,000 over a two year period. There has recently been another $10,000 of funding provided to further my research that is directly attributable to the efforts of my formal mentor.

In 2005 as part of committee work, I surveyed the entire faculty t the College on their opinions and experiences with faculty mentoring. The results indicated that they had grave concerns over the lack of mentoring during in their experiences as faculty members at the College. This mentoring program is designed to facilitate communication, enhance faculty socialization, and progress the development of new faculty research agendas.

Student Mentorship

One of the most rewarding challenges for me has been student mentorship. I have mentored students from multiple backgrounds and racial/ethnic groups. However, many African American students attend poor and underfunded primary and secondary grade school systems that do not prepare them for college; this is particularly prevalent in the South. Many are first generation college students and have fewer resources to support their professional education. As such, many need assistance and guidance though the academic process. I identify with this as I was the first and only member of my family to attend college and graduate school.

During my first year as a faculty member I started an informal mentoring group for African American students. Many needed assistance in preparing for admission to graduate school. In fact, a good percentage of black students who successfully completed our undergraduate program where unsuccessful in their attempt to enter into our graduate program. I met with the Dean and expressed my concerns and asked for cooperation in setting up a mentoring program for black students; it was granted.[1] Along with my other African American colleagues, we started to meet twice per semester as a group with black students. Additional meetings were scheduled and aimed at accomplishing particular tasks. We set up graduate readiness examination (GRE) training, writing workshops, educational planning workshops, and a review of resumes and applications for graduate school. Guest speakers were brought in as well as African Americans alumni who are now professional social work practitioners. Overall, this has been quit a successful enterprise and I have personally mentored many students who have matriculated successfully through the College. The lesson here is persistence and going the extra mile. Even though this was not an official faculty committee or sanctioned group, it was necessary in the service of students and a part of the extra efforts that are sometimes needed by African Americans faculty members at PWCU.

Many students at PWCU have never had an African American for an instructor and I have been their first. Getting past the rough edges discussed earlier, this experience has turned out to be beneficial for both students and myself. For me, it is a lesson in diplomacy, patience, and constant refinement of my teaching skills and classroom instruction strategies. For them, in many cases, it has been exposure to the black perspective and detailed information on African American history and life that challenges conventional ways of knowing and thinking.

Conclusion

African Americans considering or accepting faculty appointments at PWCUs must consider many of the issues raised in this manuscript. They must be able to observe and assess the context of organizational culture within a given academic unit and how it fits their personal and professional needs. It is important that African Americans attending PWCUs develop relationships that facilitate their scholastic and professional growth. They must understand organizational communication patterns as well as how informal networks operate. For African Americans employed at a PWCU, faculty mentorship is extremely important and therefore, gaining academic mentorship should be taken seriously. Importantly, Black faculty members must also have a sense of larger goals and the development strategies for achieving these goals. Student mentorship and collegiality can be rewarding and fulfilling experiences, but will require perseverance, critical reflection and strategic thinking.

Mainstream PWCUs that are sensitivity to the needs of minority faculty members are those that are genuinely concerned about how patterns of inequality in society repeat themselves for minority faculty members in academia. Such sensitive should anticipate clashes with organizational cultural norms that marginalized and invalidate the experiences of Black American faculty members. The goal here is to minimize microaggressions that can taint well intended actions by dominate group members within PWCUs. Although not a cure-all, black faculty members who understand and take heed of the dynamics of organizational culture at their particular academic units can minimized the normative challenges identified within the research literature that can and do occur. In doing so, they can empower themselves to promote change for the better.

Finally, mentorship can be an instrumental component of successful negotiation and career building for African American faculty members employed at PWCU. Black faculty members should not only seek out appropriate mentorship, they must also strategically select mentors that can facilitate profession growth and development within the academic ranks. It is likewise necessary for African American faculty members at PWCU who have the skill set to mentor black students that they come into contact with. Student mentorship can be a rewarding and fulfilling experience, but will require perseverance, critical reflection and strategic thinking. Like it or not, as academicians we are role models for the next generation and therefore we have the responsibility to promote the best of what it means to be African and human at the same time.

Note

1.   The Mentoring for Success Program, as it was named, did allow for inclusion of students from other ethnic groups to join and fully participate.

References

Banks, J.A. (2006). *Race, culture, and education: The selected works of James A. Banks.* New York: Routledge

Barrett, P. (2000). *The good black: A true story of race in America.* New York: Plume.

Harris, S. G. (1994). Organizational culture and individual sensemaking: A schema-based perspective. *Organization Science. (5)* 3, 309-321.

Hatch, M. J. (1993). The dynamics of organizational culture. *The Academy of Management Review. (18)*4, 657-693.

Johnson, A. E. (1991). The sin of omission: African-American Women in social work.

*Journal of Multicultural Social Work. (1)*2, 1-15.

Kashefi, M. (2004). Racial differences in organizational attachment? Structural explanation of attitude differences between white and African American employees. *Journal of Black Studies. (34)*5, 702-718.

Kulis, S., Chong, Y., Shaw, H. (1999). Discriminatory organizational contexts and Black scientists on postsecondary faculties. *Research in Higher Education. (40)*2, 115-148.

Kulis, S. (1992). The political economy of incorporation: Black sociologists in academia. *Research in Higher Education. (33)*6, 709-745.

Labiance, G., Gray, B., & Brass, D.J. (2000). A grounded model of organizational schema change during empowerment. *Organization Science. (11)*2, 235-257.

Lemelle, Jr., A.J. (2009). Social and economic organization of the black professoriate at predominately-white colleges and universities. *Journal of African American Studies. 14*(1), 106-127.

Prashad, V. (2001). *Everybody was kung fu fighting: Afro-Asian connections and the myth of cultural purity.* Boston: Beacon.

Rooks, N. M. (2006). *White money black power: The surprising history of African American studies and the crisis of race in higher education.* Boston: Beacon.

Smart, J. C. (2003). Organizational effectiveness of 2-year colleges: The centrality of cultural and leadership complexity. *Research in Higher Education. 44*(6), 679 – 703.

Sue, D. W. (2009). (Ed). *Microaggressions and marginality: manifestation, dynamics, and impact.* New Jersey: John Wiley & Sons.

U.S. Public Health Service. (2000). *Report of the Surgeon General's Mental Health: A National Action Agenda.* Washington, DC: Department of Health and Human Services.

Warfield-Coppock, N. (1995). Toward a theory of Afrocentric organizations. *Journal of Black Psychology, (21)*1, 30-48.

Chapter Nine

A Critical Auto-Ethnographic Parable of a Black Educator in a White Space

❋

Mark S. Giles

Introduction

This semi-autobiographical essay examines my educational journey toward becoming a faculty member at a Predominately White University (PWU). It incorporates the method of parable to offer a story that suggests a life lesson. Let me begin this chapter with that story,

> While investigating the vast forest near his home, a young student became confused and quickly lost his way. He failed to remember the primary instructions from his trusted teacher and mentor: "stay on the path that connects whence you came to guide your return." The student knew that his home community was not far away, but the tall shady trees, strange and colorful animals, and noticeable change in climate made him begin to believe he could not find the path leading back to his family and those who authentically loved him. After wandering for a time

and learning survival skills, the student encountered two women standing in front of two distinct paths.

The first woman was tall, slender, and appeared oddly youthful. She had long, straight, salt and pepper hair, and wore a long, beautiful, red, and gold robe, with some type of Kente cloth over her shoulder. Interestingly, she wore the identical kind of sun glasses his former teacher and mentor owned, but never wore; instead the former teacher kept his sun glasses in a glass trophy case on his office desk at all times. Those strange eyeglasses always seemed like a type of symbol the curious student never understood.

The other woman looked like someone familiar from his past, but strangely different. She appeared much older than the first woman did. This woman's hair was completely gray and long, thick, and curly. Her robe looked muted and tired as if left out in the sun too long for too many years. As the student focused on her, he noticed that she too had a pair of the same shaded eyeglasses, but wore them on a thin gold chain around her neck. This allowed him to see her soft brown eyes, which pierced through him in a compassionate, knowingly firm stare.

Suddenly, the first woman spoke in a clear, authoritarian tone: "I know you are lost and I am here to help. I have watched you for some time and sense that you have great potential. If you follow me, I will teach you new ways of knowing and understanding this great forest. I will instruct you on how to become an expert of the forest, in my likeness." In awe, the student stood silent and wondered what her eyes looked like behind the darkly shaded eyeglasses.

Just then, the second woman drew a deep breath and exhaled slowly as if her voice had to travel over a long distance before making a sound: "You are not lost. Over the years, you failed to remember how and why you entered this forest. I have watched you before you came into this space and watch you still. Although it might not seem so, you have dwelled in this space much longer than you realize. I see that you have learned many things useful in surviving challenging and hostile environment. However, if you follow the ancient one too closely and too deeply into this limitless space, and you do not return to this crossroads at the critical hour of questioning the meaning between past, present, and future, you may never remember or return to that which is most important." The two women never looked at each other, yet there seemed to be an unsettling connection between them.

After considering both statements and examining the physical appearances of the women, the student, agreed to follow the first one. For some reason, he could not take his eyes from her beautiful robe and timidly asked if one day he could earn something like it. Without acknowledging him, she reached into the fold of her robe, took out a pair of sunglasses, and said, "Put these on and as long as you are with me do not remove them. On the day you remove this veil, you can no longer serve as my protégée or student." The student followed the woman deeper into the forest. He never removed the eyeglasses. In the course of time, he became firmly embedded as one of the trees providing protection and shade for the keeper of the forest. The other woman remained vigilantly waiting at the crossroad for him to return one day or for the next traveling student who must make the same crucial choice.

The Value and Cost of Living My Blackness as Black Faculty at a PWU

"Say it loud, I'm Black, and I'm Proud!" That famous 1968 James Brown song represented a unifying coda in the late 1960s for many black youth and young adults in my Cincinnati, Ohio, West End neighborhood. Some may call it a ghetto, or inner city, but it was home. The neighborhood consisted of mostly Black blue-collar folks, Black professionals such as the teachers who taught in the neighborhood schools, a few medical Doctors, Dentists, attorneys, and pharmacists. Within any four or five block distance, we had small "mom and pop" type stores, known as Bodegas in Latino communities, that sold more groceries, dry goods, and household items, than beer, wine, and cigarettes. Neighborhood families found most of the things they needed from these small stores. Children could get the things they most wanted like potato chips, soda pop, penny candy, and items needed for playing neighborhood games. My father was a former pastor of the York Street United Methodist Church, which meant that I grew up attending a church located a

few blocks from the house. My mother made sure we were there each Sunday, no questions, no complaints, no whining. Members of the church included some of my schoolteachers, local storeowners, hairdressers, and an assortment of Saturday sinners/Sunday saints. In other words, I experienced a multilayered, reinforcing web of non-monolithic cultural contexts that helped to shape my self-identity and my understanding of my environment.

I did not need anyone trying to use some high-minded academic theories to explain what it meant to be Black in a Black neighborhood to me; I lived it. That is one of the reasons I mentioned James Brown and his big hit, *"I'm Black and I'm Proud,"* as memorable and something that embodied feelings of self-agency, self-worth, and the community pride that contributed to my early development and my current consciousness. James Brown's music has rhythm and soul and I intend for my teaching, mentoring, and scholarship to represent the same meaningful authenticity.

My autobiographical and auto-ethnographical intersubjectivity help to frame and make meaning of memories that shape my work as an educator-scholar (Roth 2005). No amount of pseudo-Cartesian objectivism can remove my past from my present. Moreover, according to Margaret Eisenhart (2005), auto/biography, despite its traditional perception as unfiltered and unbiased represents a contextualized, subjective telling of someone's life story with certain intentions at a specific moment and for a particular audience. I admit to this and say that what I share here is not a neutral, transparent account of events from my life; it is situated based on the potential audience of this article, and the purpose for me writing it. In consideration of that explanation, what I present here is not fiction; it is to be understood within the context of its purpose and what I wish to share in this social space.

This article represents a combination of critical race theory counter-narrative (Solórzano & Yosso 2002), educational autobiography and self-story (Denzin 1989), and auto-ethnography (Roth 2005). It examines and highlights aspects of my experiences as a faculty member at a predominantly white university (PWU). The themes presented in this article transform my story from a passive "woe is me" victim narrative to a creative tale of self-agency shaped by my identity and role as a black man in America who struggled to earn college degrees at PWIs and now stand in the white spaces that once blocked and supported my own progress. Sharing aspects of my journey provides insight into the ingredients and recipe for purpose in the racially contested spaces of PWUs.

My personal background represents a critical well spring of strength, a source of cultural grounding that continues to help me make choices and navigate white academic spaces that seek to sometimes welcome me for its own benefits and sometimes trap me into a pseudo-reality that is antithetical to who I am as a Black man in America. I have worked hard to maintain a critical social consciousness while challenging and surviving schooling processes and navigating the tricky forests of higher education (Shujaa, 1995). I feel lucky to have gained access to advanced degree programs. I recognize that many others who are far smarter and better suited never received similar chances. I am proud and humbled that I survived the processes of earning those pieces of parchment that indicates high achievement. However, earning a doctorate degree and entering academe as a Black faculty member takes more than luck and remembering your authentic self requires more than earning institutional freedom papers that represent the higher education promised land of promotion and tenure. However, what we do as faculty members and how we do it, demands a close, reflexive connection to who we are. Connecting the dots of one's life is never easy and for Black faculty in white spaces it is elemental and essential.

I earned my Ph.D. at Indiana University in Higher Education Administration with a minor in 20th century United States history. Since my main interests focused on African American history, leadership, and spirituality, I completed my dissertation on 20th century theologian Howard Thurman and his career in and influence on higher education (Giles, 2003). Although I received advice from my first doctoral advisor and a few other "well-meaning" white faculty members at Indiana University to avoid focusing attention on studying African American history and culture because it would pigeonhole me as an educator and scholar, I consciously followed my interests and not their warnings. I neither entered nor departed that ivory tower space thinking I would pursue a faculty career. My goal, at the time, focused on earning a doctorate and landing a stable, administrative position at a college (e.g., two or four year) or university. Since I never thought much about my calling in life, those goals seemed as good as any others. As a late bloomer in graduate school, I carried the benefit of many years of work and life experiences that shaped my identity and worldview.

Working as an academic advisor at a branch campus of the University of Cincinnati after a few years as a social worker among other jobs, I wanted to elevate myself in that particular role. I saw it as a way to help college students avoid the mistakes I made. Following that mindset, I earned a master's degree in college student personnel (college student affairs) from Miami University. A better paying job guided that choice, not my intellectual passions or disciplinary and theoretical interests. I had the intention to seek future opportunities as a college administrator, helping students, especially students of color and those from marginalized backgrounds, successfully negotiate the complexities of earning a degree. The faculty thing happened quite unexpectedly.

After earning my degree from Indiana University, I worked briefly in a diversity focused administrative role in Washington, DC, at one of the national higher education advocacy organizations. That proved to be a contradictory and conflicted experience worth sharing at another time. While working in DC, one Saturday I received a call from a faculty member from my master's degree program about their last minute need for someone to step in on short notice and teach several courses on a one-year contract (visiting assistant professor). Since the job in DC had its problems and limitations, I decided to pursue this teaching opportunity, which meant returning to my hometown area (Miami University is about 30-40 miles northwest from Cincinnati).

Teaching at the same institution where I earned my master's degree felt strange and became professionally hazardous over time. It felt strange because I never imagined myself as a classroom educator. It represented danger because I realized that I must stay in control of my emotions at all times or else face indictment of the angry Black man syndrome. In addition, I needed to navigate an uncomfortable programmatic space, which felt personally constraining and intellectually debilitating. I learned to show patience when confronted with passive racism from White students who asked me if I had a Ph.D., as if that would allow them to respect me more, and from senior colleagues who discouraged me from publishing my work in journals different from my White colleagues. Learning to understand, cope with, and counter racial micro-aggressions (Solorzano, Ceja, & Yosso 2000) became a natural way of existing within that academic white space. Racial micro-aggressions are conscious and unconscious routine, subtle, verbal and nonverbal, sometimes visual insults directed toward people of color (Solorzano, Ceja, Yosso 2000; Sue, Capodilupo, Nadal, & Torino 2008). These insults have cumulative effects that reinforce the oppression experienced by people of color. Since many Whites might claim their racist actions and comments were unintentional, the injury and lasting burden of the injury rests largely with the victim. However, I realized early on that I could help students, both graduate and undergraduate, successfully navigate some of those allegedly colorblind, equitable waters. This realization connected to what I hoped to do years earlier, to help college students, especially students of color and those from marginalized groups, succeed in college. In that way, becoming a faculty member began to close a past-present-future circle, which now offers new interpretations on my life and calling.

I never considered all of the things I would eventually discover such as navigating the faculty experience as an outsider with insider knowledge. One of the most glaring problems I first encountered was resistance from some of the white students who originally expressed high degrees of welcome, but quickly expected me to teach and think the same way my White colleagues did. Those students would regularly complain and report to my White colleagues about my teaching style and offer the kind of passive resistance to learning that other faculty of color have documented many times (Cleveland 2004; Jackson & Johnson, 2011). I survived that first year and after another year on a one-year contract, I earned a tenure track position with the same program at the same university. That was when the fun began.

One of the first pieces of advice I received from a 'well meaning' white colleague was to be careful about spending too much time mentoring and advising students of color. Her argument suggested that since I was one of the few Black faculty members in the department and within the division, students of color who wanted role models would seek out my help. However, I should avoid doing too much along those lines because my primary focus must be to earn tenure. In other words, I was there primarily to serve the needs of the department, and adopt the dominant ideology of individualism to secure my place among them. This interest convergence argument that opens opportunity to faculty of color as long as our presence and work serves the needs and vision of the White structure, assures that if those conditions go unchallenged, the current and future reality will not change (Bell 1992). Resisting the interest convergence paradigm represents a fundamental threat, which for faculty of color shows its results in unfavorable annual, third year, and promotion and tenure reviews.

That type of advice, from my well-intended colleague, cuts deeply against the grain of someone who operates from a collectivistic paradigm (Bordas 2007). I began to see that one of the dominant views of so-called successful faculty life meant submitting to and accepting an individualistic paradigm. That distinction cuts at the core of cultural difference between Eurocentric-American orientation and African-African heritage orientations. Frantz Fanon (1994/1952) argued about the permanence of racist structures and the necessity to resist them. As a Black faculty member in a white space, I too must constantly recognize the permanence of structural racism, yet find my survival, salvation, and success through multiple forms of resistance.

William Smith (2004) examines the concept of racial battle fatigue as it relates to African American faculty and students within white spaces. Smith defines it this way, "racial battle fatigue is a response to the distressing mental/emotional conditions that result from facing racism daily..." (p. 180) He identifies many issues that directly connect with my own experiences, such as how most white administrators, and some Black folks in administrative positions, downplay the "race-based stress" Black faculty experience on White campuses (p. 179). Smith identifies a multitude of symptoms many Black faculty experience due to race-based stress and cites several scholars whose work document these phenomenon. I too have experienced many of these symptoms over the past five years including "tension headaches and backaches...rapid breathing in anticipation of a conflict...constant anxiety and worrying...inability to sleep...loss of confidence in oneself and one's colleagues...rapid mood swings..." (p. 181). These physiological, psychological, emotional symptoms take its toll on the ability to perform at optimal levels, yet these very real phenomenon are difficult to prove as a causal relationship to working in a nice, white space.

Navigating Black and White Spaces

As a child of the 1960s and a teen of the 1970s, I never questioned my Blackness, I was proud of it, nor did I question or reject the community to which I belonged. I did not grow up confused as to my role within my family or my place within the few blocks surrounding my house. I feel fortunate to have experienced many of the best traditions of growing up in a positive black community without knowing just how special and fleeting the times were. It seemed as though most folks in the West End knew each other going back one or more generations, and shared a common sense of living in a type of mutually beneficial harmony. The West End held its own community cultural wealth and I benefited from it (Yosso 2005). I learned how to listen carefully to my elders and observe acceptable versus unacceptable behaviors. I learned how to protect myself. I learned who to trust among those around me, and how to cope with conflict and/or getting my feelings hurt. I did not win at everything I did, nor did I lose at everything I attempted. I learned not to trust strangers and not believe everything people told me. I learned always to apply common sense with book knowledge, and to look twice both ways, before crossing the street. I was encouraged to think for myself and take responsibility for my actions and choices.

I grew up within walking distance of several elementary schools and across the street from a junior high school. The West End had many black owned small businesses and many Black teachers who lived in the community. I witnessed Black folks in leadership and decision making positions and never questioned whether they, or I, could accomplish certain things. These teachers held the respect of all within the community. They cared deeply about what we learned in school, but more importantly, they cared about us as individuals. They cared about how we co-existed as community members.

At the same time, our neighborhood had the usual suspects of winos, hustlers, boosters, gamblers, and a few folks you instinctively knew to avoid. However, we also had certain rules and boundaries that seemed to draw respect from the mix of community members who co-existed within the shared space. No matter how tough or bad someone might have been, that person did not bother kids or old folks. The rules of engagement had some meaning even for those who made common the practice of breaking rules. Neighborhood children could play in mostly safe spaces, knowing the reality that any adult neighbor, at any time could and would scold, chastise, whip, and inform on us to parents or older siblings. The neighborhood rules allowed and mandated proper respect for elders. As children, we knew that if your mother or father, uncle or aunt told you to do something like the ubiquitous, "get in the house by the time the street lights turn on," that simple, direct instruction might as well have came from a booming voice in the clouds. Ignoring the voice and wishes of elders in the family meant certain destruction and possibly more than one beat-down. Instruction and direction with love, whether you asked for it or not, represented the norm in my community. Respect existed as a non-negotiable reality. Respecting parents and other adults was the unquestioned law and everyday there were many reminders of the importance to respect others and ourselves. I learned early that if you want respect, you had to show respect. The reverse was also true; if you disrespected someone or his or her position, do not expect indulgence or accommodation. These life lessons helped me survive white educational spaces and reminded me that in those white spaces respect and trust means something very different. Who should Black faculty trust within white spaces? Can Black faculty expect respect from an environment that historically constructed obstacles for their very presence?

I attended predominantly black schools, public and Catholic, until college. I cannot recall any intentional study of black culture or history in grade school or high school, although we learned about American history with Black folks as footnotes and background characters. Of course, we had Negro History Week during my early years, and Black History Month starting in the mid-1970s.

My elementary school had mostly Black teachers and a popular Black principal. I attended a neighborhood Catholic school from the 4th grade through the 8th grade. The nuns and priests were nice people, all white, as were the teachers. It was the early 1970s and a liberalization of Catholic educational pedagogy took hold of little St. Augustine School. They played acoustic guitars during Mass and had carpet throughout the school building. Students had to wear "house shoes" once entering the building. I found that very different and somewhat cool, because we only had linoleum on our floors at home. On some levels, a United Methodist PK (preacher's kid) attending a Catholic school should have been a major culture shock. It was not a culture shock because it was around the corner from my house, in my neighborhood. In addition, my grandmother and aunt were practicing Catholics and some of my cousins also attended St. Augustine. My Catholic school experience remained within the scope of my neighborhood context.

The real educational culture shock came when I enrolled at the University of Cincinnati (UC). For those who know Cincinnati, the West End is situated only a few miles from UC. A bus runs daily from a block away from where I grew up to the Clifton neighborhood that contains UC. Throughout my early years, I visited and felt comfortable on the campus...as an after hours or weekend visitor. I attended many football games, some basketball games, and ate at some of the fast food restaurants located on the edges of campus. I knew UC...or so I thought.

As a high school student, I underperformed doing just enough to get by and not flunk out. I operated within a comfort zone that did not prepare me for the racial dynamics or academic expectations of college. During my first year in college, I experienced the shock and strain of being the only Black student in a class, and had my first experience of blatant racism from an instructor. The details of the first racist incident are not important here, what is important to share is that it was not the only racist incident I experienced. What is important is the cultural dissonance experienced by attending a university where I thought I would feel comfortable. It represented my introduction to academic space as hostile white space. I assumed the university was a part of my home territory, only to find out that it was another world...a white space that welcomed relatively few Black students, outside of student-athletes, and even fewer Black faculty members. Many early career Black faculty stumble into assuming that there is a level playing field and our racial or ethnic backgrounds no longer matter. Environment always matters.

My idea of majoring in Business Administration, because it might help me get a good job, changed the day I visited a White accounting professor during his office hours. It was about the fourth or fifth week of the quarter. I wanted to discuss my grades and ask questions about ways to improve performance, which is what we learned to do in freshman orientation. He stated that I did not do well on a test because I had a "mathematics mental block" and should change majors. My upbringing told me not to trust this stranger; my insecurities and feelings of not belonging made me think he was correct. Maybe I was simply not smart enough to do the work. I did not seek tutoring. I did not seek an academic counselor to discuss what I wanted to gain from the college experience or what my intellectual interests were. I simply dropped the class. Although I did not know it at the time, I was experiencing my first encounter with racial battle fatigue during my undergraduate experience (Smith 2004).

Yes, it was the path of least resistance and many college students make similar bad choices for many of the same reasons. I did the same thing several times over the following few weeks and of my five registered courses for my first quarter (10 weeks) in college; I earned three "Ws" and two "Ds." Because of my first semester performance, prior to the holiday break the university promptly sent a cordial letter informing me that I was on academic probation. I found a compassionate assistant dean who allowed me to continue for another quarter if I would show improvement. I showed slight improvement the following quarter mostly because I stumbled upon a couple of Afro-American Studies courses that resonated with what I felt was most worth knowing, the African American experience, and ways to make meaning of the white space that surrounded me. By then, the James Brown song that once seeped into my consciousness as an unquestioned truth began to seem lost in time and translation.

Attending a White institution began to make me question my previously unquestioned personal pride and pride in my Blackness. Teaching in a historically and predominately white institution serves as a constant reminder that I must continually prove myself regardless of achievements and recognize the messaging that I am merely a guest in their house.

Majoring in Afro-American Studies allowed me to persevere and eventually graduate with an undergraduate degree. Remembering that I am a Black man in America and that staying connected to my roots, questioning the social, political, and cultural complexities of race and racism in the US and internationally keeps me sane and ready to excel within white spaces despite systemic obstacles. That foundational academic knowledge and experience of how to persist nourished me ever since. Working as a faculty member in a white space demonstrates that Black folks earned respect and dignity a long time ago. I stand on the shoulders of those who paved this path for me. It is my responsibility to remember how and why I got here and what I must do to remain.

I found that not knowing who I am and where I come from could destroy any shred of self-confidence and self-worth. The system was not created for folks like me. However, folks like me can enter these scary forests of academe, resist its most poisonous aspects, learn from the guides who point us in the best directions, and hold the door of opportunity open for those who follow. As a Black faculty member in white academic spaces, I consciously decided to remove my shaded glasses. I now stand at the crossroads within the forest confronted with my moral assignment to support, mentor, and advocate for students who seek to discover their unique paths in life.

References

Bell, D. (1992). *Faces at the bottom of the well: The permanence of racism*. New York: Basic Books.

Bordas, J. (2007). *Salsa, soul, and spirit: Leadership for a multicultural age*. San Francisco: Berrett-Koehler publishers, Inc.

Cleveland, D. (Ed.). (2004). *A long way to go: Conversations about race by African American faculty and graduate students*. New York: Peter Lang.

Denzin, N. K. (1989). *The research act: A theoretical introduction to sociological methods*. Englewoods Cliff, NJ: Prentice Hall.

Eisenhart, M. (2005). Boundaries and selves in the making of "science." In W. M. Roth, (Ed.)., *Auto/biography and auto/ethnography: Praxis of research method, pp. 283-299.* Rotterdam, The Netherlands: Sense Publishers.

Fanon, F. (1994/1952). *Black skin, white masks.* New York: Grove Press.

Giles, M. S. (2003). *Howard Thurman: A spiritual life in higher education.* Unpublished dissertation. Indiana University.

Jackson, S., & Johnson, R. G. (Eds.). (2011). *The black professoriat: negotiating a habitable space in the academy.* New York: Peter Lang.

Roth, W. M. (Ed.). (2005). *Auto/biography and auto/ethnography: Praxis of research method.* Rotterdam, The Netherlands: Sense Publishers.

Shujaa, M. J. (1995). *Too much schooling, too little education: A paradox of black life in white societies.* Trenton, NJ: Africa World Press.

Smith, W. A. (2004). Black faculty coping with racial battle fatigue: The campus racial climate in a post-civil rights era. In D. Cleveland, (Ed.). *A long way to go: Conversations about race by African American faculty and graduate students,* p. 171-190. New York: Peter Lang.

Solorzano, D. G., Ceja, M., & Yosso, T. J. (winter/spring 2000). Critical race theory, racial microaggressions, and campus racial climate: The experiences of African American college students. *Journal of Negro Education, 69*(1-2), 60-73.

Solórzano, D. G., & Yosso, T. J. (2002). Critical race methodology: Counter-storytelling as an analytical framework for education research. *Qualitative Inquiry, 8*(1), 23-44.

Sue, D. W., Capodilupo, C. M., Nadal, K., & Torino, G. C. (May/June 2008). Racial microagression and the power to define reality. *American Psychologist, 63*(4), 277-279.

Yosso, T. J. (March 2005). Whose culture has capital? A critical race theory discussion of community cultural wealth. *Race, Ethnicity and Education, 8*(1), 69-91.

Part III

United Kingdom Perspectives

Chapter Ten

The Experience of my Experience: Reflections on Working in "Deranged" White British Academic Space

❋

William B. Ackah

Introduction

This chapter develops and then utilises the concept of whiteness as a deranged space to account for the marginalisation and under-representation of scholars of African descent working in the British higher education system. Drawing on my personal experience the work highlights the ways in which white academic space, operates as a place of privilege and therapy for white scholars and students whilst operating under the pretension that it is a fair and neutral space open to all. This contradictory scenario is conceptualised in terms of derangement, meaning confusing, contradictory and shifting in order to avoid real change. It is argued that by articulating the abnormalities that exist within the deranged space that this may lead to its de-privileging allowing greater representation and articulation of black perspectives within the English academy.

To be a scholar of African descent within the British social scientific academy is a thing of rarity. Whereas snow leopards, mountain gorillas and other animals that are on the brink of extinction are afforded a degree of protection and recognition, scholars of African descent working in Britain have no such fortune. Few in number we are unprotected, vulnerable and on the whole seen as marginal to the development of systems of knowledge production that comprise higher education in Britain (ECU 2009).

Here, I want to reflect upon what it is like to work as an academic of African descent in Britain and to critically explore the contradictions inherent in a system that can espouse lofty educational aims and values, yet allow chronic under-representation of scholars of certain backgrounds to persist (Law, Phillips and Turney 2004). In undertaking this critical exploration I will draw on my personal experience of the English higher education system, but seek to frame that experience within a wider analysis of the struggles that people of African descent have faced when operating within the white academic space.

The principle argument that will be presented here is that one's struggle as an academic of African descent for acceptance, recognition and parity takes place within a white academic space that regards blackness as different even abnormal. Hence black struggle for acceptance within the academic space in part becomes about the making of oneself as normal, or of being able to explain ones abnormality, so that it can be considered worthy of academic acceptance. This struggle to move from abnormal, to normal, from vulnerable to protected, and from unacknowledged to recognised is an ongoing feature of academic life for scholars like myself. Yet the focus on the African self in the academic process also masks a key issue that will also be highlighted in this work. Namely that the system and processes that lead the scholar of African descent to have to continually seek recognition within the academy is what is abnormal. White academic attention and focus needs to turn to interrogating its own practices, procedures and values. Further that it needs to take the seriously the contention outlined here that the white academic space is in fact abnormal and should be theorised and critically interrogated as a deranged space.

The Oxford English Dictionary defines derange or derangement as *1. to throw into confusion, to disrupt. 2. To make insane* (OPD 1988, p 217). Theorising white academic space as a deranged space, moves us beyond viewing whiteness and white supremacist practice only in terms of power relations. It asks us to consider more critically the multiple ways in which living and operating in white spaces is confusing and disruptive and maddening in different ways for groups socially constructed and racialized as black, but also critically for those who have generally defied racialized categorisation but who nevertheless are labelled as white.

White academic space it will be argued here is a deranged space i.e disruptive, confusing and maddening. The expressions of such derangement unfold in different ways. One manifestation is the dissonance that emanates from the institutional espousal of values such as academic freedom of thought and expression and its denial or curtailment in the case of scholars of African descent (Back 2004). Another related sense of the dissonance that the space creates is where the disturbing realities of racism, oppression, marginalisation and dehumanisation that black people experience, operate as a challenge for scholars of African descent to overcome in order to produce required academic outputs. Yet these same potentially debilitating problems provide new resources and inspiration for theorising and analysis for white academics operating in the same space. A way to account for these contradictions and incongruities that operate within the white academic space and to account for its impact on academics variously described in racialized terms as black and white is in terms of derangement.

In this piece I will outline in more detail the notions of whiteness and white academic space as a deranged space. The paper will then go on to explore the implications of this space for black academics operating within it, drawing on phases of my experience as an academic in English higher education. Finally the paper will conclude with some thoughts on the utility of viewing the white academic space as deranged and its implications for academic practice.

Theorising Whiteness as a Deranged Space

Whiteness as a subject for academic scrutiny has been developing in recent years (hooks 1992; Dyer 1997; Garner 2007). Whilst this work cannot enter into a detailed discussion of the wide ranging debates concerning its utility, this work is empathetic to the view of regarding whiteness as a socially constructed relational category, that is both visible and invisible (Garner 2007, p.2) . Although whiteness is variable and its multiple unfoldings are historically and culturally specific and relational just like other racialized categories. It is argued here that the historical unfolding of racist discourses that accompanied the processes of enslavement and colonialism and the power dynamic resulting from Western European conquest of most parts of the 'non-white' world, provides those that adopt the label white with historical privilege and racialised power that has a continuing legacy and benefit (Bonnett 1998; Goldberg 2001).

Further, whiteness is not just a racialized identity that is conferred on groups of people, whiteness is valorised and embedded in the key institutional spaces that are part and parcel of Western societies such as universities, churches, financial institutions, and media and cultural industries Bhattacharayya Gabriel and Small (2002, p10). In these institutional spaces where white Anglo practices and values are deemed to be the norm, those that practice them are afforded esteem and privilege and those that are culturally, politically or ethically most removed from these practices are deemed to be at best 'developing'(Mills 2003)! What is being emphasised here is that although whiteness in analytical terms is a racialized category just like any other, the processes and dynamics that led to its construction come vested with power and privilege that were and still are not generally available to other racialized groups. Hence whiteness is unique at present, both in relation to its ubiquity, invisibleness and for its power to define, limit and oppress non white groups (Carmichael and Hamilton 1967; Mills 2004).

It is evident that in scholarly terms whiteness is beginning to be analysed and theorised about more closely with scholars confronting the diverse dimensions of the emerging arena of whiteness studies. Bonilla Silva (2000, 2001) amongst others have identified the ways in which whiteness has been unraced and invisible and that the cloak of this invisibility has been utilised as the basis to label others and maintain an identity of superiority over them (Phoenix 1996; Wildman 1996; Doane 1997). African American writers and scholars in particular have highlighted the supremacist nature of whiteness and how white people have terrorised and exploited others under this guise (Morrison 1993; Mills 1997). They have also importantly identified in creative and academic ways the impact that white racism has had on black perceptions of self, and highlighted the absurdity, nihilism and in fact multiple responses that the black encounter with white supremacist practice produces. It is principally from these writings that I draw my inspiration in relation to thinking about white space as a deranged space (Wright 1940/1992, 1957/1995; Ellison 1952; Du Bois 1903/1996; West 1994).

Turning the gaze of academic scrutiny on to white people as racialised subjects is a controversial undertaking and some have questioned its utility or expressed ambivalence concerning its impact on tackling racism (Anderson 2003; Kaufman 2006)

Others have sought to highlight the political and ethical nature of the whiteness project and to argue that the study of whiteness has to be understood through the lens of anti-racist struggle (Garner 2007). Whilst emphatic to this line of analysis one is caught in the dilemma of not wanting to reify whiteness or to confer it a special status, whereby it becomes the lens through which all studies of racialized and ethnic relations are viewed.

I think one of the ways to avoid this and not to allow whiteness to become a type of ethnic fetishization studies, is to continually draw attention to the ways in which institutional spaces dominated by whites and valorised as containing the ethics and values of Western societies are in fact sites of contradiction and derangement. The contradictions found in religious, political, cultural and academic institutions are multiple, but here attention is drawn to the disturbing gap that emerges from the publicly expressed ideals, of equality, democracy, justice, fairness, equity, freedom of speech, compassion, that emanate from these spaces and the injustice, brutality, unfairness denial of freedom, prejudice, racism and bigotry that also stem from the same spaces. The mismatch between the high ideals and the harsh brutal realities are what is abnormal and contributes to the space being deranged. It can be argued that whereas African Americans and other people of African origin and descent have articulated in various ways what their encounter with white deranged space has meant to them (West 1994, pp.133-152). The same is not true of white people and that this adds to the sense of derangement. The deranged space is the place where white pride, meets white guilt and white uncertainty. Where the perception of white as pristine confronts white as ugly and where white power meets white angst. Although the space is being outlined in dichotomous terms here, what is meant to be conveyed by derangement is that whiteness when confronted by its own incongruities both shifts, prevaricates, asserts, hides, comes to the fore, in multiple and overlapping ways. Yet through all its shifts and movements it is still not divested of its tendency to racially inferiorize the other. In fact the enduring legacy of this racialising tendency is at the heart of the deranged space.

By calling attention to the irrationalities and abnormalities inherent in white deranged space scholars can unmask the increasingly prevalent but false idea, that having disproportionate percentages of African descended peoples in white societies, in prison, living in poverty, suffering ill health or failing in schools, is somehow normal and not the responsibility of the society in which they live. By labelling white space as a deranged space and by highlighting and confronting the forms and nature of its abnormalities it is hoped that this will contribute to undermining and ultimately dismantling its power and utility for maintaining privilege and engaging in racist and oppressive practice.

The White Academic Space

The realm of higher education or the academy in the white dominated space is not immune to the sense of derangement and confusion outlined above. In fact the sense of derangement within academic institutions could be conceived as being more intense because of the contradictions apparent between the idealised notions of academic professionalism and enlightened thinking and the treatment of people of African origin and descent. Academic institutions have been complicit historically in the mistreatment of people of African descent. Some as direct beneficiaries of the proceeds of enslavement, most in the development of their disciplines through the objectification and racist analysis of black bodies. Although the analysis of African lives and cultures has changed over the course of the 19th and 20th centuries assisted in part by the interventions of Diaspora Africans themselves, the ways in which black bodies, are studied, catalogued, written about and debated over has been and continues to be shaped by the contradictions emanating from the deranged space (Chow 1993). In England whether that derangement emerges in the form of white angst concerning its own positionality in relation to black life, denial of any issues, or even a recognition of the realities of white racism. The multiple arguments, positioning, and theoretical frameworks has still not resulted in the opening up of the space to enable significant numbers of scholars of African descent to be a part of the academy (Back 1996; Purwar 2004).

It can be argued that the white academic space is not monolithic, white scholars and scholarship have contributed to our understanding of racism and discrimination and this scholarship has been utilised to bring about reforms that have enabled black people and other minorities to face less discrimination in their everyday lives. Contestation and reflection in academic circles have also brought about changes in disciplinary theory and practice in fields such as anthropology and archaeology where the sense of white invisibility and objectification of minority ethnic experiences was particularly strong. But the piecemeal movement and shifting landscape of an academic area, whether as result of development from within, or more likely as a reflection of broader social changes in the wider society actually acts as a confirmation of the deranged nature of white academic space.

Derangement as has been articulated is exemplified by shifts in thought, uncertainty, confusion, assertions and contradictions, but no substantive divestment of power or influence. Academia it is argued mirrors these traits in relation to racism. Debate, discussion, research and writing open up incremental pockets of new ideas and processes enable the academy to maintain a sense of itself as liberal, open minded and progressively seeking knowledge free from prejudice and bias. However when it comes to taking action to remedy systematic disadvantage stemming from discriminatory practices, then it is time for more anxiety, debate, discussion, but little substantive change. I shall go on to illustrate this with some examples from my experience of working in white academic spaces.

White Studies is Academic Black Studies is Therapy!

My first encounter with white abnormalities in the academic space emerged soon after I had completed my Masters degree by research where I focused on Pan-African identities in the Diaspora and their relationship to Africa (Ackah 1999). When I attempted to find spaces in which to teach what I had studied and researched within the white academic space, I found my job applications were continually rejected. I could study and learn about the black experience from 'white professionals', the white institution could take my money and inculcate me in the ways of its knowing and understanding the social world, but having gained the qualification that said I had mastered the art, no space emerged within the academy for me to teach it. Eventually the space to teach around issues related to peoples of African origin and descent came via a small black run and led community college and a black access to higher education programme run within a mainstream higher education institution, both in the North West of England. Grateful as I was in the 1990s to get some work, reflecting on those times now with the benefit of hindsight, it is evident that the scenario of being grateful for crumbs that fall from the 'masters' table was depressingly normal, in its abnormality.

I write this because black people in Britain through the seventies, eighties and into the nineties had been fighting the education system to recognise the black experience in its curricula (Coard 1971/1991; John 2006). For my own part I worked with colleagues developing curricula and arguing with professional awarding bodies as well as academic institutions concerning the validity and worth of studying black experiences and cultures in schools, colleges and higher education institutions. Mostly these efforts were met with polite interest, but ultimately the authorities questioned the academic credibility and legitimacy of such studies. Pressure from local black community activists for such studies did eventually lead to an odd module in one or two institutions, but where Black Studies or its British variants most notably came to fruition in England was in black access to higher education provision. These were courses specifically designed to boost the numbers of students from black and other minority ethnic backgrounds entering higher education institutions (White 1990). These courses accepted mature black applicants who may have been failed by the school system, and had poor examination results which would usually put higher education out of reach. It was felt however that some black and minority ethnic students had the potential to overcome previous educational discrimination and marginalisation with the right kind of focused tuition and preparation. Hence the study of the black experience, although not deemed academic enough to be studied in higher education in its own right, could be used to help boost black students self esteem. The argument was accepted that by studying their own experiences, it would make the unfamiliar learning environment more acceptable and thus assist in the process of preparing black students for academic life. So Black Studies was not legitimate as academic endeavour in its own right, but it was acceptable as a kind of self improvement therapy. Hence within the white academic space it was legitimated but illegitimated at the same time. The course could gain you access to higher education, but it was unlikely you could study it within higher education. It could boost your self esteem as a black person, but it was not worthy of universal, university esteem!

It needs to be asked what is so frightening to the white academic space about the study of Africa and its Diaspora from the perspective of Africans both continental and diasporic? Is it not abnormal to dismiss studies of the some of the most richest and diverse contributions to the human experience as mere therapy? I would suggest that this is abnormal and that the questioning of the study of black lives and cultures in higher education institutions are the actions of a system that feels threatened by areas of analysis it cannot control or police. Secondly I would argue that the querying of Black Studies in the white academic space in Britain masks the idea of academic institutions as places of therapy for white people, enabling them to cope with the angst of operating in the deranged space.

It could be argued that much of the studies of most arts and social science based subjects in higher education institutions are studies of whiteness in all its hidden complexities and multidimensional forms. And that universities confer on those who are deemed to be the producers of 'white' knowledge a certain power and prestige.

Universities operate as unique spaces where white lives can be explored, assessed, analysed, and reflected upon, in multiple ways that neither fully valorise or scapegoat the white individual. The uni or partial-versity provides options and opportunities for the white self to be seen and known and understood. In a significant way higher education acts as a kind therapy for white people as it confers status with affirmation to those who enter its hallowed theatres. Successful completion of a degree from an appropriate institution is also a passport for entry into the wider world of racialized privilege found in such fields such as politics, business, law and academia itself. It is not a surprise therefore to see that in England debates concerning who should gain access to higher education and how much they should pay for the privilege have become highly politicised (Browne 2010), or that the top positions in English universities are still overwhelmingly and disproportionally held by white people (ECU 2009).

Permanent White Universities Temporary Black Lives

One of the attractions of academia is the idea of it being a place where one has the time to think. The academic space is a place where knowledge is cherished and the quest for new ideas and new ways of thinking about the world are considered as ends in themselves to which you could dedicate your life. That was the appeal of the space to me. I was under the impression that academic life would enable me to read, think and pass on the knowledge and wisdom that I gained from undertaking a lifetime of ongoing investigation and analysis to the next generation. The reality has been somewhat different. Of the eighteen years that I have considered myself to be on the academic vocational pathway thirteen of them have been either on temporary contracts, either as full time, or an hourly paid lecturer. Two were spent outside of the field as I was unable to secure a job and only in three of those eighteen years, have I been able to enjoy the relative security of a permanent, full time position.

To live with uncertainty over such long periods of one's so called professional career is not normal. It begs the question as to what value does the white institutional space place upon you and your work, when you are permanently temporary!? The white space dangles opportunities in front of you, like fellowships, research grants and sabbaticals only for you to realise that with an uncertain status what appears to be a potentially liberating opportunity is always just beyond your reach as for the most part you need to be permanent to access them.

To compound matters as temporary one is caught in a cycle of accepting one temporary contract after another in order to pay bills, and keep body and mind together. One does this in the hope that a permanent position will arise, whilst being blinded to the fact that doing an inordinate amount of teaching and assessment and not having the time to develop your thinking and research is devaluing yourself in the eyes of the institutions that you are seeking to gain entrance to. At times you put your personal struggles down to the idiosyncratic nature of academic life and question your own abilities. Then you look around and see that nearly all the full time permanent and secure positions are occupied by white people and that of the few black people that even make it to the position of academic that their experience is remarkably like yours (Leatherwood, Maylor & Moreau 2009). With this comes the realisation that I am not the problem, it is the space that I am operating in which is problematic. It is not only academics of African descent who are diminished in this space, students too can find the space bewildering.

Within the African and African Caribbean communities that I research and teach about fleetingly within UK contexts, a strong emphasis is placed on the value of education as a means of getting bettering oneself in white societies. In recent years this has eventually translated into more and more students of black and minority ethnic origin entering higher education, even if over proportionally in a select number of institutions in urban areas close to where other members of their minority ethnic communities live. In spite of this trend which in the case of some London higher education institutions has meant that more than half their students come from minority ethnic backgrounds, the number of academics from these same communities working in these institutions is still abnormally low which provides the context for more abnormal practices. Universities become the places where white professors in positions of privilege and authority are the purveyors and holders of knowledge and wisdom and blacks and other minorities are relegated to the position of mere recipients. The university can be deemed a twenty-first century missionary outpost, inculcating the inhabitants with the wherewithal to show due deference to the white space.

As a black academic operating in these spaces you can become a magnet for some black students struggling to cope with the contradictory nature of white academic space. Some students view you as a source of potential support, as someone who can understand and empathise with their experience of being in a white institution and act as a possible advocate and advisor for them, even when you are not their teacher. This of course when you yourself are not being mistaken for a student and can access your own institutional buildings to carry out your duties! (Such is the rarity of black academics in the British system, that one is not always recognised as such even when you do have the title you can be mistaken for a student, cleaner or interloper) The white academic space makes no allowances for the type of events being described here that add extra work and pressure to black academics operating within this space (Rollock 2011). A critical abnormality that arises here is that within the white institutional space a great deal of time, energy and money can be expended examining black people as objects of research, notably abroad but when these same objects appear as subjects within institutions no special status is afforded them(Chow 1993). In fact black subjects within the academy who act 'too black' can be deemed to be problematic as will be explored in the next section.

Controlling Blackness in the White Space

I have already alluded to the fact that within English academic institutions the opportunities to study and conduct research about the lives and experiences of people of African origin and descent from the perspectives of those people is rare. That is not to say however that one cannot study anything about Africa and its Diaspora in universities in England. One can but the perspective and those controlling what is taught and researched about black people will invariably be white. The white academic institutional space in England enables and privileges white scholars with the capacity to be experts in whatever area they choose to explore, which in this case includes being experts in the study of black and other minority ethnic communities in Britain and around the world. Cultural studies, geographical area studies, history and the sociology of ethnic and race relations have been the principle disciplinary areas that have sought to place some focused emphasis on studying minorities and for our particular purposes people of African origin and descent. The abnormality of this scenario has already been alluded to in relation to the scarcity of scholars of African descent actually teaching their area of expertise in English academic institutions but here I want to highlight another facet of this deranged space that I have experienced, namely the idea of the black subject as the known object.

What is meant by being a known object in this context is the idea that many dimensions of black life are portrayed in stereotypical ways within English academic discourses and so black people are seen as familiar objects. Hence when as a black person you enter the academic space as an individual subject, you get the converse sense of students and staff assuming they know you, when they know nothing about you. Because they have studied about the poor housing conditions of black immigrants to Britain in the 1960s or the cultural traditions and religious festivals of Akan people in Ghana, people assume that you represent these diverse and often dichotomous experiences and can answer questions about them in effect be an authoritative object.

To conflate divergent black experiences in this way stems from the way in which white academic space acts as though it is the authority on all things; including minority ethnic discourses. Hence elements within the white space believe itself to have the right to interpret your experience to suit its own perception of you. Another related feature of the deranged space is that when a rare black voice as a subject does get articulated and speaks into the wider disciplinary field and is accepted as legitimate, then black voices seeking to articulate a different view are muted within the same space, as it is only willing to accept one conceptualisation of black life and culture at any given time.

In most social science courses in Britain, reference will be made to issues of race and ethnicity and in a good programme it should be woven into most elements of a degree, but in my experience, aside from the specific modules dealing with issues of race and racism, a particular module say on housing in urban spaces, or cultural production in cities, will devote one week to black and minority ethnic perspectives as they pertain to that module. With only one lesson to cover a vast spectrum of humanity, simplified and unvaried descriptions of black lives and cultures come to the fore as there is no space or time in the curricula for anything else. This contributes to the conflation and marginalisation of black and minority ethnic lives and cultures within the white academic space.

Another way in which this conflation operates is via academic boundaries. In 2009 I submitted an abstract on an aspect of black life and culture that I wanted to theorise about in ways that were divergent from the current trend in Britain where hybridisation and non essentialism in regards to writing about the black experience are in vogue. I had the surprising misfortune to have my abstract rejected and I suspected(did not have proof) that it was because it was the wrong kind of 'black' as the conference did accept a lot of work in progress type papers. The deranged space enables whites writing about the black experience to do so from a range of perspectives and the types of work that white scholars produce about black people even after the cultural turn is still broad. Whilst scholars of African descent and minority ethnic academics working in the social sciences tend to operate within the realm of ethnic type studies, and within that space there is pressure to conceptualise ones work in certain ways so that it conforms to the prevailing wisdoms concerning minority ethnic experience in Britain. I want to suggest perhaps provocatively here that the deranged space by affirming some work and denying others, by providing jobs and promotions for some kind of black and not for others contributes to the abnormality whereby people of African descent in Britain struggle to articulate diverse perspectives even when it comes to their own experience. The confining nature of the white academic space in Britain operates subtly, under the guises of academic freedom, liberalism, academic convention and quality but in reality, racism and discrimination are as much a feature of the academy as other areas of English society (Puwar 2004). As my last example will illustrate, even when the white space attempts to deal with its own derangement, these efforts are hampered by its unwillingness to cede its privilege of being in control of its own de-privileging.

Making Things Worse by Not Really Making Amends

In 1997 when the new Labour Government came into office, one of their targets was to increase the number of 18-30 years entering higher education to 50% of all this age group. To this end it established a number of initiatives and co-ordinating bodies to implement its vision of widening participation in English universities. Towards the end of the first five years of the programme, I and a number of colleagues from black and other minority ethnic backgrounds, were invited by one of these co-ordinating bodies, to look at the issue of the representation of black and ethnic minority students in higher education and related issues. When we met in 2002 it emerged that we had a lot of issues to discuss in relation to the experience of black and minority ethnic students and staff in higher education. Not least was why had we been brought together only at the very end of the first phase of the project and why when, there were funded projects dealing with issues, of gender, disability, class and other facets of social differentiation and its impact on participation in higher education, that there was no funded project on black and minority ethnic student experiences. Well as a group we decided that we would confront the relevant higher education authorities about this and as a result of our protests, we were able to secure a small amount of funding to put on a conference and commissioned a report on black and minority ethnic representation in higher education (Black and Minority Ethnic Education Strategy Group 2006).

Given that we as black and minority ethnic staff working in further and higher education were all volunteers, we managed to use the resources we were allocated wisely. The authorities utilised our report and highlighted our project to illustrate that they were working with minorities to tackle the issues surrounding BME representation in higher education, but behind the gloss, once the conference was over and the report published, no further support for our group was forthcoming and we were forced to disband. White researchers and white agencies were given funds to build on the work that we had started, but we who started the work and who had to force the authorities to take the issue seriously were denied the opportunity to follow it through. This is illustrative of the way in which, the mechanisms and processes of the white academic space produce deranged outcomes. Here was an initiative whose aim was to widen participation for marginalised groups, but which then uses methods and practices that are marginalising towards the representatives of the groups it is purporting to try and assist. On the one hand there is a 'white man's burden' to enable 'disadvantaged minorities' to gain access to higher education, but on the other there is a reluctance to give minorities the resources and authority to act independently of white control. This once highlights the often contradictory and confusing nature of the white academic space.

Conclusion

In this work I have attempted to reflect on my experience as an academic of African descent working within the English higher education system. I have drawn on the emerging field of whiteness studies to develop the idea that the white institutional spaces in which I operate as deranged spaces; that is, they are spaces of confusion and contradiction, that elevate and uphold notions of white power and academic authority, whilst undermining and curtailing attempts by scholars of African descent and other minorities to gain academic parity and a sense of academic freedom within these same spaces. Derangement is another word for insanity and at its most destructive and disruptive, the white institutional space does impact upon the psyche of those who operate within it. Drawing on my own experiences I have attempted to illustrate the insanity of living out most of my professional life on temporary contracts and in the midst of uncertainty. Crucially, I have reflected on the absurdity of studying a subject for years in order to be able to teach and research it only to find, that it was not possible to do so after completing the course. And I have articulated the frustration that emanates from dealing with authorities, who don't trust black and minority ethnic professionals to carry out work for which they are professionally and personally qualified. These reflections on aspects of my life, both as personal experience and as an analytical one highlight that the white institutional space can and does induce confusion in those who operate within its space, but that the real confusion or abnormality is that in spite of all the theorising, research and learning that takes place in the academy, that racism, discrimination and the chronic underrepresentation of scholars of African descent working within the system still persists. More analytical work is evidently needed to identify more concretely the ways in which the white space embodies ideals and actions, policies and procedures which in their unfolding, still produce outcomes that privilege those labelled white and continues to dis-empower and disenchant many who have been racialized as black. By introducing the concept of whiteness as a deranged space to account for the absurdity of this scenario, it is hoped that it will contribute towards the de-privileging and normalising of white academic space and pave the way for the improved representation and articulation of black voices within the English higher education system and beyond.

References

Ackah, W. (1999). *Pan-Africanism: Exploring the contradictions: Politics, identity and development in Africa and the African diaspora.* Aldershot: Ashgate.

Anderson, M. (2003). Whitewashing race: A critical perspective on whiteness. In A.W. Doane, Jr. & E. Bonilla Silva, (Eds.), *White Out: The Continuing Significance of Racism.* (pp. 21-34). New York: Routledge.

Back, L. (1996). *New ethnicities and urban culture: Social identity and racism in the lives of young people.* London: UCL.

Bhattacharayya, G., Gabriel, J. & Small, S. (2002) *Race and power: Global racism in the twenty-first century.* London: Routledge.

Black and Minority Ethnic Education Strategy Group. (2006). *A review of black and minority ethnic participation in higher education.* London: Tribal.

Bonilla Silva, E. (2000). This is a white country: The racial ideology of the western nations of the world—system. *Sociological Enquiry 70*, 188-214.

Bonilla Silva, E. (2001). *White supremacy and racism in the post-civil rights era.* Boulder: Lynne Rienner.

Bonnett, A. (1998). Who was white? The disappearance of non-European white identities and the formation of European racial whiteness. *Ethnic and Racial Studies. 21*, 1029-1055.

Browne (2010). *Securing a sustainable future for higher education: An independent review of higher education funding and student finance.* www.independent.gov.uk/browne-report [accessed March 19, 2011]

Carmichael, S. & Hamilton, C. (1967). *Black power: The politics of liberation.* New York: Random House.

Chow, R. (1993). *Writing diaspora.* Bloomington: Indiana University

Coard, B. (1991/1971). *How the West Indian child is made educationally subnormal in the British school system.* London: New Beacon Books.

Doane, A.W., Jr. (1997). Dominant group identity in the United States: The role of 'hidden' ethnicity in intergroup relations. *Sociological Quarterly 38*, 375-397.

Du Bois, W.E.B. (1903/1996). *The Souls of Black Folks.* New York: Signet.

Dyer, R. (1997). *White.* London: Routledge.

Ellison, R. (1972/1952). *Invisible man.* New York: Vintage

Equality Challenge Unit (2009). *Equality in higher education: statistical report.* London: ECU.

Garner, S. (2007). *Whiteness: An introduction.* London: Routledge

Goldberg, D.T. (2001). *The racial state.* New York: Blackwell.

hooks, b. (1992). *Black looks: Race and representation.* Boston: Southend.

John, G. (2006). *Taking a stand.* Manchester: Gus John Partnership.

Kaufman, E. (2006). The dominant ethnic moment: Towards the abolition of whiteness? *Ethnicities.* 6, 231-266.

Law, I., Phillips, D. & Turney, C., (Eds.). (2004). *Institutional racism in higher education.* Stoke on Trent: Trentham

Leatherwood,C., Maylor, U. & Moreau, M. (2009). *The Experiences of Black and Minority Ethnic staff working in higher education.* London: Equality Challenge Unit.

Mills, C. (2007). White supremacy as sociopolitical system. In A. W. Doane, Jr. & Bonilla Silva, E. (Eds.) *White Out: The Continuing Significance of Racism.* (pp. 35-48) New York: Routledge.

Phoenix, A. (1996). "I'm white – so what?" The construction of whiteness for young londoners. In M. Fine, et al. (Eds). *Off White: Readings on Race, Power and Society.* (pp. 187-197). New York: Routledge.

Puwar, N. (2004). Fish in and out of water: A theoretical framework for race and the space in academia. In I. Law, D. Phillips, & C. Turney. (Eds.) *Institutional racism in higher education.* (pp. 49-58). Stoke on Trent: Trentham

Rollock, N. (2011). Unspoken rules of engagement: Navigating racial microaggressions in the academic terrain. *International Journal of Qualitative Studies in Education.* 13(1), 16-36.

West, C. (1994). *Race matters.* New York: Vintage.

White, G. (1990). Black Access to Higher Education in Pumfrey, P.D. and Verma, G.K. (Eds) *Race Relations and Urban Education.* Basingstoke: Falmer.

Wildman, S. (1996). *Privilege revealed: How invisible preference undermines America.* New York: New York University.

Wright, R. (1940/1992). *Native son.* New York: Harper Row.

Wright, R. (1957/1995). *White man listen!* New York: Harper Perennial.

Chapter Eleven

'Supping It': Racial Affective Economies and the Epistemology of Ignorance in UK Universities

❋

Shirley Anne Tate

Introduction

This chapter focuses on negative affects and their psychic toll in spaces of racial un-belonging. Using black experience of racism in the workplace, it looks at the operation of the affective aspects of the epistemology of ignorance which underlies the Racial Contract in UK universities. It does this through explicating its racial affective economies characterized by disattendability, disgust and contemptuous tolerance. Such negative affects underlie the black experience of collegiality when black academics are constructed as bodies out of place and not envisaged as "friend." The argument is not about the cathartic effects of unmasking contemptuous tolerance, disattendability and disgust. Rather, it speaks to the (im)possibilities of hiring, promotion and tenure which are part of the daily lives of those who continue to work within contexts marked by the epistemology of ignorance.

For Charles Mills (1997, p.40), both globally and within particular nations, then, white people, Europeans and their descendants, continue to benefit from the Racial Contract, which creates a world in their cultural image, political states differentially favouring their interests, an economy structured around the racial exploitation of others, and a moral psychology (not just in whites sometimes in nonwhites also) skewed consciously and unconsciously toward privileging them, taking the status quo of differential racial entitlement as normatively legitimate, and not to be investigated further.

In the UK research by the Association of University Teachers (AUT) (2005) shows the effects of the Racial Contract's moral psychology of differential racial entitlement on hiring, promotion and tenure within universities. It draws our attention to the fact that black academics still struggle to be hired in UK universities in the 21st century after more than half a century of race equality legislation. Further, the proportion of Black and Minority Ethnic (BME) non-clinical professors increased from 3 to 5% from1992 to 2005 and the number of Principal Lecturers increased from 4 to 5% in the same period. However, in the UK population as a whole, 89.2%of those of working age with a postgraduate qualification were white in 2004, so the proportion of senior academics in UK universities who are from BME backgrounds is much lower than the proportion of BME postgraduates in the UK working age population as a whole (AUT 2005). The AUT study found that in my institution in 1996 professors were mostly white (95.1%) and there were very small percentages of BME professors (Black 0.6%, Asian 1.2% and 'other' 3.1%). In 2003-4 not much had changed, white professors were still the majority (95.3%) with 0.5% Black, 2.4% Asian and 1.9% 'other' including 'mixed race' professors.

This very low percentage of black professors is not unusual as across the institutions involved in the AUT study, the professoriate continues to be overwhelmingly white and male. This whiteness is also reflected at the level of lecturers (Associate and Assistant Professors). Of course, we could say that as the majority of the population is white in the UK there are no problems here. However, black people whether faculty or students, are under-represented in academic institutions when we take into consideration the fact that the BME population in the UK stands at 10% (Census 2001).

In order to show the continuing perversity and pervasiveness of the moral psychology of the Racial Contract, the paper will look at the environment of the UK where the state continues to deny racism. It will then go on to chart the everyday nature of the epistemology of ignorance through looking at affect. The argument will be that within such an epistemology of ignorance black faculty continue to be 'bodies out of place' in a racial affective economy driven by contemptuous tolerance. Collegiality is expected within Universities, but it is a collegiality saturated with contemptuous tolerance. Contemptuous tolerance underlies the white power in networks which determine hiring, tenure and promotion and keep the Racial Contract in place. This chapter concludes with thinking about marginality and disalienation as antidotes to the epistemology of ignorance and to the governance of contemptuous tolerance. First, let us turn briefly to look at the moral psychology of the contemporary UK's Racial Contract.

The UK's Racial Contract: Denying Racism

In the early 1990s in the midst of civil disobedience by BME youth across England, racism was high on the policy and research agenda. One outcome of this was finally to establish that there is a citizenship category, Black British, as well as other hyphenated identities to represent the BME descent population. Another outcome of 1990s politics has been a focus on social cohesion, where to be British citizens with rights we also have the responsibility to build a tolerant and cohesive society. In January 2010 all of this was converted by the then Labour Government's Communities Secretary John Denham, into the idea that 'race' is no longer a problem. He made this claim because in the Government's view sustained action over the past decade had promoted racial equality and better 'race relations' whereas class remained the trans-racial policy and social issue (*The Guardian*, January 14, 2010). So from this viewpoint class would be what accounts for the lack of black representation in universities, not racism. I would never discount the importance of class but to abandon 'race' is to be blind to the realities of UK society where being white still means to have skin, social and structural privileges, to be beneficiaries of the Racial Contract.

This denial of racism has also been taken up by the present Prime Minister David Cameron. In a speech on 5th February 2011 delivered to the Munich Security Conference, he claimed that multiculturalism has failed and the country now needed to engage with 'muscular liberalism'. This was necessary in order to defeat Islamic extremism and its threat of home-grown terrorism, reverse the creation of separate communities and 'hands-off tolerance' promoted under state multiculturalism and strengthen a clear sense of shared British national identity that is open to everyone (Number 10.gov. uk, 5.2.2011). Cameron sets out 'equal rights irrespective of race, sex or sexuality' as the values to be promoted along with 'freedom of worship', 'democracy' and 'the rule of law'. According to Cameron's aides, the British values set out in his speech, 'freedom of speech' and 'equality between the sexes', would be the criteria by which the government would engage in future with community groups seeking government funding (*The Weekly Guardian*, February, 11 2011). To speak of 'race' rather than racism indicates that 'race' continues to be a deciding factor in the Racial Contract. It indicates a specific racial nomos in which there is a legal, governmental and spatial order in which 'race' does not necessarily mean physical variations coded on the body any longer (Gilroy, 2004). Rather, what it points to instead, is the impersonal, discursive, imperial ordering (Gilroy, 2004) of the Racial Contract. Further, not to name racism also erases its continuing functionality in keeping the Racial Contract in place. The racial nomos of the 21st century tolerant UK is one in which racism continues to be denied or is seen only as an individual aberration.

The erasure of racism is also shown at the level of curricula where institutions in the UK do not have Black Studies programmes. What we largely have instead is a mainstreaming of 'race' achieved through the current mantras of 'interdisciplinarity' and 'intersectionality', both of which have been designed so as not to focus on racism or racist power/knowledge (Jacobs and Tate 2006; Jones 2006). So whilst there is still great scholarship on racism in the UK, its curricular relevance is being minimized. The critique, which we so clearly still need, is being lost as reflected in the fact that we have postgraduate students who write as if racism does not exist because of their undergraduate learning experiences. Such critique is now seen to be invested in the very bodies of black academics that are always already put in the 'race' position as 'bodies out of place' (Puar 2004, p. 61). Being located as 'bodies out of place' is a foundational instance of the pervasive 'epistemology of ignorance' (Mills 1997, p. 18) within the Racial Contract.

Bodies Out of Place: The Epistemology of Ignorance

In common with many black academics I am the only one in my department. I sit in meetings as the only one. I teach as the only one. I attend open days as the only one. However, being the only one does not have the benefits of being unique/ rare/ treasured. Far from it, like the few others of us that there are I am seen as either an exception or the representative of 'the race.'

Both of these ways in which I am viewed are racist. To be seen as the exception means that black people in the 21st century are still not seen as good academic 'material' but continue to be viewed as far more suited to the sports field, the athletics track or the stage. Being 'the representative of the race' means being under constant surveillance for any sign of trouble by colleagues and students. Did she get something wrong? Can she *really* read and write? Can she truly teach? Can she behave like an 'English person'? Can she *not* be 'the angry black woman'? The undergraduate students' parents wonder, what is she doing here, is she experienced or qualified enough to teach? Students on finding me alone in the lecture hall before the class starts ask me, 'when is the lecturer coming?' These sorts of incidents make us smile because of the years which we have endured them. However, they are the tip of the iceberg of racial malevolence as

> [...] on matters related to race, the Racial Contract prescribes for its signatories an inverted epistemology, an epistemology of ignorance, a particular pattern of localized and global cognitive dysfunctions which are psychologically and socially functional), producing the ironic outcome that whites will in general be unable to understand the world they themselves have made (Mills 1997, p. 18).

In my view though, they understand that world all too well. There are no mental phenomena constituted by 'white misunderstanding, misrepresentation, evasion and self deception on matters related to race' (Mills 1997, p. 19). Instead what we live with in the 21st century is not a gap in knowledge usually connoted by 'ignorance' but a *knowing ignorance* of whiteness and its racist impacts. 'Sometimes these "unknowledges" are consciously generated, while at other times they are unconsciously generated and supported [...] [but] they work to support white privilege and supremacy' (Sullivan and Tuana 2007, p.2). We cannot even call this 'self deception' or 'social deception' but rather we should be alert to the continual recoding of the Racial Contract for contemporary white 'post-race' sensibilities where tolerance is a mark of civility. This recoding continues to be necessary for ruling internal racial colonies through processes, structures and affects.

The UK though prides itself on having the best 'race' equality legislation and bureaucracy in the EU. However, we can't legislate away attitudes, racist customs and nepotistic practices which lead (a) to universities recruiting in their own white image (b) black women and men remaining in the lower levels of universities (c) black women and men being undermined by colleagues as a matter of course (d) and, at the curriculum level Black Studies and knowledge generated by black scholars being erased or not seen to be scholarly enough for inclusion in the reading list which establishes the canon, irrespective of the standing of the black intellectual. These are a reflection of the denial of racism as a problem which prevails in British social life and a university sector which nevertheless sees itself as the vanguard of liberalism, equality and tolerance, particularly so with regard to 'bodies out of place' (Puar 2004).

As a 'body out of place' I am reminded that an environment exists in universities where

> the 'current and historical epistemic and habituated embodied orders [...] configure and sustain the white gaze and function to objectify the black body as an entity to be feared, disciplined, and relegated to those marginalized, imprisoned and segregated spaces that restrict Black bodies from "disturbing" the tranquility of white life, white comfort, white embodiment and white being (Yancy 2008, p. xvi).

Within these embodied orders the history of the objectified black body is linked to the history of normative whiteness for instance as fear, desire, terror and fantasy (Yancy 2008). It is both affect and discourses which lead to the 'distortional seeing' (Yancy 2008, p. xviii) of whiteness as it time and again objectifies the black body as abject.

In common with other black academics in the UK, irrespective of gender, sexuality, location, ability and age, I can give you many examples from my own experience in which as a body out of place I was reminded of 'my proper position'. When I was in my second academic job I drove into the staff car park on campus. The (white) car park attendant immediately told me to move my car to the student car park. He had not looked at the staff parking permit on my windscreen. In my third academic job I was taking some books out of the university library using my library card. The (white) librarian accused me of stealing my library card from a member of staff. She clearly had not paid close attention to the picture on the card. In another academic job it was graduation and I was waiting to be helped to find my gown and to be robed. A colleague walked in and asked me for his robes. Embarrassed, another colleague said that I was in the department and did not work for the company providing the robes.

Incidents like these are what we have 'to sup', as we say in Jamaica. That is, absorb it, grin and bear it, suck it up, roll with the punches. There are things though which can't be supped and where we have to stand up and be counted. This happened to me very early on in my career when I was involved in a conversation over whether the course I was working on should employ a white woman who was a friend of the course leader's or a black man who was much more qualified and experienced. I am paraphrasing here because this was some time ago but here are the main points of what was said to me, 'why does our course have to bear the brunt of employing black people? I think that she should get it. What are you today, Shirley, are you black or a feminist?' It is interesting what is said in front of you when it is assumed that somehow you can leave being black behind or even that you *should* in order to be accepted as a colleague. Her either/or question illustrates the fact of blackness in academia. That is, that we are required to alienate ourselves from ourselves as we enter the university's gates. Needless to say I did not comply with this requirement and I learned the meaning of the English saying 'being sent to Coventry'.

As black, objectified, abject, we invariably find ourselves struggling against exclusion once we are within academia. We struggle with this because inclusion acknowledges that 'race' marks some as lacking in proficiency, intelligence and talent so that those left unmarked are seen as able, intelligent, proficient and having the temperament for success (Puar 2004, p. 59). Inclusion is therefore problematic because white continues to be the unmarked category, the norm against which all are judged. Black women and men are not imagined as the norm in the academy so unsurprisingly we are anomalies in 'places where [we] are not the normative figure of authority, [and] [our] capabilities are viewed suspiciously [..] There is a significant level of doubt concerning [our] capabilities to measure up to the job' (Puar 2004, p. 59). This doubt means that there is a corporeal and psychic economy set in train in which we are not automatically assumed to have the right competencies for the job irrespective of our standing in the wider academic community and within the university itself. As bearers of 'race doubt', we have to repeatedly prove that we have a right to be there, that we are not in academia because of misplaced positive action initiatives.

We have to show competence in the face of the infantilization that is the result of reluctance to accept that we are capable (Puar 2004). Such infantilization here is about being assumed to be less competent and also more junior in status than we actually are. Indeed, '[...] it is automatically assumed that black bodies cannot possibly be capable of occupying senior positions' (Puar 2004, p.60). As perceived outsiders, as 'bodies out of place', we are also subjected to what Nirmal Puar (2004, p.61) calls 'super-surveillance'. We have to be hyper-competent as imperfections are noted, amplified and any mistake is taken as evidence for de-authorization. If we make no mistakes we are seen as being outside of the ordinary and working beyond expectations because of low expectations of the group that we are seen to represent.

These examples from my experience show the problematic of being an inside-outsider within a racial nomos permeated by the epistemology of ignorance. It shows the tenuous position in which we are placed within universities even if we are tenured senior staff, a position in which we have to toe the line or else live with the consequences. The consequences, of course, range from not being spoken to, to the much more toxic, being sidelined in terms of promotion. We have to deal with the negative affects within the institution generated by colleagues without succumbing to numbing shame, blinding anger, or crushing feelings of inadequacy. How can we talk about, how can we make visible, the bad feelings in our workplaces which surround us, permeate our psyches and 'stick' (Ahmed 2004) to our very skins?

Bad Feelings and Racial Affective Economies

Academic institutions are no different from the rest of society as a corporeal schema (Fanon 1967) operates to keep us in our 'proper' racial place. This happens because of epidermalization and what our skin has come to represent as the binary opposite of the white other which, as we have seen above, makes us subject to super surveillance (feeling like an object) and infantilization (feeling small). These are just two aspects of the racial affective economies that are set in train in organizations in which black women and men dare to enter as of right, as colleagues. Here we should pause to think about the word colleague itself. The etymology of colleague shows us that it is from the Latin *collega* – *com* 'with' + *leg*—stem of *legare* 'to choose'—so 'one chosen at the same time as another.' Being chosen at the same time as another has an underlying sense of one's equality of standing in the organization. However, this is nonsense because even when we are hired in spite of being black, as 'the best for the job,' epidermalization acts to ensure that we are *less than a colleague* as well as *colleague less*.

How often do we wonder where our support structure lies in organizations? Why does it invariably lie outside of our workplaces and reside within our intimate lives? Why is mentoring not available to us and when it is available it is not somewhere to talk about bad feelings caused by racism but just about developing strategies in order to be promoted? Why do white colleagues have problems being collegial, why do they have bad feelings, if you step outside of 'the natural space of blackness' into what is still seen as the (white) sphere of influence in academic life? These are a small list of the questions that we could ask because of our daily experiences in academic institutions in which we are always already known as not equal and where the appellation 'colleague' is an (im) possibility because of the workings of the Racial Contract.

A daily struggle for us in universities is to resist our location in the space of abjection because of skin. Such abjection is transported through the negative affects of disgust and contempt. Disgust and contempt are a part of our daily affective burden even within an over-arching assumption of liberalism and tolerance within the 21st century Racial Contract. Sianne Ngai (2005) makes it clear that in the late 20th century far from being an active aspect of politics tolerance is now passive, removed from practice to non-practice. This is the case even whilst it is made a compulsory underpinning to policies and a guide with respect to acceptable behaviour. Tolerance from both the political right and left diffuses antiracist critique and returns it as laissez faire rhetoric (Ngai 2005) on racial equality, environments free from harassment and positive action in hiring, tenure and promotion. Thus, it is that,

> [...] the object of tolerance in any affluent, market-centred democracy is perceived to be harmless or relatively unthreatening. Its ability to be tolerated in this socio-political context thus becomes an index of its socio-political *ineffectuality*—in particular its ineffectuality as a mechanism for dissent and change (Ngai 2005, pp. 341-342).

The object of tolerance is us, black faculty, a group which cannot change the structures or processes of the institutions which we inhabit. Tolerance, therefore, has ceased to be a liberatory or humanizing force in 'a society of total administration' (Marcuse cited in Ngai, 2005, p. 340). It has also ceased to be liberatory in institutions like universities which espouse racial equality as well as implement the accompanying administrative mechanisms, such as ethnic monitoring forms and anti-harassment statements. Rather, a discourse of tolerance implicates disgust and contempt in the national and academia project of governing internal racial colonies. Paradoxically, tolerance always points to that which cannot be tolerated, that which is the focus of disgust or contempt. As black it is we who are tolerated, who might be given spaces to enter but who also must be controlled through words, actions, policies, bureaucracy and the affects of disgust or contempt.

Tolerance and disgust are a binary with contempt being a midpoint between the two (Ngai 2005). In contempt an object can be considered as inferior, dismissed or ignored (Ngai 2005). As black people in predominantly white spaces contempt is too often what we *feel* but cannot say with precision why that is so. Tolerance always has these two affects—contempt and disgust—as uneasy bedfellows in the 21st century racial nomos as, for Ngai (2005, pp. 336-337).

> Disgust finds its object intolerable and demands its exclusion, while the objects of contempt simply do not merit strong affect; they are noticed only sufficiently so as to know that they are not noteworthy [...] one can condescend to treat them decently, one may, in rare circumstances, even pity them, but they are mostly invisible and utterly and safely *disattendable.*

We are not noticeworthy, as blacks we are safely disattendable within a tolerance which cannot openly speak its disgust for fear that the liberal mask will slip and the naked racism beneath will be revealed. We are disattendable because that is the safest fall-back position for a whiteness which must maintain its position as tolerant at all costs. What though is being denied us and what position are we being placed in as disattendable?

To attend means to give attention, to care for and care about, to accompany, to be observant of, to listen to, to serve. We also know how we feel when we are attended to: we feel valued, liked, significant, cared for. Being *attendable*, having the possibility of attention, is replete with positive affect and feelings of self worth. If we are disattendable, not even worthy of attention, we are placed even further as outsiders, perhaps we are even *beyond* abjection, as the mostly invisible who can be pitied. We do not matter enough, we are not attendable enough, for whiteness to exert quotidian efforts in our exclusion. This is not necessary as our exclusion is always already guaranteed as absolute through the disattendability produced by racial governance in universities in terms of hiring, tenure and promotion. Indeed, disattendability is so absolute that we can even be on the receiving end of affability.

However, affability does not entail the positive affect which comes from being liked because of the indifference born of contempt. Contempt is the negative boundary of tolerance and as such can also include condescending affability and marginalizing inclusion. This is so because white superiority is never doubted so contempt need not be about 'active dislike' (Ngai 2005, p. 336). However, contempt and tolerance are not the same but it is 'contemptuous tolerance' (Ngai 2005, p. 336) that is a part of the racial affective economy of disattendability.

Another aspect of this racial affective economy of disattendability is disgust which is never far from the surface of our encounters. Such disgust generates an atmosphere (Brennan 2004; Gutíerrez Rodríguez 2010a) which is felt but which we often can never name because it is overlain by a condescending affability which we can very easily mistake for collegiality and inclusion. Disgust generates an atmosphere because it 'is never ambivalent about its object [...] there is a sense in which it seeks to include or draw others *into* its exclusion of its object enabling a strange kind of sociability' (Ngai 2005, p. 336). This strange (white) sociability is what we feel when we walk into a room which is already occupied in both the past and present *as* white, what underlies selective invitations for after work drinks or to an intimate meal or to the movies and also what determines if 'your face fits.' These are not trite examples as they are easily recognizable as facets which determine who gets tenure as well as who gets promoted. Indeed, the sense that the interviewing panel has of 'your fit' as a person who they can see engaging in these activities with them as colleagues and perhaps in time friends, can determine entry in the first place. A (white) 'race' sociability based on disgust is no longer acceptable in UK institutions as is made clear in legislative rights frameworks and their interpretation and implementation at local level. However, universities are still sites of whiteness, racism and inequality where diversity and equality are simply performance indicators (Ahmed et al, 2006).

'Race' sociability then is based on that contempt and disgust that is about affability, inclusion of 'others' and never doubting one's white 'race' superiority. This draws us ever closer within institutions to the 'very antithesis of disgust—tolerance—than to the aversive emotion it would seem more to resemble' (Ngai 2005, p. 338). Such negative affects are not only about bad feelings but also have an impact on promotion and tenure because of another affective (im) possibility. That is, that of friendship and the exclusions which this then brings from the networks which impact on progress within universities.

Friendship and Promotion

As disattendable we are outside of the possibilities of the category 'friend'—we are not the objects of 'love' or 'favour'. This is because our invisibility guarantees that we cannot be addressed as friend, never be performatively constructed as friend through this addressivity. There is no institutional memory of black women and men as friends so this is not our natural address. This is not our natural address because of what Jacques Derrida (2005, p.4) terms 'the logic of the same'. Reading Cicero Derrida (2005, p. 28) says, 'the friend is [...] our own ideal image [...].We envisage the friend as such. And this is how he envisages us: with a friendly look'. The friend is therefore a performative enactment which arises through interpellation because we have, or feel we have, something in common with someone else.

The question for Derrida (2005) is not just *what* the friend is but equally important is *who* the friend is. I want to stay with this logic of the same where we performatively *construct a friend with a look* as long as they are who-and-what we expect them to be. We envisage the friend as such at the same time as they envisage us, we bridge chasms of the strange to become familiar as we 'look in the face of' (from the French *envisager*) the friend (Derrida, 2005). If we are bodies out of place experiencing contemptuous tolerance—'the what'-, we are already *not* 'the who' of friendship. Thus, we are continually located in the *space of estrangement* through the operation of racial affective economies.

It is remarkable how the estranging sociability of racial affective economies can so easily snuff out the possibilities of positive affect even with something as small and virtually untraceable as a glance. A glance, that is, where we are not envisaged, not looked in the face, not recognized, by a friendly look, where we are made to occupy the space of stranger. A glance, therefore, is both subject and object constituting as it can be the start of a friendship or the prelude to disattendability. George Yancy (2008:22) speaks about these object producing glances of whiteness as a seeing which is 'really a form of *reading*. [...] [a] "reading" of the Black body [which] is characteristic of the epistemology of ignorance' Such an epistemology of ignorance means that 'whites suffer from a structured blindness, a sociopsychologically reinforcing opacity that obstructs the process of "seeing" beyond falsehoods and various modes of whitely comportment that continue to reinforce and sustain white hegemony and mythos [...] racist actions are also habits of the body and not simply cognitively false beliefs' (Yancy 2008, p. 22).

This knowing ignorance is cultural and not just related to individual acts so that white bodies cross spaces that black bodies have occupied differently, (Yancy 2008) and the envisaging glance of friendship is never given. White bodies are the vehicles through which racist practices are performed and perpetuated and 'racism involves habitual, somatically ingrained ways of whitely-being-in-the-world, and systematically racist institutional structures of which [they are] partly a product' (Yancy 2008, p. 22). If we see glances as envisaging friends then they can determine whether we have 'liveable lives' (Butler 2005) or not in our universities. For example, they are sometimes the only way that we know if we are valued or not, if we deserve attention or will be on the receiving end of censure. Glances are very often a symptom of the university's 'inequality regime' (Acker 2006) and reflective of the relationality of power which can determine who is in or outside of professional networks governed by friendship.

Networks and Power's Relationality

Networks represent the knowledge/practice on which organizations are based and in which the capillaries of exclusionary 'raced' power closely mirror societal inequality regimes. As we know, however, networking is the key to equality in promotion and relationships based on the logic of the same determine who gets tenure and who gets promoted. Unfortunately it is not what you have written or how well-known you are as an academic. Rather, it is most often about *who knows you* and *who you know* which determines success. Since we cannot be what Yancy (2008) calls 'whitely-in-the-world', this cuts down both who we know and who knows us, where 'to know' is to look upon us with love or favour, to look upon us as 'friend'.

How many of us have applied for promotion and were not supported by our departments? How many times have we thought 'I am glad that I was not set up to fail, glad to be spared the shame of that eventuality, glad that the news of my failure was delivered by someone who put herself in the space of friend'? How often has our failure been focused on our writing so far, our lack of research funding or our lack of administrative experience, no matter how hard we work? What is often interesting about being told we have failed or being labelled a failure though is that we do not even feel disappointment. We do not feel disappointment perhaps because we occupy a blackly—being—in—the-world which involves Said's (2007) contrapuntal reading which I would here like to term contrapuntal thinking. Thinking contrapuntally means that I always occupy the space of marginality. This is a space in which I cannot and, indeed do not, expect to be treated any differently than the black women that inspire my writing. I have no more special privileges than those members of the black community who occupy the lowest rung of the university employment ladder. I have no immunity from contemptuous tolerance, no escape from estrangement, because I am an academic.

Perhaps more interesting for thinking about networks and power is what we are often asked in this moment of failure: who did we speak to before making the application and were we being mentored by anyone? Our answer invariably is 'no-one' and 'no'. This is another failure, but is it necessarily our own or is it caused by not seeing us as mentee material in the first place because our bodies place us as invisible and our position as 'race' theorists as non-academic? Lack of inclusion in networks means that we do not get mentored nor do we get access to the knowledge/practice that are invaluable for getting tenure and being promoted.

However, mentoring can be something of a double-edged sword because it demands trust on the part of both the mentor and the mentee. How can we develop trust though in a situation which is already filled with being whitely-in-the-world in terms of disattendability, inequality and contemptuous tolerance? Trust is absolutely relational and developing trust is something that has to be worked at by both parties involved in the mentoring dyad.

However, therein lays the difficulty. How can we place our trust in someone's judgement of us and our work when we cannot be sure of their absolute sincerity, when we do not see them *envisaging us as friend?* The truth is that in our positions that is what we have to do. We have to do this even whilst we recognize that the silent workings of networks will mean that we remain outsiders in terms of promotion much longer than others and we seem to have to have more of everything than others—more books, more articles, more administrative experience. The silent workings of networks are really where the power lies that keeps the Racial Contract in place in universities. Keeping the contract in place has negative organizational impacts which spring from the fact that networks often do not lead to the refreshing of talent, changes in work practices, or transformations of organizations' views of (un)belonging. The question remains, if we do not belong can we counter the epistemology of ignorance in our work places from the spaces of marginality?

Marginality, Disalienation and the Epistemology of Ignorance

For Lewis Gordon (1995, p.11), to live a human existence means to be estranged by racism. Affective adjustment under racist conditions—the "well-adjusted slave"—is an obscenity. That even the white man is expected to be well-adjusted in his role as master in a racist society is also an obscenity. Being a 'well-adjusted slave' is clearly not an option and we have continued to be estranged by an epistemology of ignorance in which contemptuous tolerance keeps us in 'our place', excluded, marginal, 'other'. In the UK, universities continue to be 'projects of national elites' where Bourdieu's *Homo Academicus* continues to be white (Gutiérrez Rodríguez 2010b, p.52).

As black and, therefore, the focus of the governance of contemptuous tolerance which places us as disattendable, beyond abjection, those of us who dare to enter must engage in a process of 'disalienation' (Fanon 1967; Césaire 2000) in order to resist the institutional requirement that we be alienated from ourselves. That is, we have to unmake our racialized bodies and remake them, restoring them to human modes of being in the world. This is our black woman's/man's burden as we deal with the white negative affects which seek to permeate our psyches, our very souls. It is these white negative affects that we have to labor to unmask because of their invisibility, their ability to melt into thin air. These affects very often are what carry the traces of an anti-black racism based on contemptuous tolerance which attempts to be invisible by being transported through the capillaries of *what we feel* but cannot otherwise prove exists. It is thus that racism, working through affects, tries to hide its material, corporeal and psychic effects through making its noxious values so familiar and frequent that they cease to function as objects of observation and reflection; they, in short, become unreflective and so steeped in familiarity that they become invisible [...]. Racist institutions are designed so as to facilitate racism with the grace of walking through the air on a calm summer's day (Gordon 1995, pp. 38-39).

Racism then in 'tolerant' institutions such as universities is never questioned but taken as valid because of its ease of functioning as it marginalizes black others, as it marginalizes us.

However, being marginal is *the* black condition in academic institutions and indeed it is a position from which we can build critique through engaging with what bell hooks (1991) calls 'the margin as a site of radical responsibility'. It seems to me we have no other personal, political or communal choice. We have no other choice because we have to remember that we want to cease being what we have been constructed as, the exception and the representative of 'the race'— 'the well-adjusted slave'. Being marginal should cease being a concern and instead should be taken to be a sign of our success in resisting the governmentality of contemptuous tolerance which demands that we become estranged from ourselves, our communities and politics in order to be *'accepted with provisos'* within our workplaces.

Conclusion

As I write this I feel no anger, just an engaged calm. I have felt searing anger and defeated desperation in the past and I am sure that I will feel them again. To express anger is to be put in the space of the 'well-adjusted slave', a position from which we can always already be understood, known, recognized and undermined with 'see, what can you expect they are all the same'. It s the same position in which Frantz Fanon (1967) found himself when the words 'look a nigger' were spoken. Refusing such an interpellation we must, like Audre Lorde (1984), see anger as loaded with information and energy. We need to see anger as 'a grief of distortions between peers and its object [as] change' (Lorde 1984, p.129). As we grieve we must express our grievances so that they do not explode within us and so that we can engender change (Cheng 2001). Anger is productive, transformational and because we fear being put in the place of 'the other' when we express anger, this does not mean that we should be silent. Silencing ourselves means our annihilation as we preserve white racial privilege in universities. The affective components of the terrain which I dare to occupy, which refuses me psychic and emotional nourishment and which continues to set me apart is a space that is full of traps which I must continuously negotiate. I still speak from a space from which the struggle continues, a space which refuses what Lorde (1984, p. 132) calls 'racial blindness.'

Acknowledgements

I would like to thank Encarnación Gutiérrez Rodríguez for her comments on this chapter.

References

Acker, J. (2006). Inequality regimes—gender, class and race in organizations. *Gender and Society. 20*(2), 441-464

Ahmed, S. (2004). *The cultural politics of emotion.* Edinburgh: Edinburgh University.

Ahmed, S., Turner, L., Swan, E., Hunter, S. & Kilic, S. (2006). *Race, diversity and leadership in the Learning and Skills sector.* http://www.gold.ac.uk/media/finaldiversityreport.pdf. [accessed, February 25, 2011]

Brennan, T. (2004). *The transmission of affect.* Ithaca, N.Y.: Cornell University.

Butler, J. (2004). *Precarious life: The powers of mourning and violence.* London: Verso.

Census. (2001). Office for national statistics. http://www.ons.gov.uk/census/index.html. [accessed, February 25, 2011]

Césaire, A. (2000). *Discourse on colonialism,* Trans. J.Pinkham. New York: Monthly Review.

Cheng, A. A. (2001). *The melancholy of race: Psychoanalysis, assimilation and hidden grief.* Oxford: Oxford University.

Derrida, J. (2005). *The politics of friendship.* London: Verso.

Fanon, F. (1967). *Black skin, white masks.* London: Pluto Press.

Gilroy, P. (2004). *After empire: melancholia or convivial culture.* London: Routledge.

Gordon, L. (1995). *Fanon and the crisis of European man: An essay on philosophy and the human sciences.* London: Routledge.

Gutiérrez R. E. (2010a). *Migration, domestic work and affect: A decolonial approach on value and the feminization of labor.* London: Routledge.

Gutiérrez R. E. (2010b). Decolonizing postcolonial rhetoric. In E. Gutiérrez Rodriguez, M. Boatcă and S. Costa (Eds,) *Decolonizing European Sociology* (pp.49-67). Farnham: Ashgate

hooks, b. (1991). Choosing the margin as a site of radical openness. In b. hooks *Yearning—Race, Gender and Cultural Politics* (pp.145-154). London: Turnaround

Jacobs, S. & Tate, S. (2006). Susie Jacobs and Shirley Tate: In conversation. In S. Jacobs (Ed.) *Pedagogies of teaching 'race' and ethnicity in Higher Education: British and European perspectives* (pp 95-115). Birmingham: CSAP

Jones, C. (2006). Falling between the cracks: What diversity means for Black women in Higher Education. *Policy Futures in Education.* 4 (2), 145-59

Lorde, A. (1984). *Sister outsider.* Freedom, CA: The Crossing.

Mills, C. W. (1997). *The racial contract.* Ithaca, NY: Cornell University.

Ngai, S. (2005). *Ugly feelings.* Cambridge, Massachusetts: Harvard University.

Number 10.gov.uk (February 5, 2011). PM's speech at Munich Security Conference, http://www.number10.gov.uk/news/speeches-and-transcripts [accesssed February 21, 2011]

Puar, N. (2004). *Space invaders: Race, gender and bodies out of place.* Oxford: Berg.

Said, E. (2007). *Culture and imperialism.* London: Vintage.

Sullivan, S. & Tuana, N. (2007). Introduction. In S. Sullivan, and N. Tuana, (Eds.). *Race and epistemologies of ignorance.* (pp. 1-12). Albany: SUNY.

The Association of University Teachers. (2005). The ethnicity of senior UK academic staff 1995-6 and 2003-4. London: Association of University Teachers.

The Guardian. (January 14, 2010) http://www.guardian.co.uk/politics/2010/jan/14/johndenham [accessed, February 2, 2011]

The Guardian Weekly (February 11, 2011), Cameron cuts off cash to Islamic groups suspected of extremism. p. 13

Yancy, G. (2008). *Black bodies, white gazes: The continuing significance of race.* Lanham: Rowman & Littlefield.

Conclusion

Essentially, we have experienced throughout the leaves of this book the insights and personal narratives, blended with secondary sources and primary data, of twelve scholars of African heritage employed in higher education institutions that are predominately White. Relatively gender-balanced, these scholars are primarily based in US higher education, while four of them are of Black British heritage; two having experience of both nations in terms of employment in higher education settings, and two still based in Britain. The majority of the scholars are tenured and experienced in their chosen fields, while three are pursuing tenure-track employment. In short, they are by all measures and attributes successful career-focused Black scholars. In this sense, they have a lot to share concerning their careers in predominately White institutions of higher learning. Collectively they represent a window into the lives of faculty of color and how each of them has coped with the nuances of day-to-day existence and interaction in their environments is testimony to how much inner strength they possess.

Make no mistake, academia can be a vicious place for *anyone* who happens to not fit the existing cultural paradigm. One can be isolated, shunned, and made to feel like a pariah for simply holding knowledge or values that do not correspond with a majority point of view. Sociologists speak of the "in-group" and "out-group" social reality in terms of there being an included set of persons and an excluded set of persons. Once designated to the out-group status life can be made literally professionally unbearable in the workplace. Arguably, what marks higher education different from the larger society is that most folks have "clever ways" to do "nasty deeds" when it comes to discrimination. Indeed, unfairness of any kind is extremely hard to prove and those perpetuating the problem are finding more stealthy ways to camouflage their exclusionary tactics in the workplace (Twale & De Luca 2008, p.76).

Given the existing literature now circulating and the more being produced, it is important for university administrations to take heed and to better ways to protect vulnerable scholars or staff. It is acknowledged that most universities and colleges do have extensive policies that protect individuals from discrimination. Yet it appears too often that equal opportunity and anti-discrimination policy is just not effective enough due to the various ways, for example, that there can be "racism without racists" in societies like the US (Bonilla Silva 2003). To put it another way, those persons whom harbor ill-will against others know full well that "racism" or "sexism" or "homophobia" are not to be tolerated in colleges and universities. The battle to stigmatize such discriminatory behavior is truly won. However, what we now have is a form of "silent racism" that is hard to detect (Trepangier 2006); what we need to do presently is look more deeply into social psychology and how subtle forms of prejudice and racism manifest in more nuanced ways (Anderson 2010, p. 9).

What is more likely to happen in today's professional world is the isolating and shunning of an individual if she or he does not conform to the local cultural paradigm (Namie & Namie 2003). There can be a variety of ways that this occurs, but at bottom there is usually a series of subtle attacks on the individual's credibility. Once the person's credibility has been neutralized he or she will not be effective in the specific institution. That is unless there is intervention and discrimination can be proved, which is difficult to do. In fact, the literature concerning bullying in the workplace is rather pessimistic in relation to a target's chances of gaining justice (Namie & Namie 2003; Twale & De Luca 2008).

Therefore, the personal narratives in this book become a window for administrators to consider the varied but common experiences of faculty of color in predominately White space. They should not be isolated or dismissed as anecdotal as the growing literature is demanding that these marginalized voices to be heard. To be sure, there is in this collection of chapters a phenomena that reveals clearly a problematic workplace setting for faculty of color in higher education institutions. There will be a need for further research, further reflection, and further assessment of what can be done to relieve the pressure on Black faculty. Especially for those whom teach and research in the area of "race" and ethnic relations, and certainly for those in the contentious area of Africana/Black Studies.

One cannot, as often is the case, treat all faculty as being "equal" in a college of arts and science setting when in fact White faculty in traditional disciplines have far less to do in terms of affirming their statuses as valid teachers and researchers. For administrators to measure all from the same yardstick is to be facile and myopic. Indeed, in relation to Black faculty, it is another form of "silent racism" as it is a way to discriminate on the basis of "normative policy" and professional criteria. Ironically, what this book has informed, among other things, is that there can often be an implicit criteria for assessing the worth of a Black faculty member: one way for "us" and another for "them" and that reveals part of the problem faced by faculty of color. We are seemingly judged by the *same* criteria of those that have been instrumental in keeping us out of the specific institution. The rules of the "game" in academia, in other words, were written by Whites, and for Whites; certainly in relation to the predominately White university setting. To paraphrase George Orwell's *Animal Farm* (1945/1989, p. 90), it is apt in relation to much that takes place in the evaluation of the entire faculty at predominately White institutions: "all are equal, but some are more equal than others." That is the reality, we are supposedly all treated equally, but the outcome of such "equality" is skewed most often favorably toward those from the White cultural groups, and those whom assimilate to such. Regardless of this scenario, most Black faculty struggle on, succeed, but suffer quietly with "racial battle fatigue." The authors in this volume have offered how this transpires in many nuanced ways.

Recommendations

I would offer seven recommendations to improve the existing situation for Black faculty based at predominately White universities and other institutions of higher learning in the context of the US:

1) **Knowledge Appreciation:** More transparency is needed in relation to the worth of knowledge. It is not healthy to have

philosophical racism in modern universities that favors one discipline over another. It should be clear that all knowledge is specific and useful to the field/discipline it belongs, and in how it relates to the "whole" experience of university life for the student. Liberal arts and the social sciences should not have hierarchical knowledge in the modern university.

2) **Acknowledging the Problem:** Obviously it takes time for the structure and culture of an institution to change. For example, it will not be easy to make multicultural education a "normal" experience in predominately White higher educational settings. Yet without the solid support of the specific university hierarchy we cannot expect improvement in the existing workplace situation for Black faculty.

3) **Monitor and Mentor:** The monitoring of Black faculty in terms of retention and support is crucial. Too many simply leave and/or struggle on in a hellish workplace environment. Mentoring needs to be improved for new Black faculty recruits. How to teach in a predominately White classroom? How to get tenure? How to publish effectively? How to engage with White faculty positively without losing your soul? How to survive in a dominant White culture? How to stay culturally comfortable being Black in White space? These are some basic questions that should form a mentoring relationship.

4) **Revolving Doors:** If Black faculty are leaving the university after 2 or 3 years then there is something specifically wrong with the workplace environment. It is likely to be an unwelcoming institution for persons of color. Those Black faculty that remain should be consulted openly and asked to provide a basis for improving the workplace in relation to persons of color. A revolving door is a clear sign of an unwelcome place to be for Black folks. Consider if your university or college has a revolving door for Black faculty.

5) **Salary Equity:** If there is a pattern of inequitable treatment in terms of salary, usually with underrepresented groups earning less than their White counterparts, then this should be addressed. It is a clear sign of an unwelcoming institution that

fails to pay the worth of its Black faculty. To pay less for more is bordering on criminality, and Black faculty by just being a rare species exemplify much worth to a modern university.

6) **Black Men and Women:** There is a problem developing in society whereby Black men are diminishing in numbers due to various forms of societal problems. In the university system they will inevitably be scarce in the next two to three decades if something is not done to retain and develop ways to recruit young Black men into graduate school. Black women need specific help too, not least in allowing them to be themselves in cultural ways such as having their natural hair valued, appreciated, and accepted in the university setting. Black women will be the dominant force in two decades, with the scarcity of Black males coming through graduate school.

7) **Accountability:** There are insidious racists in higher education institutions. Hiding behind diversity awards; clapping the progress of one person of color, while stabbing the back of another; smiling in faces, while gossiping to hurt the professional standing of others in the given institution. There is no place for these bullies who with power create mobs to hurt one individual and favor another. It is ubiquitous, unhealthy, and has no place in a modern university. What can be done? It is tricky as they are stealthy, sly, mean-spirited, and sometimes hold a lot of power. The way to weed out such persons is to watch closely the outcome of their professional work. If the potential bully happens to have professional interaction with persons of color, it is those that have the best self esteem and a positive awareness in regard to their Black heritage that will likely be the target of inequitable treatment. The weaker persons of color may be doing all they can to assimilate, to be part of the local culture in order to avoid being hurt professionally by the bully. Therefore, the persons of color who teach and research with a degree of self worth and courage are ironically the most at risk in a predominately White university. The bullies do not enjoy minorities who are successful and have a good sense of self. Bullying in academia is on the increase, it will take all people of goodwill to eradicate it (Twale & De Luca 2008). Administrations should take

seriously Black faculty who are the targets of such unacceptable treatment in the workplace, which is not the case at present.

In terms of the UK British university system. It is conservatively estimated here that it is at least 35 years behind the progress of the US in terms of multicultural awareness and the empowerment of persons of color in the system. The situation articulated in their chapters by William Ackah and Shirley Anne Tate reveals the horrors of isolation and employment insecurity, along with the usual psychological warfare one has to engage in to be both Black and proud in a majority White workplace. Britain needs to improve so much that it will take another book to deal with its sheer lack of diversity in Black faculty and curriculum offerings.

Overall, this book is a beginning, it is certainly not the end, but it can be deemed as a starting point for further discussion and debate. It is hoped that progressive White university administrators of goodwill shall take on board what the various authors in this volume have each espoused to learn more about the lives of Black faculty in predominately White space. It is not to turn them away but to engage with them on a human level for the betterment of the modern university. There is no place for inequitable treatment in a college or university as it goes against most if not all mission statements. There needs to be a new way for ensuring accountability in terms of the improvement of Black faculty experience across the board. Let us hope that this book does not fall on blind eyes and deaf ears.

References

Anderson, K. J. (2010). *Benign bigotry: The psychology of subtle prejudice.* Cambridge: Cambridge University.

Bonilla-Silva, E. (2003). *Racism without racists: Color-blind racism and the persistence of racial inequality in the United States.* London: Rowman & Littlefield.

Namie, G., & Namie, R. (2003). *The bully at work: What you can do to stop the hurt and reclaim your dignity on the job.* Naperville, Illinois: Sourcebooks.

Orwell, G. (1945/1989). *Animal farm.* London: Penguin.

Trepagnier, B. (2006). *Silent racism: How well-meaning white people perpetuate the racial divide.* New York: Paradigm.

Twale, D.J & De Luca, B.M. (2008). *Faculty incivility: The rise of the academic bully culture and what to do about it.* San Francisco, CA: Jossey-Bass.

About the Editor and Contributors

❖

William B. Ackah, PhD is a Lecturer in Community and Voluntary Sector Studies at Birkbeck College University of London. William previously worked as a Widening Participation Officer at University of Bristol and Equalities and Diversity Manager for Learning and Skills Council. William was a co-founder and member of the Black Education Action Network. A group of education specialists and community activists working on initiatives to raise aspirations and educational attainment in black communities. William was a Board member of the Challenging Attitudes Partnership Gloucester; HMP Risley Warrington; and Granby Toxteth Partnership.

Helane Adams Androne, PhD is Associate Professor of English at the Middletown campus of Miami University of Ohio. She earned her bachelor of arts in English at the university of California San Diego and her PhD from the University of Washington in Seattle. Dr. Androne's research examines the role of ritual as pedagogy and in African American and Chicana literature.

Alma Jean Billingslea Brown, PhD is a Professor of English and Director of the African Diaspora and the World program at Spelman College. A former member of the Student Non-Violent Coordinating Committee (SNCC), she has a long history with African American activism and the struggle for civil and human rights. Her work now expands beyond the African American experience to incorporate a study abroad each summer for students who want to learn about other African Diaspora communities.

Mark Christian, PhD (Editor) is Professor & Chair of African & African American Studies, and an affiliate with the Department of Sociology at Lehman College, CUNY. He is a senior Fulbright scholar recipient, and a former research fellow at the University of London's Commonwealth Studies Institute, and currently a visiting fellow at the Department of Sociology, The University of Liverpool. He is the author of *Multiracial Identity: An International Perspective* (Palgrave/Macmillan, 2000) and two other edited volumes, and has been the guest editor of three special issue journals (2006, 2008, 2010). His research is mainly focused on the African Diaspora as it relates to the UK, US, and African Caribbean (British ex-colonies). Currently, he is the book review editor for the *Journal of African American Studies.* Among his current interdisciplinary research topics are: African American music influences on The Beatles, and the development of African & African American Studies as a field/discipline in the 21st Century.

Michael E. Dantley, EdD is the Associate Provost and Associate Vice President for Academic Affairs, and a Professor of Educational Leadership at Miami University of Ohio. Dr. Dantley received the Richard T. Delp Award for Outstanding Faculty from the School of Education and Allied Professions of Miami University. His research centers on the inclusion of African American spirituality, critical theory and transformative leadership grounded in Cornel West's notions of prophetic pragmatism in the traditional discourse of school leadership and school reform. Dr. Dantley has published in numerous journals, including the *Journal of School Leadership, Education and Urban Society*, the *International Journal of Leadership in Education*, and the *Journal of Negro Education.*

Jeanette R. Davidson, PhD is Associate Professor of Social Work and Director of the African & African American Studies Program at Oklahoma University. She is the editor of a volume entitled *African American Studies* (University of Edinburgh Press, 2010). Her work on interracial scholarship is noted. She is also an executive board member of NCORE, This committee serves as the primary planning body for the Annual National Conference on Race & Ethnicity in American Higher Education (NCORE).

Mark S. Giles, PhD is Associate Professor of Educational Leadership in the Department of Educational Leadership and Policy Studies at the University of Texas at San Antonio. In addition, he serves as Director of the African American Studies program. His scholarship interests include critical race studies, the African American experience in higher education, 20th century African American leadership, and spirituality. He has extensive professional experiences in urban community affairs, post-secondary academic support services, and diversity-focused administrative positions. He is an active member in several professional organizations including American Educational Research Association, American Educational Studies Association, Association for the Study of African American Life and History, National Council of Black Studies, and the Critical Race Studies in Education Association.

Robin L. Hughes, PhD is Assistant Professor in the Department of Educational Leadership and Policy Studies, Higher Education Student Affairs (HESA) at Indiana University Indianapolis. She is an adjunct professor in the Department of African American African Diaspora Studies in Bloomington and Indianapolis. Her research focuses on sports where she explores the development of students who are athletes participating in revenue generating sports. In addition, she focuses on race, and how it might impact faculty and students of color in higher education. Dr. Hughes is also Co-editor and co-founder of the *Journal for the Study of Sports and Athletes in Education* (JSSAE). She is the author of numerous articles, book chapters, and books that examine issues of race. Her forthcoming, co-edited book, *Dismantle This! Deconstructing Policy and Institutionalized 'isms' through Critical Race Theory*, explores how academic institutions sustain racism by structuring and perpetuating exclusionary procedures and policies for administration and scholarship.

Natasha Flowers, PhD is a Clinical Assistant Professor in Teacher education at Indiana University, School of Education, Indianapolis. She has served as a consultant for K-12 school-based programs in the areas of curriculum mapping, program assessment and multicultural education. She has also worked extensively in faculty development centers with a focus on faculty of color, diversity and equity issues in and outside the classroom. Her work embraces students and faculty of color in order to contribute to their empowerment in predominately white colleges and universities.

Mary Phillips, PhD is a recent doctoral graduate in African American Studies from Michigan State University. Her entire qualifications (BA, MA, PhD) are in African American history and culture. In this sense she represents the rare scholar "born and raised" in the field/discipline of Africana/Black Studies. As a Black feminist she has studied the Black Panther Party and the experience of women in the movement. She has also published work on the role of Black Studies in the university system.

Shirley Anne Tate, PhD is a Senior Lecturer and the MA Program Manager for the Centre for Interdisciplinary Gender Studies at the University of Leeds, UK. Her research explores the intersections of 'raced' and gendered bodies, 'race' performativity, 'mixed race' and decoloniality within the Black Atlantic diasporic context. Her first book *Black Skins, Black Masks: Hybridity, Dialogism, Performativity* focused on 'race' performativity and hybridity theorizing. Her other book, *Black Beauty: Aesthetics, Stylization, Politics,* looks at Black beauty within the Black Atlantic Diaspora as affect-laden, performative 'race' work that continues to impact on communal politics.

Martell Teasley, PhD is Associate Professor in Social Work at Florida State University. He is a retired US Army Persian Gulf War veteran, a former licensed practice nurse, and former school social worker. He graduated from Fayetteville State University in North Carolina with a BS in psychology and a BA in sociology. He earned a Master's degree in social work from Virginia Commonwealth University in May 1996 and he earned a PhD in social work in May 2002 from Howard University. Effectively managing four careers to date, he is now a regular presenter at national conferences and symposiums on a variety of topics related to educational reform and culturally competent practice with African American families. His primary concern is to provide insight aid toward the empowerment of African American communities.

Index

❋